Horatio Clare

Horatio Clare was born in 1973 and raised in Wales. A writer and radio producer, he has contributed to various newspapers, magazines and travel anthologies. He is the author of *Running for the Hills* and the editor of *Sicily Through Writers' Eyes*.

Praise for *Truant*

'The same spirit of exuberance that lures Clare into his many scrapes also infects his writing; at times it is like being cornered at the bar by a wild-eyed, raving raconteur . . . Part of the reason why Clare is so appealing as a memoirist is that he resists the temptations of self-pity and blame' *Guardian*

'Vibrant and absorbing, he shows what a good novelist he will one day make' *Independent*

'What lifts it out of the ordinary is the luminosity of his writing. His tenses effortlessly flip between the simple past and the sudden present. The pace of the prose mirrors his moods without jarring . . . Like the burning tip of a joint in the dark, the colour orange is laced through the chapters of his life: neon in the city; golden in the long dry grasses of school adventures . . . Clare is drawn to the bittersweet and painful, to the tension between the romantic ideal and the horror of reality. He is at his most outstanding in descriptions of place and landscape . . . *Truant* is keenly perceptive' *Daily Telegraph*

'Clare writes with chilling honesty' *Daily Mail*

'Engagingly written, often funny and brilliant . . . Where he is very good is in describing how dope-addiction renders a life chaotic and inconsequential, and creates in the addict an "introverted and distant", unreliable and evasive personality which must manifest, eventually, in full-blown mental illness' *Sunday Telegraph*

'Clare is a gifted writer, adept at marshalling complex information (there are lots of characters and references but you never get lost as you read), as well as a brilliant mimic with a marvellous ear. His replication of drug-addled non-sense talk is pitch perfect yet never boring. (This really is an achievement.) His recall is also extraordinary and so is his candour. Finally, there is no special pleading: he accepts responsibility without demur. But over and above this, what's most remarkable here is Clare's cool, lucid and detached exposure of the great lie we tell ourselves about dope. For those interested in this debate, *Truant* is a must-read. Get your stoner friend a copy. It might just save their life' *Irish Times*

'Clare inveighs against cannabis eloquently' *Evening Standard*

'Clare leaves behind the Welsh valleys of his childhood, so tenderly written about in his debut memoir, *Running for the Hills*, and grows up, getting expelled and finding drugs along the way, in this laugh-out-loud-funny follow-up' *Harper's Bazaar*

'Here he enters much darker terrain as he recounts his headlong tumble into drug abuse, and the sadness and the madness that it wrought . . . In this brave, compelling, beautifully written book, he tries to make sense of why he and his friends fell into drugs and how and why he managed to fight his way back' *Good Book Guide*

'Upfront, upsetting, a clever reassembling of [Clare's] drug-and-madness fragmented years. Lyrical, funny and acute, the story is blisteringly observed . . . This will strike a chord with parents and students alike' *Good Housekeeping*

Truant

Notes from the Slippery Slope

HORATIO CLARE

JOHN MURRAY

For S

First published in Great Britain in 2007 by John Murray (Publishers)
An Hachette Livre UK company

First published in paperback in 2008

6

© Horatio Clare 2007

A CIP catalogue record for this title is available from the British Library

ISBN 978-0-7195-6917-3

Typeset in Bembo by Servis Filmsetting Ltd, Manchester

Printed and bound in Great Britain by Clays Ltd, Elcograf S.p.A.

John Murray policy is to use papers that are natural, renewable and recyclable products and
made from wood grown in sustainable forests. The logging and manufacturing processes
are expected to conform to the environmental regulations of the country of origin.

John Murray (Publishers)
338 Euston Road
London NW1 3BH

www.johnmurray.co.uk

Contents

HAMLET I am very glad to see you – good even, sir.
        But what in faith make you from Wittenberg?
HORATIO A truant disposition, good my Lord.
HAMLET I would not hear your enemy say so . . .

Hamlet, Act 1 Scene 2

truant noun & adjective. ME.
    [old French . . . prob. of Celtic origin (cf. Welsh *truan*
    wretched (person), Gaelic *truaghan* Irish *truaghán*
    wretched).]
noun. 1 A person begging through choice rather than
necessity . . . an idle rogue.

Oxford English Dictionary (2002)

This is a true story but not always a rigidly factual account: some conversations and incidents have been reconstructed where they could not be entirely remembered. Names have been changed and identities disguised.

Prologue

I KNEW A pigeon once, a beautiful racer. He landed on the mountainside where we lived, exhausted, after a storm. I found him crouching in the yard, very weak but not frightened of being handled. He had a numbered ring like a pilot's licence around one leg. He looked thoughtful so I named him Aristotle.

It felt a great honour that he had come to our yard for refuge and it was a wise move: we lived high above the valley on an old and primitive hill farm. We saw many more animals and birds than people. We were kind to them. I carried Aristotle into one of the barns, took him a saucer of water and fed him on linseed cake which I carefully picked out of the dog food. We worried that the rats might get him but he flew up to the rafters, where he perched and preened and thought for a week. Then one afternoon, a day of broken skies, wind and sudden sun, he flew out on to the roof of the stable, cocked his head and seemed to take his bearings. The view from the stable roof was magnificent, plunging down into the valley's quilt of coloured fields and rising in a surge to the mountains on the other side. He studied it.

'Look, look!' I said. 'Aristotle's come out!'

He shuffled his feathers.

'Ah,' my mother said, 'he's probably getting ready to go.'

Had I been a little younger I might have been upset at this, for I loved birds and I was very fond of him. But I was a big boy now, eleven years old, and I understood that Aristotle had a mission and a calling: he had places to go and races to win. His visit had been a blessing which could not last. I was going away soon too, off to school, to broaden my horizons. There are things we have to do, I knew.

There was a shudder of wind and the sunlight broke through again, bright, almost white under the rain clouds. Aristotle jumped into the air with a clap of his wings and climbed swiftly, now as high as the sycamore tree, now higher.

'Goodbye, Aristotle!' I cried.

And then the bird did something which seemed extraordinary. First once, then twice, then three times he flew a circle over the farm, at the same height, faster and faster, his slate-blue back and pale underwings flashing in the sun.

'Look at him,' I marvelled. 'Isn't he wonderful!'

'It's a salute!' said my mother. 'A lap of honour.'

Then with the merest tilt of his wings he broke the circuit, became a spot, then a speck, arrowing for the skyline, and was gone.

Later that afternoon I sat on my swing and thought about Aristotle, and a girl called Rhiannon, my first crush. Aristotle was a racer, a traveller, an athlete. He was small and thin but he was strong. He was self-possessed. I wanted to be like that. I wanted to fly out across the world, to be battered by adventures, to win glory and, one day, the heart of Rhiannon. What was likeable and admirable in men? The things they knew. Things they had done. Experience and the memory of distant lands. Daring and expertise, knowledge and the ease of tested strength.

Now it seems odd that I should have conflated a racing pigeon, a girl and idealized visions of my future but as I sat on the swing, twisting around in slow circles under the larch trees, above the valley, it was not strange at all. My mind was a carnival of disparity: fighter aces, snow leopards, pirates, eagles, Biggles, a fox called Rufus, my father, Indiana Jones, Jack and Cem (heroes of Robert Westall's books), Just William, my brother Alexander, snipers, my best friend Matthew, pheasants, Princess Leia . . . Fantasy is too weak a word for it: these figures were an audience to all my doings and actors in most of my private thoughts. I was going away to school and beyond, but I was taking them with me: to honour them, to pursue them and add to them, as well as to do well and please my mother.

I liked the idea that great adventures in stormy realms might one day wash me up, like Aristotle, on a distant hillside, and I hoped vaguely that the gentle hands which revived me might be Rhiannon's.

Whatever was out there, beyond the mountains, I thought I was ready for it. I was scared but I knew I wanted it. And whatever happened I would have my imagination, and the mountains would still be here. I could always come back, I thought.

My father wrote to me, just before I left, with a few words of warning about public schools. He did not approve of them, he said. They were exclusive and privileged and they taught a particular view of the world. Many people disapproved of them, including people who had been to public schools. But he was proud of me, he said: I had won an Assisted Place, which meant the government would be paying my fees (my mother had no money) and he trusted that I would work hard and do well. He warned me to beware of snobbery and elitism.

On my first evening in the little prep school, after I had said goodbye to my mother and she had departed, hiding her tears, I was standing with a few others, self-conscious in my new grey uniform, when a party of boys from the town passed the gates, jeering and hooting. One of my new peers, the incarnation of everything Just William had led me to expect of prep school boys, owlish in his glasses, plummy-voiced and mischievous, sneered.

'They're just doing it because they haven't been well brought up,' he said. 'They haven't got good parents.'

'You snob!' I flared.

He pushed me and I pushed him back. We tussled. He punched me in the stomach and I put him in a headlock. His glasses fell off. I gave his neck a squeeze and held my fist under his nose as a warning. Then the door to the dining room opened and boys began pushing and shoving to get into supper. I let him go. My heart was beating fast but I was proud of myself. I had stood up against snobbery and elitism. My father, my friends from primary school, my brother and the whole carnival of real and imagined figures in my head had seen the incident, and approved. I was not going to be warped by public school. I was going to stand against it, if necessary. I felt I had made a good start.

The carnival stayed with me, no less noisy and no less luminous, only the figures changed. By the time I was seventeen my head was full of girls known and unknown, actual friends, present and distant, poets and writers, and the creations of poets and writers. Coleridge was as real to me as the imaginary love of my life, who shared my head with my first proper girl friend, Lara, and Allen Ginsberg, Jack Kerouac and Christabel, Coleridge's devilish witch, and Byron.

I was not a complete fantasist. Actual figures – my friends, family and teachers – had the most say and sway over me, but the invisible ones mattered too. They may not have had as many votes over my conduct but their votes counted, and there were a lot of them. I read the work and the biographies of poets and wished that I might be one. Hell-raisers like Byron and Hunter S. Thompson, wild youths like Shelley, romantics: I loved the words for their sounds and inferences as much as their senses. A hell-raiser wore a leather jacket and created uproar in bars, fought and fell about laughing. A wild youth tore through things passionately, leaving delight and scandal like a missile trail, and a romantic wore a three-quarter length coat and walked abroad under a new moon, studying nature like a spell book, seeing mysteries, nourished by the sight of towering clouds, sensing truth and divinity in the life of a hedgerow or the tilt of a midnight breeze.

This dreamy solipsism had three points: above all I wished to delight my friends, to attract girls and to become a writer. The order of importance varied from moment to moment. And now, at seventeen, I was not restricted to dreams: I could act. There was a physical road which led to the carnival, a path of actual places and vital experiences. You had to become a lover. You had to go to Paris and New York. You had to have your heart broken. You had to run out of money and not care. You had to find rock bottom despair, as well as ecstasy and bliss. You had to try everything. You had to live as much as possible in order to know and to feel as much as you could: where else could writing come from? I wrote poetry but I was under no illusions about it. Though I was not a great romantic writer I might still be a great romantic.

At my age many of the gates of experience were still locked. I could not dance at the Ritz until dawn. I could not take a ship to the Antarctic. Even catching a bus to Denver, like the figures in Ginsberg's *Howl*, would be tricky. So I started with the things which were available to me. I started with booze, and drugs, and sex.

*

4

If a good childhood instils positive hopes and dreams, it also imparts reasonable and realistic fears. If you are good you will do well. If you are bad you will get into trouble. You must work hard or you will fail. You must be honest or you will be distrusted, be kind or you will be disliked. In addition to these formulae, my unusual childhood, which was full of freedom and beauty (we lived very close to nature), had given me plenty of adult responsibility. I had worried about how little money we had. I had worried about my mother's health and happiness: I had sometimes panicked in case something should happen to her when she was out with the sheep, miles from shelter and safety. I had worried about my brother's progress at school.

But after I went away to school, my mother sold the farm and we moved down to the valley. She and my brother were safe. And now that I was far away, and growing up, the anxieties of my childhood lifted off me. There was nothing I could do to help my mother and brother: now I only need worry about myself. And I was not worried about myself. I was confident. My fears fell away. I would be the author of my own fate and my own code. I set myself few rules.

Six years later, in the new year of 1997, I left mid Devon, where my first job on a local newspaper had ended in disgrace, not exactly on the run from the police (I was out of the country before they knew they wanted me) but certainly a fugitive from justice. I had done two things and while I did not much regret the first, the second was appalling. At the time I was on a manic high, laughing desperately, drinking so fiercely I never seemed to be drunk, smoking and rampaging and in only intermittent touch with reality. The carnival had all but taken over.

I thought I had been behaving in the same way everyone I knew behaved. (I was a drug addict, but if you had told me that, I would have laughed and tried to put you straight.) I thought I was in step with my peers; I thought I was normal. And I think that this is the most frightening thing about this story. Though I took it to extremes, in the main I was perfectly in step. I was normal.

But now I knew I had gone too far and was sure to pay for what had happened. Horrified by it, I ran. I packed a small bag and fled to the station, to London and to Heathrow with more than enough money for a plane ticket (I came into an inheritance at this moment, unfortunately) and nothing else but disgrace to my name.

I must have looked exactly the way I was that night, drinking miniature vodkas and eating dope all the way through the flight: I had not really meant to carry the little brown block of hashish on board, it was simply that I never went anywhere without it. I was not quite mad enough to try to take it through customs at the other end, so I ate it.

Guilty and lecherous in an unclean white shirt, elusive eyed and red faced: I felt like scum, as I pretended to be another innocent passenger. I felt like an actor in a film, but not the hero. I felt like a minor villain, and I marvelled that my life had become the story of a black sheep. It was not clear how it had happened. I thought I had tried to be good. But at some point one of my cousins had taken to saying 'Hello, trouble!' when we met, and it was appropriate. I was trouble. I was an adult only on paper – aged twenty-three – who had already given a DNA sample and prints (twice) to the police, receiving two cautions in return. One was long spent but the other was fresh. Now that I was in trouble again, the police would know I had 'form' but a jury would not, in the event of a plea of innocence. I have never so pled.

I

Sapiens qui prospicit

(Wise is the man who looks ahead)

1987–90

IT WAS A night flight. The wide aisles, the ranks of seats and the humming of the giant aeroplane's vast and harnessed power filled me with a lurching excitement which curdled in my stomach around a clot of guilt. I have never forgotten a sermon given by the head-master of my prep school about conscience. Conscience, he said, was like a sharp-pointed pyramid inside us. When we sinned the points of the pyramid dug into us, pained us, urged us to make redress and to be better. If we ignored it and continued to sin the points would eventually become blunt and rounded until we were able to behave monstrously without regret, whereupon we would be entirely lost. You cannot recover your conscience, he said, it will not regenerate and cannot be repaired. You must guard it, heed it and treasure it: this way you will become better people.

My pyramid's points felt sharp but I recoiled from their digs and jabs as if tightening my muscles against them, soothing their scores and cuts with duty-free alcohol and the sandy taste of surreptitiously chewed hashish. The period between transgression and retribution is terrible. You cannot go back so you go on, faster and faster, filled with a kind of recklessness, a mad, silent laughter. Part of you wants to be caught, to settle accounts, but another part whispers 'Run, run! Don't look back!' You feel a kind of silent roaring inside you, like the angry gust of the great burners that fill hot air balloons.

Other travellers hoisted their luggage into lockers, took off their coats and settled themselves. They were glamorous and successful-seeming; there was a professional kind of cool in the cabin. They were business men and women, employed, achieving, productive people. What was I? A writer who had never been published; a journalist with-out a paper; an adventurer with no cause; a sinner in headlong flight from wrongdoing. I felt sick and excited. The plane roared and hurled us all up into the night. I was restless and excluded, craving contact.

'May I see the cockpit?' I asked a stewardess, 'I'm a nervous flyer but if I could meet the pilots I'd feel much better . . .'

She gave me a look I came to know well, a querying, penetrating look, part bemused, part suspicious. The more you are subject to it the more you behave as though you deserve it.

'You don't look the nervous type,' she said, slipping me a handful of miniature vodkas. After the meal when the lights were dimmed and the passengers slept I hunched under a blanket and lit a cigarette. All around people dozed; no stewardess appeared. I do not remember anything of immigration or customs. I took a taxi to a random hotel and came round there later, alone in New York, fully clothed on the bed with all the lights on. I had one friend on the east coast. I called Ben.

I first remember Ben at the trials for the school rugby team. Our new home stood on the side of the hills overlooking a wide Arcadian vale; below the railway line the town surrendered to miles of fields and orchards which faded away beyond the river Severn into a green English distance. We were thirteen, only days into the life-changing immersion of public school, but for most of us its rituals were already familiar. We had learned hierarchy, tradition, chapel and rugby at prep school. It was all new to Ben. I stood with my best friend Rupert and others from prep school on the windy games field and watched a tanned, dark-haired boy duck, dodge and run fast past would-be tacklers. When caught he fought vigorously. He did not seem to understand that anger on the rugby field was reserved for the annual inter-house competition, for yourself if you did not play well and, occasionally, for other school teams. Who was that, getting so worked up? An American? What's his name? Hardiman? We hooted it, taking the piss encouragingly. 'Give it to Hardiman! That's it, Hardiman! Go on! Go! Pass!' He had never played the game before but we could see he was a definite for the team.

Next he arrived in Set 1, the scholarship classes my friend and I had started in – key subjects were streamed by ability and Ben had started low down, presumably because he had made no effort with his entrance exams. He headed for the back row as if trying to avoid attention. He sat slumped, gazing at the proceedings darkly from under his fringe, his expression wary, occasionally amused. He flipped a pen in a clever way around the knuckle of his thumb. When forced to speak his voice was quiet and, to us, comically American. It was a laconic and entertaining performance, however many times you saw it: weekly, even daily he would offer an excuse, a denial and an apology for undone homework. He was strikingly good-looking, we agreed. He was not tall and not quite all-American; he had a European diffidence, having been raised among expatriates in Germany, where his father worked.

We believed he had been out with beautiful girls (I had barely spoken to any girls at all since primary school) and was probably not a virgin. Virginity was a great concern among us. Like several others I claimed to have lost mine during the holidays. My fantasy deflowering took place on a beach with someone who looked rather like Cindy Crawford. I think she was French.

I was a chatterer, a giggler, always laughing with my friend Rupert. I sat near the front in most lessons, keen and excited. We were a loud, competitive class, except Ben, who disguised a certain shyness with a studied, slow-moving calm.

'Too cool to talk, Hardiman?' the history master goaded. Ben did not give himself easily: obtaining his attention was, we found, an unusual pleasure. His eyes focused on you for slightly longer than you were used to, the gaze seeming to come to rest somewhere near the centre of your self. (We were all self-obsessed and had enough education to be consciously confused: we were just discovering words like 'ego' and 'ego trip', we gossiped and sniped about one another's 'images'.)

He smoked more or less constantly and so was more or less constantly in trouble: smoking and drinking were serious offences. It seemed unfair that he should be punished for an addiction, but then unfairness was routine and inherent in 'the system' (another phrase we used a lot): the first law of public school was Thou Shalt Not Get Caught. He was forever getting caught so we called him a waster, though if he drank more than us it was only because he had more friends in the years above and therefore more access to booze and parties.

*

9

Ben insists that Winona is his woman, the one for him. They are going out, basically. He is so firmly convinced of this that we are persuaded. For years if we read or hear about something Winona Ryder has done or someone she is seeing we gravely inform Ben: 'She's going out with so-and-so now, you know. You've got to dump her this time . . .'

He looks up, slowly raising an eyebrow. 'So-and-so?' Something crosses his expression, something hard to name. Bemusement? Pain? Then his focus comes back to you. 'Really?' he says softly. 'Is that true?'

'Yes! It's in *Sky*. She's taking the piss now – dump the bitch!'

He spits, a thoughtful white pellet projected several yards with an economic twitch of the mouth and a kind of wincing sound. 'Wch.'

He drags on his Marlboro, studying you. 'You read *Sky*?'

'You can't let her carry on like this. Kick her ass!'

'Hey – just cool it, 'k? Or I'll kick fuckin' *your* ass.'

'She's gone off you! She doesn't love you any more.'

'Nah. She does though.' Then, thoughtfully, 'It won't last. I might have to kick fuckin' so-and-so's ass if he doesn't get *off* her . . .'

'I'll do it for you.'

(Patient look, one eyebrow minutely suggesting you've lost it.) 'Cheers.'

'I don't know what she sees in him . . . wanker . . .'

'Wch.'

'Johnny Depp! Even looks a bit like you, just . . .'

'*Dumber.*'

'. . . not such a hopeless waster, I was going to say.'

He inspired widespread amazement and envy when as a mere second year he received a message from Sarah Harvey. Sarah Harvey was held to be the most beautiful girl of all those in the little town, in which there were three girls' schools. She was a tall blonde from Bermuda with gilt skin and tearing green eyes. She did not go out with school boys – College boys, as we thought of ourselves. She was in the Upper Sixth at the Girls' College, three years older than us. At the station once I saw her realize she had forgotten something and decide that there was time to get it and catch her train if she ran. She slipped off her shoes, gathered up her skirt and took off, away up the hill, running easily and fast.

Sarah – 'Sarah' (I still hear her name in a soft American accent, Ben's accent) – was the fairest of them all. Miles better than any of those who smouldered and simpered on our study walls, better than Belinda Carlisle, Kim Wilde, Linda Lusardi or Wendy James; if he had been caught in bed with Sam Fox we would not have been more impressed. It was unusual for any girl to show interest in a boy in the year below her (it was believed such things could not work, as if all those peer trysts ended in marriage, and the couple could expect to be teased for 'cradle-snatching'): three years below was unheard of. The message said that Sarah was a photographer. Would Ben let her take his picture?

He smoked, spat (he spat a great deal around this time), wondered whether he should charge, go nude, tell Winona . . .

Our English master is a tall and distinguished man, dark browed and affectedly mordant, elegant as a vampire, one of the few who can match any boy's cool. His classroom is up under the pitched roof of the main school building, a Victorian gothic construction, turreted and imposing. Through the windows you can see across the cricket pitches, the railway line and the garden-of-England view. This man has a reputation for favouring the most able or interesting pupils while having little to do with the rest. To earn approval or a high mark from him is a great thing among us. His charm is enhanced by his wryly intellectual manner, a quietly provocative, dark-polished irony. He is thought weird and slightly fearsome. None of us had found English so interesting or so difficult before we met him.

'Hardiman,' he says, slowly, as if inspecting the syllables.

'Yes – sir.'

The master raises his Victorian-gothic eyebrows. Hardiman returns his glance, frowning slightly, as if in confusion.

'Where is it?'

'Sirr?' (As if not in on some mild conspiracy.) 'What's that?'

(Muffled giggles from various boys. Sigh from the master.) 'Your ess-ay, Hardiman.'

'Ah.' (Long pause.) 'I – ah – seem to have misplaced that, sirr.'

'Mis*placed* it?'

'Yes. Sirr.'

Roars of laughter, but not from the master.

'You mean you haven't done it.'

Pause. Ben studies the distance, the desk, tries not to let our snorts and comments put him off. 'I wouldn't say I'd done all of it.'

'It's almost two weeks late. When can you do it?'

'Ah – soon.'

'Tonight?'

'Errr – that might be *pass*-ible – yes . . .'

'Good. I am on duty in Number 5 tonight. You could come and do it there.'

'Ahh –'

'You're in Number 8, aren't you?'

'Yes. I could do it there . . . preferably . . .'

'Yes. Well, I'll talk to Mr Smith. I'll find you somewhere quiet in Number 5, all right?'

'Sirr.'

'Hall starts at seven fifteen, doesn't it?' ('Hall' is two hours' home-work every week night, in silence, no leaving your study.)

Ben hesitates. Someone else shouts: 'He doesn't know!'

When finally he hands it in the master dangles the slim sheaf of paper distastefully between finger and thumb, holds it up and sniffs it, making a face. The writer looks up.

'It *stinks* of smoke.'

The class laugh; Ben winces: he stinks of it, too. Two days later the essay comes back marked: 42/45. Straight A. There will be one 44 in the next two years. I doubt Ben got many better marks in five: I did not. I only glimpsed a splinter of the notes for it – '. . . or Tom Faggot . . .' – and wondered where that fitted into three sides of literary criticism.

'So what happened?'

'Excuse me?'

'What fucking *happened*, Hardiman?'

'Christ dude, what are you on?'

'What happened with Sarah Harvey?'

'Who wants to know?'

'Oh please! Just tell me . . .'

'Nothing happened. Now get lost, man. Hit the road.'

'Are you really going out with her?'

'Going *out* with her? What's that?'

'Are you?'

'I wouldn't say that.'

'You are! I don't believe it! You – dog!'

'I'm actually just going to meet her so if you don't mind, you're a real fun guy an' all, but you have to go now – now! Before you get us all busted. Fuck off home, wouldya please?'

It is the summer of the Stone Roses. My friend Rupert says, 'Get this!' and the basement of his House fills with the longing, triumphant notes of 'Waterfall'. I cannot hear the words properly but the soft-edged, yearning chords fall like hot rain through the beckoning beat. *She'll carry on through it all – she's a waterfall.* Yes! I think, yes, yes! She will, she is. I am in love with a waterfall, a girl called Thea. She is the only American in the nearest girls' school. She is bright, she is beautiful, she has a loud, ready laugh and a hands-in-pockets, head-back look which makes me want to kiss her feet. I am not good-looking, not like Rupert or Ben, and near her I feel wretchedly ugly. My solution is clowning. I can make her laugh. I jump off the bridge into the river Severn at Upton which impresses her mildly but does not make her fancy me: the after-effect of the plunge marred by a large smear of sea-green snot. I ride back to the college in the evening on a borrowed bicycle and see Ben and Sarah together on the common, in the last of the sun. Sarah's golden hair and Ben, dark in his faded jeans, make them look like two lions doing a shampoo advert on a perfect set. The climate and flora of this part of England are absurdly fair in the summer – one patch of the common is known to everyone as 'the Timotei fields'. I stop. Ben pads over.

'Good *look*, dude. What have you done?'

'Jumped off the bridge at Upton.'

'Way to go. Was Thea there?'

'Yes she was.'

'Ha-ha-ha! You're *such* an *ass*. Nice work. That must have been fun.'

'Oh it was – just brilliant!'

'And may I ask what you're going to do next?'

'Probably have some supper.'

'Yeah? . . . *Wch* . . . Good. Very good. Enjoy your supper.'

I wave at Sarah, and she waves back. There is Sarah Harvey, summer herself in a field of gold, and there is Hardiman. I am proud of him. He seems to have honoured us, his friends, with this extraordinary conquest, effected with such ease. I long to sit in a field of long grass with a goddess but though I do not have anything like Ben's looks or his cool the fact that he has done it means it can be done. If Sarah Harvey is possible the fantastic is possible, everything is possible!

Sarah's photographs showed Ben in a coat and hat in a graveyard. He did not charge her, go nude or tell Winona. Nor did he tell us, until years later, that he found the whole thing terrifying and embarrassing, that he was out of his depth. We are all out of our depths. Thea kisses Rupert, which breaks my heart, but instead of soaring off into the sunset he looks abashed and awkward. 'She's got the sex drive of a bull,' he reports. I am not sure what that means.

The dormitories are silent, I am padding around in the dark, long after midnight. I slip into an empty study and stare through its window. A bright moon soothes the stars and casts a sheen over the vale of Evesham. I feel my way through a pile of someone's tapes and put one into the stereo. I turn the volume to zero, start the tape, and move the volume up, ever so slowly. A thin, distant voice begins to sing, and his song seems to laugh and lament at once, chiming exactly with the moon, the night and my mood: contrary, lonely but not alone, defiantly soulful. A voice which has lost much, found something, and longs for and points towards and promises something else.

Hey Mr Tambourine man play a song for me, I'm not sleepy and there is no place I'm going to . . . There is a prickle in my spirits, then a rush. Suddenly I am in exactly the right place, perfectly balanced between the huge, distant moon and the dark study, between sleep and waking, between my tiny, enclosed life and the vast dim vistas of my

dreams. *To dance beneath the diamond sky with one hand waving free* . . .
The night I discover Bob Dylan I know with absolute certainty, as
sure as my first love, my first orgasm, my first kiss, that everything has
changed, wonderfully, dangerously and for good.

Our English master gives us William Blake's *Songs of Innocence and
Experience*. 'The road of excess leads to the palace of wisdom,' we
read. The master's method is to sit back and cast his gaze slowly
around the room, raising a laconic eyebrow. 'Well?'

It looks self-explanatory. I cannot seem to grip Blake: what can
you say to his smooth and mighty aphorisms? 'The fool sees not the
same tree that the wise man sees.' So what? I think, and return to the
first. Oh give me excess, give me a road! It does not occur to me that
the fool and the wise man see not the same wisdom, that wisdom
might be a terrible thing, gained in the way the fool achieves it, a slim
and bitter compensation for all he has lost and wasted on the way.

The next book is *Out of the Shelter* by David Lodge. The shelter is
literal, an air-raid shelter, and figurative, the sanctuary of the hero's
childhood. A boy our age goes to post-war Germany where his big
sister is working, dating Americans, riding in big cars and thriving in
a foreign and adult world. On his first day she gives him a cigarette
but somehow it goes out. 'Cigarettes don't go out!' she says. He ends
up on a bed with his hand down a girl's knickers. I read and reread
the passage; his hand circling, creeping the last few centimetres
through the electrifying brush of her pubic hair, a marine smell and
something like a shrimp in a warm rock-pool trembling under his
fingertips.

Our English master watches us wryly. We are bursting out of our
shelters: some of us are erupting out of the pores of our own skins,
our acne like rhubarb and custard. My classroom notes are covered
in biro sketches of naked women and hand grenades. We are tormented by sudden knee-weakening erections: one of my friends,
Tom, is struck by a spontaneous orgasm on the way to the Art
Department. 'I thought I was dying or something,' he says, awed. 'I
wasn't even thinking anything in particular, just walking across
the lawn and then fuck me, I'm coming! Out of nowhere. *Really
coming!* . . . In my pants.'

The world is coming out with us. One evening the house television room rings with whoops and cheers, as if the rugby team has just scored a dashing try: the Berlin Wall is being overrun. Another night the TV room explodes in a storm of noise, an ululating roar, shot through with groans and cries. Now what? We rush into pandemonium: everyone has gone mad. They are on their feet, howling. Chairs have been overturned, boys are punching the walls, the air, each other; they clutch their heads, claw their faces and pump their groins towards the television, howling and laughing hysterically. Vanessa Paradis is performing her song 'Joe le Taxi' on *Top of the Pops*. She looks about our age and is wearing a T-shirt without, apparently, a bra. 'She's – pure – Girls' College!' roars Stevens, one of our meatheads, a muscle-bound boy who excels in the cadet corps. He seizes a chair and bashes it repeatedly against the floor. 'Pure – Fucking – Girls' College!' She may be gorgeous and she may be French but Stevens is right: she is also one of us, just not mewed up in an English public school. Ainley storms forward and pretends to snog the television, making rutting noises. We shout at him to get out of the way but we sympathize entirely: there is a thin glass screen between us and the world and we are desperate to rut through it.

Marijuana comes first as a rumour, a dark and forbidden something, out of the question but barely beyond reach. 'Drugs', we are taught, are a kind of living death. The slippery slope, the beginning of the end, the first step to heroin and hellfire. Just say no, they tell us. Cannabis will lead you to other drugs, they say, to cocaine, to heroin and to death. 'Drugs' seem remote, not the kind of thing nice children do, except someone's cousin you have never met who is 'hooked', a vague and spectral warning exchanged among parents. We feel quite safe. We do not know any 'pushers' and anyway we are much more interested in alcohol.

Alcohol is a dangerous drug, they admit, but when you are old enough, in the Upper Sixth, you will be able to buy it legally and as long as you are careful and learn to use it responsibly there should be no problem. Until then stay away from it, they say, or you will be in serious trouble. Naturally we do everything we can to obtain it: of all the prizes of maturity which are denied to us – women, freedom, self-determination – alcohol is the easiest to access. All we have to do is fake some ID or persuade an older boy to buy it for us. We all know someone in the years above who does 'offie runs' for his peers. If he likes you, and perhaps for a small commission, you can order something too.

In the basement of Number 8, Ben's house, with him and a thin wild boy called Miles I get drunk for the first time. I am fourteen. We sit around in the semi-dark, under the damp arches of the gloomy cellar, our clothes bruised with dust, the other two smoking (I am opposed to this habit of my mother's which I loathe, which had killed my uncle in his mid forties) and all of us drinking. They have cans of lager; I have a two-litre bottle of cider which goes down easily, sweetly, until suddenly I am giggling, stumbling drunk.

At six o'clock the next morning I am face down in the shower bringing up strings of surprisingly yellow bile. I do not say never again: on the contrary, intoxication was great. The vomiting was unfortunate but not an unreasonable price for the hilarious evening in the basement. Intoxication without vomiting would be even better. Most importantly, I can now say that I have been drunk and thrown up. I want to be able to say all sorts of things. I want to say I have tried this, I have done that, I have kissed her . . .

'What does it look like?'

Our dormitory is going to bed. In one corner Garston is cursing me and picking his way through the minefield of cod liver oil tablets I have sown in the carpet around his bed. He douses himself with more Kouros in an attempt to cover their smell. (All of us have an aftershave, though we are only shaving twice a week.) Next to him Spod (so called because he has a huge nose and a giant penis – we believe there is a correlation) is taking out his contact lenses and making sure his hair band is within easy reach. Once the duty prefect has put out the light Spod will pull on his hair band, pinning back his fringe, thus, he claims, preventing zits forming on his forehead. In the bed opposite mine Cox is rereading the autobiography of his hero, the great goalkeeper Pat Jennings. I am trying to talk to Olly, whose bed is in the far corner. He is folding his clothes lovingly.

He has an entire wardrobe from Next and, he tells us, great dress sense. Olly is tallest, loudest and strongest of us. He, Cox and I are from south Wales. Their parents have flourished under Thatcher. Olly's father runs a building business. When he wants to goad me, Olly capers around chanting, 'Maggie Maggie Maggie!' Most of the boys in my house have huge stereos and expensive clothes but there is no snobbery or elitism about them: they are the sons of self-made men who intend to go on to make their own fortunes.

We are living in the age of cash and flash and success, the triumph of the individual. Our magazines are full of yuppies, fast cars, ever cooler Walkmans, glossy babes and stories of boys not much older than us who have made fortunes out of illegal acid house parties. 'Designer' is the current craze. Designer clothes, designer stubble, designer aftershave, designer cars. 'Shut your mouf and look at my WAD – loadsa MONEY!' shouts Harry Enfield's character, and Olly sometimes copies him, only lightly ironic. We are all fans of the Wedding Present, the Inspiral Carpets and the Clash. *Daddy was a bank robber, he never hurt no-body*, we sing. *When they kick down your front door – how you gonna come – with your hands on your head – or the trigger of your gun? O-oh, the guns of Brixton* . . . we chorus, as if 'they' are a woolly amalgamation of the police, whom we have never met, our teachers, the system and adulthood.

Olly pauses, catches sight of his face in the mirror, swoops in, studies it, touches the scar which runs parallel to his nose. He turns his head a little.

'Fuck me,' he murmurs, absently. 'I really am *incredibly* good-looking.'

For once no one laughs or abuses him, except Garston, half-heartedly.

'Fuck off, Chamberlaine,' Garston dimples. Olly looks up, a wolfhound buzzed by a bee. Nicholas Garston has dark, almost feminine looks. He is pudgier than the rest of us and one of the few who really does need a shave. He has a chaotic strength. 'Set 6 for everything, thick as shit!' Olly sometimes shouts at him, but Nick Garston just laughs. I realize, when I pay him any attention, that Garston knows a bigger, glitzier, more sophisticated world than we do. He has been to raves, for one thing; he can even do rave dancing, scissoring his arms in the air and rocking hectically in what looks like rhythm.

'Fuck off yourself, Garston, you yid!' Olly shouts gleefully. 'Hooknose!'

The Life of Brian is a craze. Cox can recite entire scenes, doing all the voices perfectly in the dark, after lights out. Garston is Jewish, which means nothing to us beyond the connection with the film.

Garston raises a fist as if to punch him. Olly bares his teeth invitingly. Garston declines.

'Chamberlaine . . .?' I prompt.

'What? Dope? It's a bit like a rubber – yeah, yeah, an eraser – but brown.'

'What do you do with it?'

'You hold it over a flame and it goes soft and then you crumble it into a fag and smoke it.'

'What's it like?'

'It's really funny. Like, I dunno, it makes you laugh – you laugh a lot, you can't stop. It's hilarious. And then really mellow. We should get some. It's great. You would be really funny on it, you fucking nutter . . .'

'Shit!' Garston cries, stooping suddenly. 'You're suchafuckingtwat, Clare!'

'Piss off, Garston, they're good for you. Is it very different from being pissed?'

'Yeah. You don't hallucinate or anything but it's like' (making peace sign and putting on hippy voice) 'everything's beautiful, man!'

'How long does it last?'

Olly shrugs. 'Depends, but if you just had one joint, maybe an hour.'

'I'd like to try it.'

'Yeah . . . I'll bring some back next time I go to Cardiff . . .'

Olly never does bring back any dope from Cardiff. When finally I see some it looks nothing like a rubber and it is not brown. I am in School House in Miles' study with another friend, Rob, wondering how much of Miles' collection of cult and classic literature he had actually read, admiring the tie-dyed sheets which cloak his study walls, mulling the reek of his joss sticks, undecided whether I like it or not, and listening to the House of Love and the Cure.

'*I've been looking so long at these pictures of you that I almost believe that they're real, I've been living so long with my pictures of you that the pictures are all I can feel . . .*' keens Robert Smith, the singer of the Cure, and my spirits keen with him. I imagine I am in love, in love with the one girl in all the world for me, who has left me, and my heart synthesizes the agony perfectly, so that I am half imagining being tearful and exhausted, and half feeling it.

It is Saturday night so I am wearing my poncho. I had been watching my father's collection of Clint Eastwood tapes and fancied myself as a taciturn loner, riding into one-horse towns, squinting into the sun and impressing women. My mother thought it a lovely idea when I said I wanted a poncho for my birthday. Unable to find a shop which sold them, she bought a beautiful, soft tartan blanket, cut a slit in the middle and stitched its edges with blue thread. It is deliciously warm and comfortable and I think it makes me look great. Everyone else thinks it ridiculous. Olly and Cox laugh themselves sick.

'Freak! Weirdo!'

'Clint!'

'Twat!' they agree.

I shrug and grin and wear it anyway. I have decided that I will have to be a loner and an oddball until my destiny comes to find me. (She is an Italian goddess in a Valentino advert I have torn from *Sky* magazine: I am convinced that wearing a blanket is exactly the sort of thing which will make her fall for me, hopelessly and for ever.)

The door bucks open and Miles lurches in.

'Fucking *Ruddy's* got some!' he cries.

'Got what?'

'Dope,' Rob says, with one of his thoughtful looks. Rob has a kind of dreaminess about him; he purses his lips and shakes his head slowly.

'In his study behind his stereo,' Miles announces breathlessly. 'Let's lift it.'

Rob looks dubious. He and Miles regard Ruddy with an affectionate disdain, the same way Olly looks at Garston, the way all hustlers look at victims, bemused by their folly and aroused by their weakness. Ruddy is small with a squeaky voice, the ludicrous floppy fringe we all wear and the face of a pretty girl. He smells of smoke and toothpaste. Like Garston he seems to fall into trouble by accident rather than deliberate mischief.

'Come on!' Miles leads the way. 'I'll watch for him, you get it.'

Rob and I invade the study, Rob palpably reluctant. He shifts about uneasily while I investigate. Behind the stereo Ruddy has driven a pin into the wall. Dangling from it on a blue thread is a film capsule. Inside the capsule is a tiny bag of what looks like dried herbs.

'This stuff?'

'Yeah,' Rob says, fingering it.

Miles' head appears. 'Got it? Give it here.' He stuffs it into his pocket, glancing up and down the corridor. 'Right, go! Go.'

We flit out of school and take the Chimney – a long, tight path which climbs straight up towards the common and the crowded woods which gird the hillside. At the top we cross a road and plunge into bushes.

There is nowhere more desolate and strange in the limited compass of our world than this interzone where the town meets the country. Man's chemical light dripping through the branches and running down the trunks; litter lying in the boles of trees. This is where they would dump the bodies, where the animals and birds move seldom and silently, where few penetrate and no one lingers. We have travelled only a few yards into it when Miles, panting, halts.

'Enough – stop. Can't see a fucking thing . . .' He crouches down and moves around carefully until his hands are in a patch of the orange wash from the street lights below. I watch as he rolls a cigarette between his finger and thumb, squeezing the tobacco into his palm. When the paper tube is empty he pulls out the bag of herbs and pours it into his hand. He mixes the two substances and starts to stuff the blend back into the paper tube.

Rob and I grin at each other, our faces pallid in the gloom. For the first time I feel that marvellous anticipation I will come to know so well. What will happen? What awaits, moments away? What knowledge, what bliss, what horrors attend us, gathered like goblins in the straggling wood?

Miles has finished. He straightens up and lights it. He draws on it a few times and passes it to Rob. Rob takes his turn. Any second now it will come to me. We would be expelled for this. Expelled! There is no more terrifying word in a public school boy's lexicon but we are not afraid. No one is going to catch us out here. Rob passes it to me. It feels loose and fragile, the butt is slightly wet. I put it to my lips and squeeze my cheeks in as smokers do, then I open my mouth and gulp in air.

'Horatio,' says Rob, doubtful and amused. 'Do you know how to inhale?'

'No!' Miles puts in.

'Well, I don't smoke.'

I try again. Rob coaches me. I make gasping sounds. It tastes of chemicals and heat. Miles stretches out a hand. My head spins slightly. I feel something, a sickly twinge which passes. The thing will be finished before my turn comes again and I am secretly relieved. I watch the way the smoke puffs across the shafts of street light; a beautiful, hypnotic thing.

The heart of the school and the start of its day is Chapel. To ensure our attendance we are each issued with a card bearing our name: we hand it to one of the prefects guarding the door, who will return it to the Housemaster, who will check it against his list: woe betide you if your card fails to come back to him. You will get an 'Ernie', which means rising before six and going to see Ernie, the Head Porter. Ernie will give you a rag and polish and send you off to buff up some fittings. Olly and Cox turn this spectacularly to their advantage one morning when Ernie fails to supervise their activities in the Masters' Bar: they fasten their mouths around the nozzles of the beer taps like delinquent babies and reappear at breakfast, staring drunkenly and laughing.

The prefects eye us as we file in. Are our shoes polished, our shirts clean, our ties neat, our hairstyles in some sort of order? Hovering near them is 'Bomber', a young and energetic chemistry teacher infamous for his love of discipline, attention to detail and the relish and expertise with which he sniffs out malefactors and busts them. His chilly, penetrating expression suggests he knows your innermost deviancies. 'If he did not exist we would have to invent him,' our English master retorts, when we moan.

'Newell!' Bomber cracks suddenly. 'Come here, Newell.'

Newell is wearing brown suede shoes, the rebel's favourite. His top button is missing, his shirt hanging out and his tie is a road-killed snake, dirty and awry.

'Aw, whaa . . .?' he whines, indignant. Bomber's freezing glare sweeps over us and our sniggers die in our throats. Bomber is very tall and Newell is short. The master looms over him like Zeus.

'Boy, you are a *disgrace*. Back to the house and change. *Shut* up. Go. That's an Ernie, Newell. And take your card with you.'

That's a double Ernie. The rest of us slink in to give thanks to God.

The pews are raked up on either side of the aisle, facing each other. Six hundred of us minus Newell squeeze into our blocks, house by house, prefects dotted among us like riot police, glaring and hissing and threatening the whisperers. The masters sweep down the nave as if borne by the air billowing in their black gowns, bob to the altar and turn, gliding up to their perches in the alcoves behind us. The feel of their eyes on the back of our heads stills us. Cox assumes an attitude of prayer. A smile spreads slowly among the boys on either side of him: Cox has brought his Pat Jennings book.

The organ's meditations die away. For a moment there is silence. We are drawn up, arraigned and made ready, almost as still as the figures in the stained glass windows above us. The brightest will go to Oxford, Cambridge or Edinburgh. The Foreign Office, Whitehall and the Treasury expect them. Others will go to the newspapers, television, the BBC. Business and industry will take a slew of us; the City, law and accountancy will account for dozens. Some will be soldiers, one or two will be sportsmen or artists; many more will be managers and consultants.

From where we sit, the traditionally trouble-making scruffs of the Remove, the world is a brutal pyramid. Below us are the Foundation Year, the 'splits', only just out of prep school, their voices creaking, their little balls just beginning to drop. Below them are the unfortunate masses, not clever enough to win scholarships, not rich enough to buy their way in. Above us are the Hundred (who have girlfriends), then the Lower Sixth (a law unto themselves) and the Upper Sixth, bound up in A-levels and university interviews. On top of them are the Head Boy and his deputy, the

Masters, the law-givers, the Deputy Head and the Chaplain, the Head Man and our parents, towering over us in ever richer, more powerful and shorter ranks, all the way to the government, the cabinet, Margaret Thatcher and Ronald Reagan, answerable only to God.

Now the organ proclaims Him and the doors bang shut. We come to our feet in a rustled rumble and heads turn as one. First come his outriders, two College Prefects, then the Head Man himself, features immobile as a gargoyle, set in a righteous scowl. I look over at the Number 8 boys. No sign of Ben: he has a friendly prefect who will slip his card into the collected pile, granting him an extra hour in bed. Cunning Hardiman, I envy him. The familiar tension rises in my chest. I want to scream in Chapel, to shatter the silence, to loose outrage, confusion and disgrace, to set them at the pyramid like a pack of wild dogs. Sometimes I pretend I suffer from amnesia and screaming fits. I imagine they have all been told that I sometimes howl then instantly forget it, and they have learned to ignore me. Perhaps I was screaming just now, howling obscenities at the bastard Head Man (hence his expression); perhaps the straight-faced throng are in a vast conspiracy to deny my maniacal raving, to hold me close to their blazered ranks and their bored, bored eyes.

What fools we were, what fools, gorging on toast, bloody toast, on girls, on the idea of girls, which was the same thing, all the grass forbidden, the night time out of bounds, chained to games, doing press-ups in an October gale, the PE master shouting 'Gor! Look at you, your girlfriends don't have much to worry about!' Well no, we thought, they bloody don't. Orange juice, bloody orange juice – Ben would go through a carton of it every sullen Saturday night. We tramped and tramped the slow rising streets, zigzagging up and down the hill, looking for girls and the good time and realizing finally that neither existed, until we found the station, where with them we drank rotten coffee (for the image) and hot chocolate for the sugar – oh God, the sugar! Filling all the café tables with our longings and grimacing at every train, at their noise and the fact that we weren't on them, or getting off – getting off! Did you get off with her? – getting off or on with a traveller's bag and a narrow look to take it all in, the girls, us, the Barry Manilow poster that was there for years, and wishing for a ticket to take us the hell away.

One December night in the Winter Gardens, staring at the duck pond, we sat in our suits, Ben's cigarette the only thing moving and at least three rules like broken glass around our feet (out of the House at night, out of the Grounds at night, Smoking) and all for the love of E. J. Major (oh God, E. J. Major! Justin's fatal, gorgeous sixth-form sister) who was smoking in solitude a few feet away. 'Shall we do it?' we whispered. 'Hell yes, let's do it!' and calm as camomile we did it on three. We upped and sauntered, one, two – and flung ourselves headlong into the duck pond, shattering the black stillness in shallow dives, into the judder and punch of the rocky bottom and the hysterical cold, the ducks having kittens, their shit webbing our fingers as we reeled back in triumph to E. J. Major, Ben asking politely for a cigarette while her shoulders shook. 'You're both out of your minds,' she laughed and we were, we were.

'Well,' we shivered. 'We've got to go to Stratford now, see *Coriolanus*,' and off we shogged, dripping majestically, heroes at last.

'D-do you think she w-was impressed?'

'Oh f'sure!'

'Th-that was b-brilliant!'

'Uh-huh. *Genius*.'

I left *Coriolanus* at half time and went to an off-licence with Nick. Parading the length of the shop, homing in on the sherry, I realized I was 'smoking' (still not inhaling) and stubbed the thing out on the sleeve of my coat, dropping the butt calmly into my pocket. I grabbed the sherry and approached the till, presenting the bottle and a tenner.

'No,' laughed the man behind the counter. 'Just *no*.'

Our glorious, terrifying French master gives us *L'Étranger* and *Waiting for Godot* while professing himself impatient for our 'intellectual balls to drop'. In Camus and Beckett we discover the absurd and the existential. The French master waves his arms: 'Ah mean,' he says, ''ave you ever looked at a tree? Really looked at it, as if you 'ave never seen a tree before? 'Abit! You see it through 'abit and you do not see it!

'Abit is the screen between you and the universe!' We wrestle with 'abit, and questions of being and morality in the absence of God.

Our English master teaches us to read with scrupulous attention: beyond the words, in the structure, in the form of poetry, in what it implies, alludes to and does not say is also its meaning. Turning these discoveries on our own existence, we find that school tradition insists that hierarchy is underwritten by an ineffable righteousness, by an unquestionable authority, by something like God. Except that it is questionable, and what is this 'God'? We sing the plodding school song in Latin as if to underline that understanding is granted to the few and defined by the ignorance of the many. School politics suggest we should love Thatcher, whom I have been raised to loathe, fear socialism and dread the possibility of a Labour government (it is whispered that they would shut us down, cast us into the bear-pit of the state schools and confiscate parents' Range Rovers through punitive taxes). School culture allows the torment of the strange, the weak and the fey; it fears homosexuality, detests nonconformity and is suspicious of difference.

Unable to alter or resist the system we settle for irritating it. Cigarettes and booze are a pedestrian solution but we begin to find other protests. Two boys in the Hundred borrow a milk float and joy-ride it along College Road until they reach the bend, where they find the wheel will not turn: this float is equipped with a steering lock. They wrench at it and the wheel comes off. Attempts at guidance without the wheel are in vain. A policeman appears. The hijackers take refuge behind a parked car. Underneath it, they watch the policeman's boots advancing towards them. The story leaves a deep impression on me. I imagine them stuffing their fists into their mouths to stop their giggles, vainly trying to dam the glee and terror of the moment.

One evening towards the end of term the boys in the year above us, who have done their GCSEs, emerge like flying ants, by strange consensus, carrying files and boxes full of notes. Everything is to be burned in the brick incinerator between our house and Number 4. Number 4 are our closest rivals and they are wild. While we in Number 6 are governed by a kind and decent man, their housemaster, known as Smeg, is a former Royal Marine who rules by fear. Punishment for infringement in Smeg's maths class is physical. While the rest wrestle with matrices, one or other of us is either in the corner doing press-ups or running pointlessly around the Triangle. Smeg's effect on his house is marked: when they let off steam it is something to see. Number 4 come pouring out with their files and fling them on the pyre. One of our boys produces an aerosol and throws it in. We run, squealing with laughter, and it goes off. We dance around, egging each other on. Suddenly there is a ripple of alarm among the watchers: a lone figure charges out of Number 4, sprinting towards the fire. He clutches a squat blue canister.

'Shit!' someone shouts. 'Butane!'

Unburned notes flutter to the ground, the grass is strewn with abandoned files and the paths thud with the footsteps of fleeing boys. There are a couple of breathless beats and then the detonation: a furious bang, a giant *whump!* and a mushroom of flame gusting into the evening air. We all dive into our studies, hearts thumping, ears pricked for the approach of a retribution which does not come.

Our English master invites five of us for drinks. We make our way up the hill to his flat. It is another trembling summer evening. Most boys are playing games while the lucky few meet girls: summer is the lovers' time; you are more likely to be caught but every grassy bank is a bed. Olly is lying on the common with Claudia. I watched him woo her at the end of term disco: he marched up, opened a palm to reveal two cigarettes and nodded at the door. Masterful. Cox is giving a virtuoso performance of Crockets, a House version of cricket played with different rules for different kinds of tennis balls. Cox's bright eyes zero in on each new missile and with serpentine speed he strikes, dispatching them according to the code. A cheese (a dead ball with no bounce) is smashed away over the roof of the racquets court; a flaming onion (a cheese soaked in lighter fluid and ignited just before launch) is smacked straight back at the bowler, trailing smoke like a meteorite. There is not a ball in creation that Cox cannot command.

'There's Pimms,' our English master intones. 'Form an orderly queue.'

We grab glasses and shuffle up. The Pimms is an orange-red resin colour topped with a creamy froth and spears of green mint. There is a sad-sweetness in the atmosphere I associate with all this time. Our English master is leaving, going to be head of department in a famous school near London.

'Do smoke if you want to, Ben,' he murmurs. 'Have any of you seen *If*?'

We watch as Malcolm McDowell's schoolboy hurtles around the countryside with a girl on the back of his motorbike and later machine-guns masters, pupils and parents from the chapel roof. 'Better form another orderly queue.'

The queues become more disorderly as the Pimms goes down. The sun sets. Beyond the windows the chinking blackbirds and the wooing pigeons fall silent. Above the hills the sky turns russet, violet and satin blue at last, that echoed twilight which seems to carry the light over its span in midsummer, as though the air wore day's bright shawl over night's dark gown. It is goodbye now. 'Be well,' our master says, quietly.

The following term my list of favoured teachers is down to three: my housemaster, the History man and the French master. The rumblings in our group grow louder. To hell with this place and its bullshit. To hell with the way it makes us see girls as sex objects: they're turning us into tossers. To hell with the system. We get caught drinking sweet German wine in a car park and are punished according to our records. I am 'gated', banned from leaving the school grounds or from wearing anything other than uniform or games kit; Ben is 'rusticated': suspended for two weeks.

I am desperate to leave, to go somewhere else for sixth form. My mother has heard of an international school in south Wales. A Bulgarian girl shows me around the grounds of a castle on the coast of the Bristol Channel. The students wear their own clothes. They call their teachers by their first names. They are all on scholarships: rich and poor live as equals, side by side in mixed houses, boys and girls together. Here there is no tortured, arcane traditionalism; in place of the school motto, 'Sapiens qui prospicit' (wise is the man who plays cricket, as we thought of it), is an ideal, International

Understanding. There is Service instead of Games: I could drive lifeboats instead of playing bloody football! There are hundreds of beautiful girls! I apply for a scholarship.

In the Spring term we learn we are to be given a week off to revise for our mock GCSEs. This means no homework, which means 'hall' is free time (unless you actually need to revise for these mocks), which means Olly and I wait for the corridors to go quiet and the duty prefect to settle into *Mein Kampf* (everyone was always 'doing the Nazis'), then climb out of our windows and set off for the girls' school up the hill. We were looking for girls, not drugs.

'Up the road?' he whispers.

'No, through Smith's garden is better.'

'Smith! That bastard's a Jerry . . .'

Olly is living in a deliberately juvenile war film but the parallels are perfect.

'Shh! What could possibly go wrong?' (It's one of our catch-phrases.)

'And he's got a jerry dog!'

'If you shut up it won't hear us. Here's the fence . . .'

'Alarmed?'

'Me or the fence?'

'Get on . . .'

The grounds of the girls' school are thick with shrubbery, deep shadowed under looming trees. We flit from bush to bush, duck in and out of rhododendrons, Olly levelling his fingers like a pistol every time we round a corner. And then there is the bench, huddled shapes and murmur of voices. Pip, Paula, Claudia and our mate Nick.

'Jerries!' Olly hisses and leaps out, 'gun' drawn. Swearing and giggles. We sit down. They have dope, a tiny lump of darkness in the dark, but no cigarette papers. They are using an envelope. It passes from hand to hand. Again I fail to feel anything. I still have not learned to inhale but it is darker this time and I do not think anyone notices. Olly and I go back to college and find we have not been missed.

A few days later we have a divinity lesson with the new chaplain, who has discipline problems. I filch the whiteboard cleaner, which squirts water. I do Rupert in the ear. He does Quentin in the face. Shermer, a wild boy, cuts loose with it. Uproar. The Reverend 'Lippy' Lewis loses his temper. The entire class is in detention. The lesson will be restaged next Tuesday at 7 a.m.

Come the Tuesday we are all too dazed to make trouble. Lewis drones his thoughts into respectful silence, but as we are nearing the end, and thinking about breakfast, the door opens. Mr Blackstone, the Deputy Head, a man who emphatically does not have discipline problems, looks terse.

'Excuse me, Mr Lewis. Reynolds and Clare, the Headmaster's Study. Now.'

We stand. Everyone grins uncertainly, including Lippy. Reynolds looks guilty but then Reynolds always looks guilty.

'Way to go, dude,' Ben says admiringly.

I cannot imagine what this is about. We march along the corridor and up the main stair. Outside the dreaded study is Olly Chamberlaine, looking pale. They haul me in first.

They are sitting in a semicircle facing an empty chair. 'Sit down,' Blackstone says.

There is the Head Man, my housemaster, Bomber and the Head Boy, who looks as if he might be trying not to enjoy himself. They are all smart, in their shiny ties, like businessmen, except my housemaster, who will always look like a friendly history teacher in thick glasses.

'Last night,' the Head Man begins (oh thank God, I wasn't doing anything last night, they can't touch me), 'the Drugs Squad were called to the Girls' School.'

I see it. I feel my face flush. 'Several girls have admitted to smoking cannabis cigarettes, and they have told the Drugs Squad that you were involved last week. Now, I want the truth. You are in a serious position and the best thing you can possibly do is be straight with us. Did you smoke cannabis?'

I can feel my pulse in my neck. The rest of me has drained away through holes in my shoes.

'I don't know.'

'What do you mean you don't know?'

'Someone passed me a cigarette and I took two drags on it but nothing happened.'

'Did you know it had cannabis in it?' Blackstone demands. I can see he is trying to help but I have already gone too far.

'I wasn't sure.'

The Head Man resumes. 'But you thought it did?'

'Yes.'

'Who gave it to you?'

'I can't remember. One of the girls.'

'Who did you give it to?'

'One of the girls.'

'Did Olly and Nick smoke it too?'

'No.'

'This is a police matter now. We're trying to help you and I seriously advise you not to lie. Did they or not?'

'No.'

'Go and wait outside.'

They have a go at the other two, one at a time, then haul us all in together.

'I think one of you is mostly telling the truth and the other two are lying. The girls have said you all smoked it. I believe them. Now I want to get this straight and hear the truth from all of you.' He looks at me. 'Did you smoke it?'

'Yes.'

'Olly?'

Olly looks him in the eye, head up, and says clearly, 'Yes, sir.'

'Nick?'

Nick is flushed with anger. 'Yes . . .' he says quietly, almost trembling with the effort of not telling them to fuck themselves.

'Thank you. Go and wait outside.'

We stand outside his office staring across the Triangle and the cricket pitches. Chapel has finished and boys are heading to their first lessons. It is a bright spring day. Mr Corbin appears, the only suave maths teacher I have ever met, who coaches the rugby team.

'Smoking dope? Is it true?'

'Yes, sir,' Olly answers.

'How many of the rugby team involved?'

'Us three.'

'Bloody *hell*,' he says. 'Idiots!' He stalks off angrily.

'Fair enough,' Olly says thoughtfully, watching him go. 'He's got to find a new Flanker, a new Number 8 and a new Centre by this afternoon. We just need a new school . . .'

'I'm sorry,' I start, 'I should have denied it. I said you didn't . . .'

'Don't worry about it. They didn't believe us.'

'Fucking bastards,' Nick hisses. We stare out of the windows. No doubt our housemasters are putting up a fight, but we all know what is going to happen.

We are isolated from the rest of the school, eating lunch with the housemaster's wife and, bizarrely, Sarah Harvey's current boyfriend, who is a friend of the housemaster, and who regales us with stories about riding on the roofs of trains. It all seems unreal. We are confined to the forbidden areas of the school, the masters' studies, hallways and sitting rooms where boys do not go. In the afternoon we are interviewed by the Drugs Squad. On the way to meet them we are escorted past the rugby team, where we should be, in the coach, waiting to be driven to the match. They stare at us through the windows, their expressions a kind of woeful fascination. Olly gives them a V-sign and there is a ripple of silent laughter. Cox is in tears. Suddenly, though it does not stop feeling unreal, it becomes terrible.

The Drugs Squad are two small men in leather jackets. They do not seem very intelligent, which is fortunate as we have decided to lie to them. We do not want to drag anyone else into trouble but we believe it will be worse for the girls if we say it was our first time: we imagine they will pay an extra price for introducing us to it. We therefore need to concoct a previous history which implicates no one. I tell them I tried it one New Year's Eve on the beach at Brighton, supplied by a man whose name I pluck at random from an Alistair Maclean novel. They let me go eventually, but as I reach for the door handle one of them says:

'Oh Mr Clare, just one more thing. Have you got any drugs in your study?'

It seems such a clichéd trick I stumble for a second, unable to take it seriously. Then I remember I might actually have some drugs in my study: drying on the radiator are ten or so wispy little mushrooms which I had been hoping might turn out to be magic. I hesitate. 'Drugs in my study? Er, no!' I splutter. They seem satisfied.

Olly notices the officer charged with taking his statement is not at ease with written English and chooses his words thoughtfully: 'We conglomerated in the Girls' School at about half past eight . . .' We do not know what Nick's strategy is but the door flies open at the end of his interview and the three of them tumble out, red faced, Nick with a defiant glint about him. 'That kid's got an attitude problem!' one of the officers blurts. We grin, proudly.

We return to our houses for sentencing. My housemaster looks tired. There is no bombast or anger about him. He says simply, 'All three of you are being expelled. You will be allowed back next term to take your exams but when your last GCSE is finished you must leave immediately. While you are here you will be gated. The police are only going to give you a caution because this is your first offence. You had better telephone your mother. If possible she should come to pick you up tomorrow.'

'Yes, sir.'

'I am very, very sorry,' he says.

'Me too, sir.'

'I'll let you talk to your mother. You can use my phone.'

He withdraws and I dial the number. I can hear it ringing. I feel sure she is there. I imagine her crossing the kitchen towards it. She picks up.

'Hello?' she says, happy and excited, hoping it will be me or my brother.

'Hello, Mum.'

'Hello, darling! How are you?'

'Not good, Mum. Something bad's happened. Really bad . . .'

'Oh God, what?' The breath has been squeezed out of her.

'Me and Olly and Nick went to the girls' school last week and the girls had some cannabis and we tried it . . .'

'Oh *God*.'

'The girls got caught doing it and they gave our names.'

'Christ. Are you being suspended?' Her voice is a whisper now. The shame of it, suspended.

'We're all being expelled, Mum. I'm sorry. I'm so sorry . . .'

'Expelled!' she gasps. 'You're being expelled?' She starts to cry. 'I can't believe it. I just – can't – believe it. After everything . . . you're being thrown out?'

'Yes, Mum. I'm so sorry.' For the first time I really am. The sound of her crying makes me cry.

'How could you?' she cries. 'How could you be so stupid? What on earth are you going to do now?'

'They want you to come and get me, Mum.'

'When?'

'Tomorrow.'

'Well,' she says, eventually, in a voice which sounds flat and beaten. 'That's that then.'

Our middle-ranking school did not produce prime ministers. One famous name became an actor feted for his portrayals of decent, loveable men crushed and harried by the world. He was invited back once to present prizes at the end of term and asked by the Headmaster if he had enjoyed his time there. The actor replied that not until his psychiatrist's bills passed the amount his parents had spent in fees would the damage the school had inflicted upon him begin to be repaired. By far the most famous alumnus was Aleister Crowley. He was supposed to have sacrificed a cat in the college chapel: like much that was written and said about him in his lifetime this is probably untrue. It is not possible to say how much of the school's formative effect on his thinking was responsible for his creed: 'Do what thou wilt shall be all of the law.'

I had been well taught. Essays and exams would never frighten me and I knew I loved books, and writing. I had kissed four girls by the time I left, which made me feel like Casanova. I had made friendships which I believed would last my whole life long. I had, in sum, entirely erroneous and inflated ideas of my own sexual and intellectual prowess, and an optimistic view of my chances in the world. Many sixteen-year-old boys feel this way, public school or not.

My moral development was no more unusual, except perhaps among the privileged, where I had been. Authority, be it the Police, Thatcher, Religion, the Law or Public Opinion, seemed to me always questionable, if not plainly hypocritical and odious. If you 'toed the line' and 'kept your nose clean' authority would not molest you, went the deal – but it was a bargain I was unwilling to strike. I hated those expressions. I loathed the image of all of us lined up, like bloody Cadet Corps, with our toes just touching the line. It made me want to hurl myself over it, whooping and capering like a gibbon until they shot me. What were you supposed to do with lines if not step over them? And 'keeping your nose clean', a favourite expression of my housemaster's wife, seemed quite disgusting, as if my nose was constantly, naturally dirtying itself, and in order to remain on the housemistress's good side I should be continually cleaning it, like a cat licking the back of its paw and rubbing its face. I felt like daubing my conk with charcoal in protest.

In spite of itself, public school taught me that not only was breaking the law tremendous fun but that it might also, in various circumstances, be morally right. Why should sixteen-year-old boys not meet girls their own age? Why should we not wear brown shoes, walk on the grass, smoke cigarettes, drink occasionally? Why not jump off bridges, listen to Dylan all night, skip chapel and football?

My parents had inadvertently helped form some of this streak in me. My mother was a rebel and a romantic but I had reached the argumentative age. We had always been close but now I tried to assert myself, often by disagreeing with her. Had she said do not obey stupid rules, I might have obeyed them just to defy her. My feelings for my father were more complicated. He had always stressed the importance of thinking for yourself, and of not marching in step just because everyone else did. I felt a mixture of resentment at his having left my mother, my brother and me when we were young, and adoration. Sometimes I despaired at the thought that I would be like him (he had many relationships but never a happy marriage), but more often I wanted to be like him, to be clever and competent and strong and successful (he was an award-winning journalist). I felt my defiance somehow came from him, and honoured him. I did not realize that it might be directed at him.

On the night of our expulsion our housemaster gathered the house and spoke to them. Olly and I sneaked along a back corridor and listened. They probably all knew by now, he said, what had happened. A tragedy for us and our parents, a tragedy for the school, and a heavy blow for the House. It was no secret, he said, that Olly and I had been heading for great things. He expected I would have been made Head of House, and Olly our College Prefect. Now our school career lay in ruins. An example had been made of us, in accordance with the rules. Let it be a lesson to them all.

Olly and I slunk away, shamed. We had let the house down, let our friends down, let our parents down, let ourselves down. We were the lesson and the example, we were the figures who would be held up by parents when they wanted to caution their children: look what happened to Chamberlaine and Clare. What a waste.

The police gave us 'cautions', which felt like tattoos. We were marked. Smoking pot. Expelled for drugs. Thrown out for taking cannabis. The images these phrases conjured in my mind were outlines of long-haired, dopey-eyed, hard-core rebels who think it is cool to smoke. The kind who lead others astray, boys with stashes of porn mags and hoards of cash extorted from smaller boys. I wondered if this was how others would see me.

The morning after the sentence was passed I woke in the dormitory and for a moment I did not remember there was anything wrong. First there was nothing but blankness, coloured at the edges with the fading fragments of dreams, then came a nagging feeling of misgiving, a memory that somewhere something was wrong, and then it all came bursting back. Expelled.

I washed and dressed, amazed by how calm I felt, amazed that I had slept. The state of disgrace, the first time, is a curiously muffled condition. You stand in the eye of disaster: ignominy and shame, anger and curiosity swirling around you more than through you. Disbelief softens them all: until that point you have felt a measure of control of your own destiny, you feel you have been the author of your own life, which now suddenly has escaped you, running off at an appalling tangent. You would never have written it like this, so it is as though someone else has seized the narrative, and now the voices that surround you sound hollow, and the sadness and distress in people's faces seem to be reacting to misdeeds that are not entirely yours. For the first time you see yourself through other's eyes and cannot quite credit the prospect. Shock absolves you of reality. You know that underneath it all you are the same person you were before, it is just that your body, your outward form, your name and face are now disgraced. You hear what people say, but part of you is confused about who they are talking about.

'Oh what a silly boy,' said my mother's friend. 'Silly, silly bugger.'

'How stupid,' said my aunt. 'I hope he's learned his lesson.'

'I'm so sorry, I'm so sorry,' Rupert cried, hugging me. He was terribly distressed for me, more than I was: I hugged him back.

'It's all right, it's OK,' I said.

'The important thing is not to let it get in the way of your GCSEs. You need to concentrate on getting the best results you can,' said my father.

My mother, father, brother and I were summoned to see the Headmaster together: it was as though we were all being expelled. I was soaked with shame. My father was very calm. I tried to tell him how sorry I was and tried to dam the tears which seemed to well up from my stomach. He put his hand on my shoulder and murmured a message from his girlfriend. 'She says not to worry too much,' he confided. 'It happened to John Lennon.'

'How will you fill the places?' my mother asked the Headmaster.

'Marlborough have expelled three for the same thing,' he said. 'We're taking them.'

We climbed into my mother's car and pulled slowly away from Number 6. Miles, Rob and Ben were standing on the edge of the cricket pitch. They were miserable and angry; their rebel uniforms – shirts hanging out and ties adrift – looked more beaten and scruffy than cool. They watched us go.

We made the national press: a boy with journalistic ambitions in Number 9 telephoned the *Sun*. The story appeared in a little box buried in the middle of the paper: 'Toffs Out for Puffing Pot' – it felt like front-page disgrace to us. It added to the feeling of unjust ignominy. We were not 'toffs' and we had not 'puffed' anything. We had barely sniffed it.

★

From then on it was as if my outward manners were shutters concealing a broken pane. Whenever I was forced to reveal it, I felt myself take a dip in the opinion of my interlocutor. All that privilege, and you sat around smoking drugs, I saw them thinking; there must be something not quite right with you. From then on I felt culpable and defiant: I was guilty, but felt myself unjustly branded: I had never even been 'high'! I perceived a gap between the law and justice, a perilous outlook for a young man. I left public school with twin convictions of resistance and guilt. And I felt I carried the mark of dope with me, and always would.

2

Honey Dew

1990–92

'THEY KICK YOU out,' said Evelyn Waugh of public school, 'but they never let you down.' During the period of exclusion running up to the exams my masters could not have been kinder, setting exercises, marking work and recommending further reading by post. My housemaster wrote me a reference I never saw but which made a strong impression on the authorities at the International School. Selection was a weekend-long assessment in which groups of candidates were examined by a series of ex-students over two days before a final interview. The ex-students were formidably grown-up figures. Our first had come down from Oxford sporting a little beard, a sports jacket, jeans and the kind of horizontally laid-back attitude I had not encountered since Ben.

'Statistically,' one of our group informed the rest, before we began, 'only one point five of us are going to get in.' Chris had a public school manner and a hooded sweatshirt I associated with Stone Roses fans. It turned out that he had come from a tough London day school. He certainly was not going to settle for being the point five. We looked around the group, and at each other, and prepared to slug it out.

Our assessor's opening gambit, faced with our ring of bright, fresh faces, was very dry. 'So,' he said, parking himself on a table, swinging his legs as if already impatient, 'do any of you have anything interesting to say?'

We stared. We half-smiled. We looked at each other. 'Anyone? Anything interesting happen to anyone recently?'

I could see the pain in Chris's face. He terribly wanted to open his mouth, but he could not quite coax himself into the yawning trap. My pulse thudded in my ears. I knew what was going to happen, as if I were watching a man climbing on to a ledge. It seemed that the ex-student knew about me and this was some sort of test – a set-up. I had known the moment was going to come but I had not dreamed it would be so soon, or so public. I felt dizzy with a precipitous feeling, standing on the balustrade, knowing I now had to jump. All or nothing, then.

'Well,' I said, matching the assessor's easy tone, as the heads turned and the ex-student's eyebrows lifted in laconic invitation, 'I've just been expelled from public school for drugs. That was quite interesting . . .'

He looked, in spite of himself, impressed. The group grinned, Chris broadest of all. No one could possibly mess this up more than that. The ice was broken and soon we were swinging along, discussing the row over Salman Rushdie's *Satanic Verses*.

'Anyone actually read it?' the ex-student demanded.

'No, but I've read the extracts they printed in the *Sunday Times*,' I lied.

'Yes, me too,' said Chris instantly, his deep voice lending him a bass-note of veracity. Our eyes met. We carried on.

They gave me a thorough going-over in the final interview, demanding I convince them that I would not 'experiment' at college. I made them a sincere promise, they accepted it, and when to my amazement and delight they let me in, I kept it. It turned out to be easy, one of the most extraordinary things about an extraordinary school. At a time when every public school was lying about being drug free and every sixth form college was fuming with the sweet and sickly reek of it, there really were no drugs here.

The moment I arrived I wanted to leave. My mother had driven me down from our home in mid Wales to the south coast, to the castle by the sea. She pulled up in the car park and we watched, unmoving in our seats, as coaches full of new students stopped at the outer gate. As each coach arrived it was greeted by wild cheers. Dozens of second-year students milled around, shouting and laughing.

'I don't believe it,' I said, slowly. 'They're holding up banners.'

'Crumbs,' my mother giggled. 'I can't make it out, can you see what they say?'

'It looks like "Welcome",' I grated. 'Turn around! Get me out of here . . .'

We both laughed. 'Happy clappy . . . hippy hell!' I groaned. Public school had taught me how to deal with bullies, sarcasm, teasing and fights. The idea that new kids might inspire kindness, warmth and excitement was entirely outside my experience.

'Well,' my mother said brightly. 'Better go and make the most of it!'

I winced, to entertain her. I was looking forward to it. I had decided to come here against my parents' preference (they thought another public school would have increased my chances of going to a good university, which meant Oxbridge) and I was determined to make the best of it.

'Have fun, darling,' she said, hugging me. 'I hope it's wonderful.'

I met my new 'house parent' – there were no 'masters' here. He was a burly, saturnine man. He introduced himself to me firmly.

'I know about what happened. Just as long as you understand there's absolutely nothing like that here . . .'

'I do, yes.'

'And you're going to behave yourself, right?'

'Yes.'

'Good. Make sure you do and we'll get along fine. If you don't I will come down on you like a ton of bricks, right?'

'Yes.'

'And don't tell the others, there's no need for them to know, you can just get on with it like everyone else.'

'They already know, sir. A couple of people have mentioned it . . .'

'Oh. Well. Just don't make it an issue. Fresh start, right?'

'Yes, sir.'

'Stop calling me sir. I'm Alan.'

It was the nearest thing I had to a bollocking for the next two years.

There was Chris again. 'They let you in then?' he boomed.

'And you, they must be mad.'

'And Craig and Cameron and Cathy, actually,' he said. 'Five out of six. Statistically that's . . . really very good.'

In the dinner queue another first year introduced himself. His name was Robin. He manfully overrode an evident impulse to comment on my ridiculous name. 'Where are you from?' he asked.

He had a boyish face and an open, inquisitive look. His clothes were very trendy, huge trainers, massive jeans, puffy jacket.

'Near here actually, south Wales. And you?'

'Same.'

'Right,' we smiled.

'Are you feeling a bit nervous about being away from home for the first time?' he asked, in a friendly way.

'Well,' I replied carefully, 'I've been at boarding schools since I was eleven so – not really. I'm sort of used to it.'

'Ah, right.'

'Are you nervous then?'

'Well,' he said, 'my dad's actually the Principal and I was brought up here, so – no, I'm not!'

'Oh, right,' I said. We turned away, both anxious to talk to an extremely pretty girl who called herself, with a laugh and an Irish accent, 'Jane from Spain'.

From that moment Robin and I hated each other. Public school twat, he thought, wide-boy yob, I countered – both of us too nervous to admit we were. We were in the same English class. I thought I was good at it, lolling backwards, testing myself with degrees of pins and needles, mentally rearranging the order in which I would sleep with the girls in the class if I was forced to sleep with all of them – I was still a virgin – while Robin slumped forward, experimenting with different kinds of graffiti.

We do Blake here too.

'Tyger tyger burning bright . . .' reads the teacher.

'Some bastard set him alight!' concludes Robin.

In the first couple of weeks he was caught out after 'lights out' – no lights were turned out but you were supposed to stay in your house – and given an official warning. Too many of those and you would be out. I felt a surge of fellow feeling, but also the counter-urge, the righteous disapproval of one who has got away with it. He started going out with a girl in the year above in my house. Some of the second years resented him for it, jealous and disapproving of his exuberance, his refusal to be modest, quiet or studious.

The same applied to Chris, whose manner was so upright and who was so keen that he made me think of that generation who were

sent to the trenches to fight like lions and die like cattle. I called him
by his surname, Wilson. The same few second years disliked me: our
principal crime in their eyes was that we thought we were cool.
Wilson – with his boom and bluster, his ever-ready statistics, his will-
ingness to challenge anybody on anything – probably was cool in
some true sense, though all his school life he had been the bright
one, the well-read, ambitious and idiosyncratic one, which had led
his classmates to tease him, fight him and bully him. Wilson was
quite incapable of keeping his mouth shut at the sight of anything
he thought wrong, stupid or just remarkable. The state school he
had attended in north London sounded brutal. His delight at his new
circumstances was unconfined.

Robin and I had both hung out with the rebels in far softer
schools. We were now the leaders of invisible gangs of our far-off
friends, instantly antagonistic, both claiming the high ground of cool.
It took a while for the college to show us how idiotic, defensive and
adolescent our postures were. But we were brought together by cool.
We had a very similar idea of what was and what was not. Old prams
definitely were.

On the last night of our first year I am at the top of the main drive
which slopes downhill, the width of the campus, to the castle. I have
an old pram. With another friend I am racing it down the drive, over
the sleeping policemen. Robin appears. The year of English lessons
has led us as far as cordiality.

'Woah! Where did you get that?'

'Sea front. Salvaged her.'

'What a beauty. That looks great . . .'

'Completely brilliant,' I confirm. 'Try it?'

'Oh yes, absolutely!'

My friend said he had had enough and went back to the house.

Robin and I take turns launching each other down the hill at the
speed bumps. We fall off, cackle and do it again. We discover the
optimal speed at which you can hit the bump before you wipe out,
and that wiping out is the best bit. From then on we are great friends.
Through Robin I come to meet and properly appreciate Gambo,
another Welsh boy, the son of a former teacher at the school. Gambo

TRUANT

has his own idea of what is cool: a suede jacket with tassels. He has
a vast directory of noises: hoots, whoops and warbles. Robin and
Gambo have known each other since they were small children,
campus kids, raised at the college. They are both gifted impression-
ists: frantic Liverpudlians, filthy Frenchmen, Jamaicans, Bluesmen,
Southern Rednecks, spaced-out Dutchmen, sex-crazed Germans:
the school provides an international paradise of material. They speak
extraordinary languages, like 'Europong', in which all vowels are pro-
nounced with different 'European' accents.

'Yor speuk da eurpong lingwoch?'

'Yeurs. Ee hof spakin eet sonce eu wasa baaii.'

'Vera got. Ah wash to himp yeur mither . . . ha meech wid thot
kist?'

Now we are friends they home in on me like hyenas.

'Give us a cigarette, Gamb.'

'Tch. Bloody scrounging loser.'

Robin looks up. 'Tax us a fag, we used to say in Bath . . . Oi Clare,
you freak, how would you ask for a cigarette at *public school*?'

Unthinking, I answer honestly. 'Um, "Crash us a tab, Piers . . ."
or whoever.'

'Sorry? Whaaat?'

'Oh fuck.'

'Did you just say *crash us a tab*? "Eew God, Piers, cresh us a teb,
for God's sake . . .!" Ha ha ha!'

They love language. During an argument over which pub to go
to, Gambo shrugs and says, 'We need to hit a laughing clairvoyant.'

'What?'

'Hit a laughing clairvoyant.'

'What are you on about, you fool?'

'Strike a happy medium,' Gambo says, patiently.

Robin blends and mangles words and expressions, remixing them
like a chaotic DJ. He is a supreme storyteller, waving his arms, throwing his whole body into the narrative, changing the expressions on
his face as if he had a set of rubber puppets to act all the different
characters. Denying ignorance of something he cries, 'I'm not green
behind the ears!' Indicating a heap of mess he says, 'Throw it on that
pile of shack' – a cross, I think, of shit and cack.

44

We excel at harmless fun. We dive over bushes, jump out of windows, leap from a speeding bicycle on to a swinging rope, throw things off cliffs, squirt each other with soda bottles, trip each other over, complete a perilous circuit of the castle roofs, practise 'accidentally' falling over, go ghost-busting in the castle at night with hoovers, plunge down steep hills on a child's tricycle: acceptable behaviour at twelve and more than twice as funny at seventeen. In search of a caffeine high Robin makes and drinks multiple cups of espresso, then insists we go cow-rolling. The cows hear us coming and make off.

We live in a paradise of diversity and novelty. No one's 'culture' is quite the same as anyone else's. Everyone has different music, different politics and different clothes: the college 'look' is a chaotic blend of whatever we would have worn at home crossed with Palestinian scarves, Kenyan cotton, cheap Welsh wool jumpers and thick checked shirts. Everywhere Robin, Gambo and I look, there are beautiful girls. We embark on a two-year festival of kissing, sometimes more. No one has to make an effort to be different or to fit in. We are all different, so we all fit.

Facing us across the Bristol Channel is the coast of Somerset. On a clear day you can see the jut and curve of the wooded cliffs between Minehead and Porlock, and all the way down to Linton in Devon. There, I know, Coleridge went walking. He found refuge in a farmhouse one night, took opium and dreamed up 'Kubla Khan'.

> *In Xanadu did Kubla Khan*
> *A stately pleasure-dome decree:*
> *Where Alph, the sacred river, ran*
> *Through caverns measureless to man*
> *Down to a sunless sea . . .*

The beat and imagery of the poem, its visions, the thought of Coleridge striding through the night and plunging, as if through a portal in this world, into a realm of mystical archetypes, into an eternal, parallel chiaroscuro of darkness and flashing lightning, and surfacing through waves of opium sleep like a swimmer clutching an unearthly treasure – this poem lights my spirits with longing and something like lust.

> And all should cry, Beware! Beware!
> His flashing eyes, his floating hair!
> Weave a circle round him thrice,
> And close your eyes with holy dread,
> For he on honey-dew hath fed,
> And drunk the milk of Paradise.

That is exactly it! That is what I want. Oh, how I long for them to say that of me. I want flashing eyes! (I already have the floating hair.) Honey-dew. The milk of paradise. Opium. What a beautiful word that is. Opium, as if the O itself is a round red door to the dens of the other world.

As I walk the Welsh cliffs and stare across the channel it seems that Coleridge is still there. From where I stand it could still be 1797 over on the other side. The prophetic incantations of the poem are as alive now as ever they were. Waning moons, gardens bright with sinuous rills, holy and enchanted groves surround me. I bury myself in the first volume of Richard Holmes' biography of Coleridge, in which I find this passage, from a letter the poet wrote to his friend John Thelwall.

> I can *at times* feel strongly the beauties, you describe, in themselves, & for themselves – but more frequently *all things* appear little – all the knowledge, that can be acquired, child's play – the universe itself – what but an immense heap of *little* things? . . . My mind feels as if it ached to behold and know something *great* – something *one & indivisible* – and it is only in the faith of this that rocks or waterfalls, mountains or caverns give me the sense of sublimity or majesty!

I absolutely know and understand the aching for something great, one and indivisible. I know that worshipful ache, a kind of keening of the soul produced by the apprehension of beauty and power which weather and light bestow, as they act upon the land and sea. Beside it the universe of material life does seem a heap of little things. But there is never time to brood. There is no time for teenage angst. There are always more books to read, lifeboats to launch, girls to chase, the pub at weekends and, every night if you want it, there is dancing, lots and lots of dancing.

For some of my peers the ache is answered by God. Every Sunday two friends, a white Zimbabwean and a black Bermudan, take the college minibus to church. But I and most of my friends are not for God. We look to the world, to each other and ourselves, to the cult of the individual and the affirmation of the group to supply our needs. Besides, when it comes to God, as to all enshrined authority, I am with Shelley. One autumn day I sit in the library as stormy winds thrash and bend the treetops in the valley below the castle, and read Shelley's 'Ode to the West Wind'.

> *O wild West Wind, thou breath of Autumn's being . . .*
> *Wild Spirit, which art moving everywhere;*
> *Destroyer and preserver; hear, oh, hear!*
> *. . . Be thou me, impetuous one!*

You do not need drugs when intensity like this is all around, blowing out of the angry sky.

The formula for a drug-free school seems simple, though not necessarily simple to replicate. The college was founded by a group of ex-servicemen. After what they had seen of wars the founders had decided that the best chance for peace was to mix the world's children at an early age, in the hope that they would discover that they were much less divided by their cultures, beliefs and prejudices than they were united by their humanity. There were seventy-six nationalities in a student body of 350. My first experience of a student-organized event is a seminar about German reunification staged by East and West Germans. There are members of staff there, but they are sitting in the audience, like students, to listen and learn. It is a revelation: we can be teachers, we have things to contribute. When the first Gulf War breaks out I watch it in the television room with the whole world.

'Just one aircraft carrier!' my Lebanese dorm-mate prays. 'Just let him [Saddam Hussein] hit one aircraft carrier.'

'Why, though?'

'Just to show the bastards they can't always push us around!'

His family had fled the American-backed Israeli invasion of Lebanon. He would probably work in America one day, but it did not stop him wishing it a black eye.

I witness how easily an Israeli and a Lebanese can get on, and also how vehemently a Greek Cypriot can dispute with a Turk. Indians and Pakistanis, white and black South Africans, Americans and Iraqis are not just friends, but best friends.

Rather than hammering us into the straight and narrow, as public school had attempted, the college shows us something of the breadth of the world, its variety and its difference. Rather than forcing us to break rules if we want to meet the opposite sex, the college throws us into mixed houses (with strictly separated dormitories) and lets us get on with it. The message inscribed on the plaque on the way up to the library was ascribed to Kurt Hahn – the one appeal to the young, he claimed, which never failed: 'You are needed!'

Whereas at public school there was a queasy undertone to the feeling of privilege – the majority were there thanks to their parents' money – we have arrived in this beautiful place through some merit and a great deal of luck. You are fortunate beyond measure, they tell us, you have a responsibility to make the best of it. Provided we hurt no one and keep the two iron rules (no drugs, no sex in the dormitories) we can do as we please with our free time. No one thinks it cool to risk your scholarship by smoking dope, so no one does. The cigarette smokers can smoke in a designated place (which takes the rebellion out of it) and if we are old enough to buy booze, or can stand up to the gentle scrutiny of the local landlords, no one minds if we drink.

The fact of our being there seems a mighty benediction. An extraordinary thing had happened to all of us: a dream-come-true, a jackpot, a bull's-eye. The real world, we know, is tough and unlike this, but we understand that it can deliver miracles, riches of people and place. You can be very lucky. To feel that, then, was the greatest blessing of all.

*

There were rebellions, but they were as likely to come from the top as the bottom. One day in our second year the Principal summoned us all into the hall.

'There's a lot of *talk* at the moment,' he said, looming over his lectern like a great Welsh bear, the lilt of his voice rumbling off the stone walls, 'about *stress*.

'A lot of you have been saying you're *stressed*. No doubt you are. It's a stressful time. And I'm sure the staff are stressed. Even *I'm* beginning to feel stressed, and I don't like it. Obviously we all have a lot to do, and that can be stressful. But I'm not having everyone running around, made *miserable* by it. So. For today and tomorrow *all* lessons are *cancelled*. You can do whatever you want with the time, but if you have some catching up to do, I hope it will help. That's all.'

There Principal and teachers are excellent, but the secret of the college is the extent to which they insist that the students educate each other. The service side, the social work, the environmental work, the extra-mural centre, the arts and photographic service, the farm, the lifeguards, coastguards and lifeboats are among its most distinguishing features, and though there are staff supervising them all, the skills each new intake requires are taught by the year above them.

The responsibility involved in taking a small rubber lifeboat into a stormy Bristol Channel, or coaxing a child with learning difficulties into abseiling down a cliff, is considerable, and entirely in the students' hands. No staff member will be on the boat when you launch on a real rescue: it is up to you. The second years feel these responsibilities keenly: for the sake of the evident importance of the work and in honour of the now ex-students who had taught them, they are adamant that we first years should pay close attention, concentrate and get it right.

I am busy: between the International Baccalaureate curriculum (we all do six subjects in place of the three or four most A-level pupils take), friends and girlfriends, editing the weekly newspaper, crewing the lifeboats, first aid, swimming, drama, rugby and reading, I have neither time nor inclination for serious transgression. Of course there are escapades after lights out, occasional drinking sprees, and, in my second year, at long last, there is love and sex, but the school's structure and ethos allow these things to take place discreetly, make them experiences and decisions for which the responsibility and consequences are ours.

These are two of the happiest and most productive years of my life. Had I not started smoking cigarettes in my second year they would have been, by my extremely varied standards, an unmitigated triumph. Being expelled from public school for drugs proved to be one of the best things that had ever happened to me, which makes it worse, really. Because as soon as I left the International School, at pretty well the first opportunity, I looked for dope again. I still had no idea what drugs were like and I still wanted to find out.

I went to London to meet my public school friends. Ben's sister, Jen, had a flat in Chelsea, the only place I could see them: school tradition said that the expelled were forever banned from the grounds. Weekends there are riotous (I and other of Ben's 'little friends' caused plainclothes police to break into Jen's spare bedroom; we put the TV in the bath; I first broke a bone while staying at her flat) but they are not usually drugged.

We have no idea how to score: instead the idea of drugs, the hope and promise of drugs, like the thought of women, makes us grin and giggle and drawl. Anticipation is the best fix of all. Leicester Square, we believe, is the place. We hold long discussions over who should go, pressurizing each other in turn. Finally Mark gives in. He heads for Leicester Square with Nick. They find a man. He slips them a little package with two lumps in it for twenty pounds. They return.

'What did you get?'

'This.'

'Oh man! Is this what it looks like?'

'Er – it's definitely liquorice.'

'Ha ha ha! Disaster!'

'I quite like it, actually. And – we got this too.'

'Oh gad, what now? Oh! Oh – well done. This is – excellent.'

'Thank you. Very pleased with it . . .'

A twig.

The next night Ben and I try King's Cross. We head for Games Zone, an orange hell of silent men and loud machines. Heads turn as we walk in. My legs feel shaky, my head light. My vision narrows and I pretend to be interested in the Pinball. In seconds we are approached.

'All right, boys, all right,' the man says. 'Give me twenty and wait here.'

'We'd rather come with you.' Ben is trying hard to be competent, to be cool, to be on the same side as this furtive man.

'OK . . .'

Up a dark street. Down slithering stairs. A grille. Men moving behind it, whispering to each other, peering out. They pass out two little lumps of silver foil. We retreat, clutching one each.

I unwrap mine with clumsy, greedy fingers.

'What you got?'

'It's . . . it looks like – Ha ha! Shit. It is. A Rolo.'

'A Rolo?'

'Chocolate coating, toffee centre. Do you love anyone enough to give them your last Rolo?'

Ben unwraps his. 'Please, please, just a little piece of – ah shiiit. That dude definitely fuckin' loved us. I got another one.'

'I would probably feel more sorry for you if you did not have such a ridiculously exaggerated limp. I can't take it seriously.'

'Neither can I.'

It is a Sunday lunchtime, we are heading for the tube to Paddington, to bid Rob farewell. I am crabbing along, swinging my leg wide and pivoting on my heel, trying not to apply pressure straight down. My ankle is purple and green and swollen. When I get the stride wrong it sends up a sickening bolt of pain. I did it, drunk, on a flight of steps on Friday night, running for a tube. I would certainly have taken it to hospital had it not been one of these weekends. The pain has forced me to spend a lot of time in the bath but that was better than missing anything.

'Here, stick this in your face.'

Ben has retrieved a tiny blue square from his wallet, the size of a match head. He gives it to me carefully.

'What, I just eat it?'

'Yup. Well, you hold it under your tongue first.'

'For how long?'

'Long as you like.'

He fishes out another blue square and puts it in his mouth.

'Right . . .'

The acid begins to hit in Paddington. Suddenly the voice reading out the stations seems huge and catastrophically funny. Moreton in the Marsh! What is it doing there? On the tube I realize the carriage is menaced by a host of dangling silver snakes, swaying to the rhythm of the train. They are rubber hand grips, coiled in metal springs, and I suppose I know this, but they are also lunatic serpents, and how come no one else is bothered by them? I giggle. Another passenger looks uneasy. Is it me or the snakes? If I catch Ben's eye I will have hysterics. Changing trains we have to go through a long curving foot passage, faced in red glazed brick. Because of my limp I fall behind and I can hear Ben's voice telling me to hurry up but the foot passage has turned into a circle and I am limping through a red-glazed forever, following a voice. I start to laugh. We emerge at Marble Arch, separated from the park by an infinitely wide river of cars.

'OK, we're going to play in the traffic now. You ready?'

'Um, err – Aaaaaggh!'

'Good. Come on.'

If there is a pattern to the traffic I cannot see it. If there is a safe way of doing this I do not know it. I push myself off from the kerb as if my body were a punt and I a boatman. Cursing, laughing, limping, I veer across the torrent of machinery, hunching my shoulders so that anything that hits will bounce off. We gain the other bank. A crowd of people surrounds men on boxes who rave and gesticulate. A man stands watching them and as I watch him I see that his head is split into two halves – up to his eyebrows he is normal, above them, instead of hair, he has fur! A perfect fur head. I try to look elsewhere, alarmed, but my eyes cannot stay away from him. A fur head, how extraordinary. It must be a trick. Or an implant. Or his mother had it away with a bear, or –

'Wow!' I exclaim. 'Cosmic!'

'What have you seen?'

'That man . . . do you see that?'

'The guy with the hat?'

'Hat! Shit . . . I can't tell who's mad and who isn't.'

'It is kinda tricky. Except for you. Come on.'

We lie on the sticky grass. The sky is an electric grey. Lots of boys are running helter skelter up and down, trying to avoid a ball which chases them. Suddenly they all wheel together like starlings and take off after one guy who runs for his life. Then they all go down on their knees and bow towards a tower block. We stare at the tower block: what is it going to do? Mills and Reynolds are not on acid, they are real, they are normal, they are – Christ! They are goblins. They have goblin faces, long, sloping cheeks, blotchy with colours I have not seen before. Their eyes are calm, they seem perfectly at ease, but their mouths protrude miles, their jaws are huge, chomping mandibles. I try not to attract their attention.

Later we go back to the flat. Jen is there with two of her friends. Things seem to calm down.

'I think I'm back,' I say to Ben. 'But how do I know?'

He laughs quietly. 'That's the thing. I don't think you ever really come back.'

I rejoin Robin and my first proper girlfriend, Lara, a Canadian. We are going inter-railing: we have bought tickets to the whole of Europe for a month, for £175. I have a tent, we all have the inter-railers' huge rucksack and sleeping bag, and in addition Lara has a little bag bulging with Canadian flag badges, a whistle and a metal pen-shaped thing which fires flares.

'Everything a good Canadian needs for going abroad!' Robin yells delightedly, waving the flare-pen. 'This is *de luxe*!'

Lara is a quiet, studious and well-brought up girl from Toronto. She has visions of seeing something of Europe's art and history. Robin and I are not really thinking about culture.

In London we meet three more friends from college who are going inter-railing too. We set out on the boat train from Victoria in a state of high excitement, Robin and I quite drunk and daubing our eyes with Lara's mascara, so that we look like Goth highwaymen. Amsterdam is our first stop: 'to see the Van Goghs', we tell our parents. We go from café to café. We meet an American with a hash pipe and a high, comically wheezy voice.

'How long you guys bin here, man?'

'We just arrived.'

'How long you stayin'?'

'Not long, we're not sure, we might just train it out tonight, save the hotel bill.'

'That's what happened to me, man!'

'What happened?' Robin asks.

'I came for a day, six months ago. And here I am!'

'Ah, right . . .'

'Say, can you guys spare a bit of hash?'

'Sure.'

'What's that over there?' I ask Robin.

At another table a man has made a huge bulb of paper and stuck it into the end of a tube. Robin looks dubiously impressed. 'It's called a tulip. Jack-rammed with hash.'

'It's the only tulip I've seen in Holland.'

The dope makes us feel drowsy, disconnected and uneasy.

'Let's get the hell out of here while we still can.'

We leave that night. Over the next month we cross and recross Europe. We sleep on the luggage racks when there are no seats, and get terrible giggles at Robin's bat impression. (This is a bat which swoops down from the luggage rack crying 'Swoop!' and 'Roma! Roma!' in the vain hope of fooling other travellers into abandoning their compartments.) We are kicked awake by the police in Prague's main station and thrown off the train to Sicily for not having reservations.

On Corfu some of our party have a shouting row with a hotelier. That night Robin and I take one of the hotel mopeds for a spin, howling through a hot darkness cut with sudden rain.

I sit behind Robin as he drives. He says something.

'What?'

'I said I wish I wasn't so drunk!' he shouts. Then he says something else.

'What?'

'I said I wish I was wearing my glasses.'

'Jesus, that's it. Take us back, I want my own moped.'

The next morning the hotelier chases us off the island. We barely wash. We climb into the cellars of the castle in Heidelberg. We develop a game called Tampon Ninja: dipping them in water and zinging them at each other. Robin, our 'Italian speaker', nearly gets us beaten up in a Florentine taxi when he confuses the vocabulary for 'How much?' with 'What did you say?' He pretends to understand the driver's increasingly irate replies and asks the question again: *sí, sí,* but what did you say? I catch a sunburn on a Greek ferry which has people stopping to take photographs of me. We are pursued around the Continent by a South American pipe band and posters of Phil Collins, who is on a European tour. In Rome we write odes to a particularly damaged-looking pigeon as we wait for McDonald's to open. I get us so lost in Venice with such confidence that Robin says 'Right, that's it,' quite quietly. He takes off his rucksack and throws himself at me, fists windmilling. We drink a lot and smoke fags, relishing the first Camel of the day at 07.08 in Paris St Lazare, reeling across the platforms, pretending we are being kicked in the stomach and simultaneously beaten about the head. We smoke hundreds of Camels but no more dope. It is wonderful.

Because we fear nothing, nothing can go wrong. When a train strike maroons us on a platform in Patras, we sit down on our sleeping bags and shrug. 'Let's just chill here,' Robin says. We while away twenty-four hours without a hint of displeasure, composing poetry and putting the tunes of George Michael's songs to stories of our journey. I come up with a formula for complete satisfaction: 'I want full strength Camels, high alcohol beer, red meat, strong coffee, Irish linen sheets, high-calorie, full-fat, full-cream, big nicotine, maximum volts, four season, goose feather, high caffeine *shit*!'

'And *possibly* a shower,' Robin adds.

3

Freight Trains

1993

A s summer shrinks away the hangover from college sets in. We know we will not see many of our friends for years, if ever, and we cling to those we can. We are not a special selection any more: we are among millions of young people, searching, scheming, setting out, returning, starting again, setting out again.

Gambo and I sit in his beloved yellow Beetle, eating chips, with all the rain in Wales running down the windows.

'You know it's bad,' he says, 'when you're halfway through the chips but you're looking forward to the cigarette.'

And so begin the wandering years, which stretch out through all my twenties. The wandering years, when you find yourself on trains in the middle of weekday afternoons, going to or leaving your parents, skint or topped up with a couple of tenners, semi-autonomous, semi-educated, semi-legitimate. Watching as the tracks give way to the backs of small houses dull-shining with rain, then bramble banks, old cars, sheds and empty fields. Everyone is away, turning the handle of the world, and here you are, misfit.

The Economist runs an advertising campaign on station billboards: 'No one ever got rich and famous staring out of the window.' Thanks a bunch, you clever sods.

'Do something useful!' our parents said. Rob and Rupert, my friends from public school, went to teach English in the Gambia. They came back ill and stoned. It was not clear if they had been any use. 'Do something!' our parents said, then 'Do anything!' I served beer and washed dishes and looked forward to the next train.

The line leads to the sofa of a friend's flat, or to their parents' spare bed, to the yellow-lino years, to empties under the strip light and white bread sagging in damp-floored kitchens. Or to a girl, to whom you pay the three-hour, three-night or three-week stand, your clothes spilling from your bag, your base a tiny untidy occupation in one corner of her dim room: you smile and are friendly to friends of hers you will never see again; you are a temporary curiosity, some guy someone's flatmate brought back.

And the places. Flats in Surbiton, Ealing, Caterham, Esher. The nights squeezed into narrow beds or panted out on cushions on the carpet, fading too quickly into the slow churn of next mornings. The world of the couch-surfer, the perennial guest. There is a slip in translation between you and the discourse of everyday things: houses, plants, shops, jobs, cars, everything referring to a normality not yours, as the light broadens, tilts, and the day slips from potential to waste, the panic of the morning's papers already two days old. And the hours at bus stops, the miles of small brown houses and little grey parks, the deferred time, the length of a bus ride, a train ride, a life. A car's world, an adult's world, a what-are-you-looking-at world, as you stare at passers-by. No division between holiday and work, no job expected to last beyond the next corner, all free time, no free time. Another few minutes burned in a cigarette, two fifty-seven on a Sunday afternoon, walks by the river on days not fine. The ache of something like redundancy – not an absence of work, we do not mind that, but an absence of cause, of purpose. And always those little whispers: 'How wonderful to be young! The best days of your life!'

In the best moments it does not matter. We are young, after all. We are all potential. Our time stretches far beyond our horizons and only the next few days and weeks are in focus. In the worst moments is all the melodramatic exasperation of our teens, salted with the knowledge that at eighteen and nineteen we are not really teenagers any more. We feel quicker, stronger and sharper than anyone older or younger than us. We are beautiful. We get the jokes. We are a treasured and mystifying demographic. Banks, fashions, music, films, courses and careers all compete for our attention. We decide what is cool, but all we are really interested in is each other.

Our language reveals us: what we really want is carnage, a party where everything goes to hell, where we have it large and everyone is up for it, mad for it, on fire, where we get destroyed, wrecked, trashed and fucked up, and somehow, ideally, pull. The vocabulary of our pleasure parallels a phraseology of war.

So back and forth across the country we track, pinning our time to each other, comparing hilarities and uncertainties in laughter and booze. It often comes down to a walk to a pub, where we swim with the old men, the perpetuals, the tobacco fish, in a submarine fag-smoke gloom. It is like being a poet without a pen or paper. All this seems telling, seems important, signifies something – but what? I keep striding along, my head up, eyes searching everything for something. A carload of lads approaches me in Abergavenny, the little town near my mother's house with a station, gateway to the rest of the world, and it slows, and they roll the window down.

'Oy!' one of them shouts. 'Chesney Hawkes!'

I laugh. They nailed it. Floppy-haired nit, head up his own arse, probably humming '*I am the one and only . . .*' – Chesney Hawkes.

Neither I nor any of my friends had the slightest notion of what we might do with our lives, and it did not seem to matter at all. The next step was university, obviously. In our advanced society you could take as long as you liked to reach adulthood – the material adulthood of jobs and homes. You could linger over education into your mid twenties, into your late twenties if you could fund it. Further study was the answer to everything and a deferment of all. A student grant would give you three years to work out what you might want to do, anyway. I wanted to be a writer, I loved books: I would read English.

Robin and Gambo said they had no interest in academics. They talked about making money. We rattled around south Wales in Gambo's beetle, sniffing out the best greasy spoons, eating chips for supper, watching comedy videos and going through our college year books, laughing and leering and comparing stories of conquests and defeats. Robin and Gambo went on a business course, planning to open a café, but it never happened. We never had any dope. We might have relished it but we did not go looking for it. We all took a year off.

I wash up in the kitchens of a local hotel and take driving lessons. Just as my test approaches I am invited to New York, to see Ben and Wangechi, a Kenyan girl I idolized at school, now studying art in Manhattan. I skip the test and go. Wangechi is sharing a room in Greenwich Village. She has the top bunk, her room-mate the lower one. We try to be very quiet. Ben arrives.

'Well, I hope you've got some dollars,' he says.

'Some. Why?'

'Because I've just spent all mine on this . . .' (A caricature, by one of Washington Square's pavement artists, which looks nothing like him.) 'And this.' (A little bag of dope.)

'Good *man*, Hardiman.'

I introduce them. I feel so proud of my lover and my friend: I am over-excited and they laugh at me. They get on immediately. And the fact that he has dope tops it all perfectly. We are all pretending to be laid back, grown up and sophisticated. We make no fuss as Ben rolls a joint. This time it works. Everything in sight seems richly coloured and pleasing. Everything either of them says is funny and clever. I can actually feel their affection for me, like warmth on my skin. I giggle. I start jiggling my knee. 'Make it stop!' I shout. They laugh. We listen to Tom Waits.

> *Operator, number please, it's been so many years,*
> *Will she remember my old voice, while I fight the tears?*

I could almost groan at the resonance and depth of it all. I look at Wangechi and Ben and love them both. They talk about drawing. Wangechi produces a pad of paper and two charcoal sticks. They both draw me.

'You're better than half the artists on my course,' Wangechi tells him.

'That's not right,' Ben drawls, looking at her picture.

She raises an eyebrow. 'Oh no?'

'That's how you see him, really?'

'Yes.'

'Nah. That's beautiful.' (Looking sceptically at me) 'He's an ugly fucker.'

'Oh shut up, Hardiman. Come and look at the fire escape.'

We have another joint on it, watching as a middle-aged couple make out on a couch behind one of the lighted windows opposite.

'I think they're going to do it.'

'Nah, they're not.'

They are lying side by side, arms entwined, twitching sometimes like landed fish.

'They are too! He's going for it . . .'

'Mmm, but she's not sure.'

'She is. She wants it! Go on, son, get in there.'

It confirms everything I imagined about dope: that funny and revealing things happen when you smoke it, that lighted windows appear in the darkness of the everyday, that it gives access to a raunchy and enticing world. Ben exhales.

'Is this bad?'

'What, this?'

'Uh-huh.'

'No, it's great. Very educational. Watch and learn.'

'We're voyeurs, dude.'

'We're artists. And they're exhibitionists. They could draw the curtains.'

'They *made* us watch, officer.'

'If they actually do it I'm going to cheer.'

'Humans mating . . .' Ben says, thoughtfully. 'It's not that attractive, is it? Kinda sweet though.'

'It's not like the movies.'

'Christ, do you think they're *lyin'* to us?'

But this is all like the movies. New York is the first city on the planet. Her glittering towers, her streets like bright valleys are even more cinematic, more dramatic and more glamorous than the movies. I can scarcely believe the majesty of the steel and concrete canyons, the filmic beauty of the yellow taxis, the dramatic low prowl of police cruisers, the infinity of colours and shapes in the bagel café, the lava flows of food, of goods, of choice: the way you can buy shoes at midnight, the way the harmonies of Tom Waits and Bob Dylan exactly capture the soul of this, the stories of lovers and friends who cannot stay long, the lines between us as thin as telephone wires, as pure as music.

For her course Wangechi has to make a structure out of pasta that will support a kilogram of weight. For hours we fiddle with pasta and glue guns, breaking to smoke and kiss, real New York artists, real New York lovers! Going to bed before dawn, trying not to wake her room-mate. New York becomes a city of small hours. We go up the World Trade Center and stare at the million tiny lights, at the infinity of motion, the vast intricacy of the city stretching across rivers and islands. I hold Wangechi's cool hand. In the lift on the way down I tell Ben not to jump.

'Why?'

'Because of the speed of the lift.'

'What?'

'You'll hit the ceiling.'

Other passengers look at us, wordlessly.

'You don't have to worry about that, dude.'

'I am worried about it.'

'Nah. See, the ceiling's rubber.'

'Oh! So it is.'

The other passengers look up, despite themselves.

With the final throw of his presidency, George Bush sends troops into Somalia. We watch the television and scan the newspapers.

'There's nothing here!' I cry. 'Barely even in the *New York Times*.'

'What?'

'There's no debate, no protest, no questioning. There's nothing. And the TV! It's just chat shows. Arsenio. Whoopi. Letterman. And adverts! You have adverts every five minutes. You have adverts, then they say they're going to show the film, then more adverts. You have adverts for adverts.'

Wangechi shakes her head. 'War and adverts? This is not my doing, my dear. This is Mzungus doing what they have always done.'

Ben and I lounge on street corners, vaguely hoping something will happen, smoking glamorously.

'You on the game or what?' I demand.

'Wch. Might be.'

'Me too. Let's sell our asses.'

We prop the wall up, posing, eyeing businessmen in a frank and suggestive way. They look offended. Softening our stares somewhat, we cast querying looks at hurrying women. What great toy boys we would make. No one bites.

'Fuck it, we're going to starve before we pull. Let's kill someone and take his wallet . . .'

On the last day Wangechi and I carry a yellow pasta crane through the streets. It seems a perfect metaphor for us, a fragile oddity in all the noise and business of the world. Then we say goodbye. I fly back to Britain, lovesick, wondering what I am going to do now.

'Come to St Etienne and teach!' Chris boomed down the phone. 'There's a really nice guy here, an American. We're going to get a flat. There are plenty of jobs.'

'What's the town like?'

'It's the Sheffield of France. Slag heaps like Madonna's tits. There's a rugby team. French girls. You'll love it . . .'

The first night we drank a bottle of J & B whisky and told Robert, the American, increasingly exaggerated stories of our heroics on lifeboats. Robert was ten years older than us, balding, and an auto-didact. He had been mostly interested in cars until he had discovered French literature: now he taught English in France half the year and French in America for the other half. He spoke the language beautifully and he could hold his booze. While Chris and I reddened, stumbled and slurred, Robert sat neatly with ankle on his knee, laughing and drinking until we passed out and he was able to read Paul Valéry in peace. Very early the next morning I woke knowing I was going to be sick. In my mind I drew a map of the small flat and plotted a course between the bed and lavatory. Nine tenths of the way along it I threw up into Robert's beautiful new black leather shoes. He did not hold it against me.

In a freezing January of cold skies and a bright hard sun we found a flat in the middle of town and configured it to suit us. We would have no television. We would paint it all black and white. We would throw steak knives at the bathroom door until we were all supreme knife-throwers. One drunken night Chris appeared with a large round sign he had stolen from a shop: on a couple of boxes it made an excellent table. We looked longingly at the tables and chairs outside McDonald's but never quite dared to pinch a set. We planned lessons: our job was to provoke our pupils into speaking English. Chris favoured devices like playing them Bobby McFerrin's 'Don't Worry Be Happy'. I staged debates. My white middle-class students shared their parents' view that the town's large Arab population were a species of dole scroungers. I accused them of racism and ignorance and insisted they defend and justify themselves in my language. Chris and I harangued our classes with the ideology of our international school: you can change the world, we insisted, if you want to. In the evenings we read, sometimes by candlelight. Chris was deep into Denis Healey's autobiography. Robert introduced me to Kurt Vonnegut. We made friends in bars, kebab houses and cheap restaurants all over town. We played rugby for the town under 21s and made more friends, including a boy called Ludo, who was huge, and obsessed with the letter O. Wherever you went in St Etienne there were signs missing O's. The local supermarket chain, Casino, suffered particularly badly. It all went very well, then one day a dealer turned up.

I cannot remember where he came from, he is just there one evening in our kitchen, a pale-looking youth with curly black hair, a cheap coat and a little black rucksack. His name is Stéphane, he lives with his mother – he instructs us not to call him after 9 p.m. so that we will not disturb her – and he carries an automatic pistol in his rucksack.

'Why have you got a gun?' I demand.

'So no one can rip me off,' he says.

'Let's have a look.' I heft it. It seems to be the real thing. 'Is it loaded?'

'No.'

I point at the bathroom, my finger curling around the trigger. 'Wait!' Stéphane shouts. 'It is loaded!'

Chris comes out of the bathroom (it is in one corner of the kitchen). 'Christ! Wilson, you cunt, I nearly fucking shot you. Take this thing and get it out of here.'

'H, you cunt! I can't believe you just did that!'

'I didn't realize you were in there and he said it wasn't fucking loaded!'

Robert has his face in his hands. 'I love the way you guys talk,' he gasps, through his laughter.

'What, the accent?'

'No, the language! "Wilson, you *cunt*" – Ha ha ha! "H, you cunt" – we just never talk like that. We don't use that word.'

'But it's a fantastic word!'

'Not in the States. It's really, really bad. You never hear it. Only drunks and wife beaters . . .'

'It's pretty bad in Britain too,' Chris declares. 'You wouldn't say it in public.'

'No. It's a term of endearment among friends.'

We pay Stéphane for his dope and Chris shows him the door.

'Living with his mum and carrying a fucking gun,' Chris says, shaking his head. 'What a cunt!'

'Mmm,' says Robert sniffing the dope, a little brown lozenge like an eraser, exactly as Olly described it years ago. 'Stony . . .'

Now in place of the books and the candle-lit arguments about politics and the mini-lectures on economics (which Chris spends patient hours trying to explain to me) and the painstaking hours of writing love-letters (I am pining for Wangechi while Chris is involved with a Norwegian girl from our year, now back in Norway) there is dope.

Another friend comes to stay for a week. Theo, a German, had been in the year above us at college. Theo is very tall and very loud. His face is framed by extremely long hair, his features dark and delicate like a pretty girl; but his hands look as if they could snap your back and his reactions, speed of thought and movement, are terrifyingly fast. His mastery of English is such that people cannot be sure where he comes from. Spreading confusion is one of his great pleasures, along with causing violent surprise, solving problems, flirting with women, ridiculing anyone he likes and provoking anyone he does not. He spent a lot of our first year creeping up behind people – for a six foot four monster he can move horribly quietly – manoeuvring his mouth to within a few centimetres of the back of one of their ears, and screeching, a terrible sort of BEEEOOIIW! which would make the victim scream or swear and jump: Theo would giggle insanely and fend off their involuntary attempts to punch him. Now he is in his first year of Politics, Philosophy and Economics at the University of York, and he is an expert on dope.

'NOO! Man, that's horrible! If you made a joint like that at York you would be laughed out of town. Start again. You've got to toast the tobacco first.'

'Toast it?'

'Give it here.' He takes the lighter and runs the flame gently up and down the length of the cigarette, browning the paper, careful not to blacken it.

'There.'

'Why do you do that?'

'Tastes better. Now. Skin up and get it right!'

'Skin up . . .' I mutter, wrestling with the thinner, wider, harder to manipulate rolling papers, OCB, which are the French equivalent of Rizlas.

We spend the next five days sitting around our kitchen table, arguing about who should go and buy the pasta this time, who should cook it, whose turn it is to skin up, getting stoned and playing *Blockbusters*, with Theo in the role of psychotic host and regulator.

'Go on then!' he roars.

'What? Oh, OK. What K is an ignorant German cabbage eater . . .'

'NOOO!' he screams, frantic. 'It's still me. Wake up! Ha ha! – ask me for a letter.'

'It certainly is you. Oh, OK. B.'

'Ask properly!'

'Jesus. May I have a B please, Theo?'

'Yes, you may. What B,' Theo begins, his eyes narrowing, 'what B is the registration number of the college lifeboat . . .'

'B554!' Chris shouts, banging the table.

'You didn't buzz,' Theo hisses, threateningly.

'Buzz!' I scream.

'You didn't bang with your buzz,' Theo snaps.

'Oh fucking buzz!' Chris shouts, banging the table.

'Yes, Mr Wilson?' Theo queries, suddenly civilized.

'B554 *American Ambassador*,' grins Chris.

'NOOO!' Theo howls. 'You interrupted the question, which was what B is the registration number of the college lifeboat which replaced B554 *American Ambassador* when it was being refitted, eh? EH?'

'Oh fuck OFF!'

'BUZZ!' I shout, banging. 'It was B540.'

'Yes, Mr Clare, but a bit fucking late. It's no use banging now. Mr Wilson does a forfeit.'

'Oh bollocks . . .'

Theo rubs his hands together manically, crowing, while Chris grins defiantly.

'Your forfeit is . . . wipe your bollocks on the floor.'

'Fuck off.'

'OY! Protocol!'

'OK, fuck off, MR SCHMIDT!'

'That's better, Mr Wilson. Now, wipe your bollocks on the floor.'

The first days, weeks, even months of marijuana use have a golden charm about them. You are filled with a silly, sunny, toppling feeling which bubbles into laughter at the slightest thing. Your sense of the absurd is sharpened and heightened: as well as being surrounded by your newly stoned friends who are unusually susceptible to giggles you are also funnier than normal. The world is a comical and amusing place. Strange things happen. You are in a tiny club with the people you are smoking with. You know exactly what you are all feeling; it is as though you are all visiting earth together and laughing at it. The jokes and absurdities which crop up between you are difficult to remember or retell but all you have to do is get hold of some more sweet-smelling Moroccan hash, skin up once again and pass it around. The emotion in music is heightened, the lustre of colour is deepened and brightened. But because you get used to it, because your brain is cumulatively affected by it, you are subject to a law of diminishing returns. The escapades and incidents require more cannabis to seem as funny and telling as they did at the beginning, and over time the defamiliarization of the world ceases to be so amusing. Each time you light up part of you is in pursuit of the happiness, silliness and strangeness that you felt at the beginning. Thus a habitual smoker becomes a chronic nostalgic, in search of vanished sensations. Each time you do it you feel a twinge of those wonderful early days but you can never have them back. To be a stoner is to be a perpetually hopeful and perpetually disappointed romantic.

When I started out I was ignorant of this, and as a confirmed romantic I had a strategy for dealing with any intimation of disappointment: should anything start to pall, push it harder.

Friday night in St Etienne, the little industrial city runnelled between the knuckles of the Massif Central. It has been raining heavily all across the south: the rivers boil white, the gutters gurgle, the roofs and roads shine black with water. Chris and I have been smoking. We are standing on the side of the ring road with our thumbs out. The approach of each car dazzles us. In Chris's face I see my own pallid skin and reddened eyes. Another car soars past us in a sizzle of light and speed.

'This is hopeless. I wouldn't stop for us. Need to think of something else, Wilson.'

'Hmm.'

'Take me to the sea! I wanna see the sea!'

'I'm trying, dammit!'

'I must go down to the sea again, to the lonely sea and the sky . . . Perhaps we should try the station.'

'Try what at the station?'

'We could jump on a freight train.'

He looks at me speculatively. 'Mmm. We could go and have a look, anyway.'

I loved the station, stoned, at night. I loved the silence between trains and their terrific infusions of sound, the solitary figures waiting and the faces of travellers in the carriages, coming from somewhere, going somewhere and peering out at us. Let us not forget, on platforms, when even the grey floors seem harsh with sudden noise and our shoes feeble against the grime and cold, and the drunks' spunk and the black gum flat as pebbles, that from the window of the late train, in the eyes of another narrator, face staring hungrily through the glass, we are the very soul of adventure, night poetry, stark in our film star pallor, beautiful in our arbitrary scattering, evocative, momentary, under the station lights.

'What are you staring at? Let's go down there . . .'

Chris leads the way to the far end of platform one. We are both quiet and purposeful, our excitement slyly suppressed. It feels as though we are about to pull off a heist. There are wagons from Italy, Switzerland and Germany. The entire continent is there, just out of sight, beyond the signal box, beyond the lights, the whole of Europe waiting like a promise in the vanishing point between the electric web of overhead wires and the dark steel of the track.

On the other side, about ten lines away from us, is a vast freight train. It is so long that we cannot see either end of it: we cannot see, in the darkness, where the engine might be. It is standing still.

'*That* baby.'

'Indeed,' says Chris.

We reach the end of platform one, far out of sight of the SNCF men around the station buildings, and set out towards it, nipping over the steel ribbons like grasshoppers.

'Which way do you reckon it's going? If it's going?'

'Well, we want it to go that way,' he says, pointing south-east. 'Then there's a chance it might go down the Rhône to Marseilles.'

'If not Slovenia.'

We reach it. The train is a series of huge hoppers; it could be a coal carrier. Each wagon has a small platform, a little gantry with a small rail at one end. We climb on to one.

Chris raps the side of the hopper. The huge iron bucket booms.

'Empty.'

'What now then?'

'Just wait and see, I guess.'

Even as he says it there is a noise like a shot, a series of shots, racing towards us down the train. Suddenly the gantry jumps beneath our feet, the couplings just below us crash and grab at the tiny rail.

'Woah! Easy, driver!'

The train is poised now, we can feel the tension through our feet.

'I think we're off.'

There is a long creak and we start to move.

'Shit. Wrong! What's this way?'

'Er, the whole of France.'

We are rolling quietly through the station. We huddle down.

'Too late to jump off?'

We look down, doubtfully. We have reached running speed and are still accelerating. 'Yeah,' Chris judges, 'too late.'

'Hell then! Bring it on!'

'Yee-Haa!'

Now we are between high brick walls and the noise is beginning to grow. Now we pass a train going the other way – a blast of wind and pressure makes us squeal and swear. The gantry bucks as the train gathers speed. And now suddenly the world goes black and we are clubbed to our knees, smashed, beaten flat by a savage, bucketing roar, the most enormous and terrifying sound. The tunnel is like being eaten by a dragon, like being swallowed into his howl. All the huge iron hoppers are wild drums bounding down a black pipe, their furious echoes reverberating off the walls, roof and floor, the vast and broken booming of the wagons fighting the iron crash and scream of the furious wheels. It is a physical assault in complete darkness in which our bodies have disappeared. I raise a hand in front of my face and there is nothing, no movement; I scream and there is no sound. I can feel the screaming but not the scream. The terrible noise comes from all sides, all directions at once. I hear a tiny piping: perhaps Chris is screaming too. There is a flash of golden sparks, so brief and bright they are gone before they come, as if time is playing backwards. There is nothing left of me but ghostly scraps, staring blind eyes, hands clinging to the cold rail, no mind, no senses but blasted, useless ears. I am a nothing, a sensation of terror in a hammering black vortex. Then we are out. We are both still screaming, obscene strings of fear and thrill. We swear and pant, gasping for breath.

'Mother of . . .'

'Son of a . . .!'

'That was ridiculous!'

'Unbelievably intense!'

*

Soon the city is left behind and we are out into a wide valley. There is a river and fields, there are isolated level-crossings where the headlights of cars flash over us. Our complete helplessness, our fate and direction in unknown hands, is also a victorious thrill. We have stolen into a secret world of night trains and junctions, empty stations and silent sidings, discovering all this adventure as if we have picked the lock on a door. The wide night and all nocturnal Europe for nothing! There is not a boy of our generation who has not seen a hundred war films: as we roll through silent France we are in one, at last. It has stopped raining and now it becomes cold, then very cold. After a while the train slows and we begin to snake through sidings, across junctions.

'Looks like a station.'

'Shall we disembark?'

The train stops. Chris cranes and peers along the track.

'Er, H, don't want to alarm you, but there are a bunch of men with dogs coming this way.'

'Don't wind me up.'

'Seriously, there are men with dogs up there.'

'Right, that's it.'

We jump down and scamper away, up an embankment and on to a road.

'Where are we, Wilson? This isn't the sea.'

'Nice river though. Let's find a drink . . .'

The bar is warm and plush; black polished wood and thick red carpets; couples sit watching a woman play the piano. It is like strolling in from outer space. It is still like a war film. It could be 1942. I look out for Vichy informers. We ask a man where we are. 'Roanne,' he says, evenly, as though this is a reasonable question. We drink whisky until the bar closes, then wander down to the river. A huge yellow moon hangs in a mauve-blue sky.

Back in St Etienne Robert listened to our story, shaking his head.

'We're going to do it again.'

'Again! What? You've gotta be kidding.'

'No. We're going to do it again, tonight, but this time we're going to do it properly. Come!'

'Uh, no. Definitely not.'

We were much more picky about our wagon on Saturday night. We found a flat car with small sides in the middle of another endless train. Some way behind us there was a line of white delivery vans, factory fresh, ready for transporting to showrooms.

'Paris or the coast!'

I tried to fend off the terror of the tunnel with a cigarette but the howling wind blew my lighter out. In its sparked flashes I saw Chris grinning. It was a colder night but we were prepared for it. We were wearing multiple layers of clothing and we had a sleeping bag. Chris had whisky, I had cigarettes, papers and dope. The moon was a cold white and France stretched out around us, miles of silent country, hedges and trees silhouetted against silver fields. We were bolder. When we needed a pee we walked down the flat wagon and stood up, pissing into the slipstream, cheering and waving as we passed through the headlights of the level-crossing cars, swilling whisky to keep our spirits up. We danced a bit to keep warm. We lay down as we passed through stations. Now and then the train stopped at signals. We whispered and wondered if we had been discovered. Then the jolt ran through the couplings and we were off again. It grew colder and colder as the hours passed. I shivered for a long time, then stopped. I wondered how many steps into hypothermia we had taken. We had both learned a lot about it on the lifeboats but I could not remember now how many stages it had. Five? Seven? We had both been quiet for a while. Stopping shivering was a bad sign, I knew.

Chris had his arms wrapped around his knees and his head sunk down behind them. Suddenly he looked up and said, 'H, don't take this wrong, but I think we have to hug.'

'Good idea. No kissing though.'

'Oh shut up.'

'Come here then, big boy.'

We huddled into a ball with the sleeping bag wrapped round us. It was better. We travelled for a while like that, shivering again. Then Chris started laughing. 'This is ridiculous. It's too bloody cold!'

'It's a wonder people put up with it.'

'Whisky.'

'Hypothermia.'

'Fuck it, whisky.'

'Perhaps we should break into one of those vans,' I said suddenly. 'What do you think?'

We both looked up at the vans, and we jumped. The hair on the back of my neck stood up. One of them, the first in line, was indicating right.

'What's that?'

'Someone in there!'

The van seemed to be chasing us across France, indicating right. The dark windscreens looked at us, dumb and severe.

'That's a bit spooky, isn't it?'

'Bloody spooky!' Chris laughed. 'Must have been the vibration.'

'Or a ghost. Help, Wilson – a haunted van!'

'Help!' Chris boomed. 'Help! We're being haunted by a van!'

'I'm tempted to break in just to switch it off.'

'It would be a hell of a lot warmer . . .' Chris pondered, wistfully.

'. . . but the shit if we were caught . . .'

'Yeah. No. We'll just have to take it. Whisky . . .'

The train settled into a stride. For hours we went without pausing or slowing.

'It's really getting on my nerves. What sort of van is that?'

'I dunno. Renault?'

'I'm not buying one.'

'If it starts beeping I'm going to take action.'

'If it starts bloody anything at all I'm getting off.'

'If we ever get a chance I'm getting off.'

'We should be wearing wetsuits. Why aren't we wearing wetsuits, Wilson?'

'Oh God! Wouldn't you love to pee in a wetsuit now?'

'God, yes. The heat . . . oh the pleasure . . .'

'Hey, slowing down.'

'Thank fuck.'

It was no longer much warmer when we slowed but at least the wind dropped. The tracks fanned out on either side and we came down to a running pace.

'Where do you reckon this is?'

'I dunno. It's almost five. We can't be far from Paris.'

'If we've been heading for Paris. Ho, shit! Chris!'

'What?'

'I've just been seen. That signal box.'

'Sure?'

'Definitely, definitely. Guy looked right at me.'

'But did he see you?'

'Yes. Fairly sure.'

'OK, we better assume he did.'

'Off then.'

'Yup. Jump.'

'It's going kinda quick, isn't it?'

'It's not going to get slower,' he said, with his amazing certainty – unjustified at least forty per cent of the time, by my reckoning. 'Jump!'

'You OK, H?'

'Fine. You?'

'I'm good.'

'Actually I can't feel anything. Where are we now?'

'Quite a big town.'

'There's the station. Christ, I'm cold.'

'I'm hungry,' he announced. He lifted his nose. 'I'm hungry and I can smell food!'

'You're always hungry. Orleans! It says Orleans.'

'Hmm. What do they eat in Orleans?'

'At five in the morning?'

'Their pillows, I expect. But smell it? Can't you smell it?'

I could smell it. A sweet, sugary, buttery smell.

'Someone around here,' Chris announced, 'someone around here is making croissants. And I'm going to find him and offer him any amount of money he wants.'

'Which way?'

'Here. Down here somewhere.' His nose lifted, inhaling cold draughts of the pre-dawn air. 'It's getting stronger. Croissants, pains choc, patisserie, coffee, I can smell it all! Oh! I can taste it! God, that's good.'

'Which way now then, Fido? What happened in Orleans? Didn't we burn Joan of Arc here . . . no, that was Rouen. But something happened here, the maid of Orleans . . .'

'This way. There – oh yes! Done it!' There was a steel door in a wall, ajar, with light and warmth spilling out, and the wonderful smell.

'Allo?' Chris boomed. 'Allo? Bonjour?'

A small man in a dark blue coat appeared. We looked at one another in silence for a moment. He took in our bulky jackets, pallor, sleeping bag, near-empty whisky bottle and drug-reddened eyes. He was carrying a huge tray of unbaked croissants, neatly lined up like a regiment of golden crabs.

'Ah bonjour!' Chris cried, warmly. 'Veuillez-nous excuser, m'sieur, mais l'arome de vos croissants est vachement formidable et mon ami et moi – si possible, si nous vous ne derangeons pas – voudrions les acheter . . . s'il vous plaît?' I tried not to giggle. Chris looked so hopeful that in normal circumstances it would have taken a monster to turn him down, only now the baker's merest objection to alcoholic tramps would surely undo us.

The baker nodded tiredly. 'Combien?'

'Quatre! Non, six! Will that be enough? Better make it huit, huit, s'il vous plaît. Vous avez des pains au chocolat?'

'Combien?' said the baker, with a little more interest. We were digging handfuls of francs out of our pockets.

We collapsed on to the train back to St Etienne, sticky, with the vertiginous feeling of having been awake all night, thoughts slow and muddled, things toppling numbly across the slow shimmer of vision. We moved like divers through the doldrum-calm of exhaustion. I had boosted myself with a final spliff before departure. The orange seat covers of the coach seemed to pulse. Chris was stuffed to the ears with pastry. He wanted to sleep.

'Wilson!'

'What?'

'Don't go to sleep!'

'Why not?'

'You'll feel worse when you wake up. You'll reset your clock.'

'Goodnight.'

'Wilson!'

'Hmmm.'

'Wake up, Wilson! Talk to me! Look, maybe we can see that signal box.'

'Shhh.'

'Wilson! Wake up!'

'Mmpff.'

I prodded him. He opened an eye like a dead slug. I giggled and prodded him again.

'H, if you don't fuck off, I'm going to punch you.'

'If we both sleep we'll miss the stop and wake up in bloody Italy.'

'We won't miss it.'

'I'm going to stay awake for the common good.'

'Good for you.'

It was very, very hard not to prod him again. I was reduced to the level of a three-year-old, a bad one; a stoned imp in me would not let up. It was as if prodding him was the only way of achieving any sort of peace. 'Know when to stop,' my mother always said to me. 'Know when to stop!' It was a perpetual struggle. Even when the knowing was possible, the stopping was almost beyond me. I sat on my hands and fought the urge until something happened, and I started awake again, and looked out of the window, and there was St Etienne.

'Wilson!'

'Hmpff? For fuck's sake, you c –'

'We're here.'

At midnight, at dawn and in the silence of Sunday afternoons I walked the estates of St Etienne, the graveyards, the freight yards and the valleys which led up into the massif where snow-melt rivers roared. These places were magically atmospheric, playgrounds for the imagination; with a bit of dope I peopled them with the spectres of distant friends and dream lovers: it was as though I was doing this with them, seeing for them and through them. I loved the slow rhythms of the station café in the middle of the afternoon, and the quiet of bars closing down at midnight, their light-spill crossed by the tired shadows of waiters putting chairs on tables. I loved the faded photographs and the flowers wilting on the gravestones and the mysterious doings of the outskirt factories at night. I thrilled to the raddled faces of the men drinking at the bus station and the smart clip-clop of women hurrying to the Lyons train. Dope magnified the beauty of the present, slowing time, leaving me aghast at the wonder of ordinary things. It was not that I could not have felt this way without the drug, but it seemed to clear away everything else, to focus the mind through the eyes, to attach stories, implications and fantasies to the merest thing. The moment expanded to fill all thought's horizon: the past was nothing and the future whatever you wanted it to be. I felt as though I was part of my mental carnival. I was a figure in a Bob Dylan song.

We fell into debt. Chris was spending too much, partly supporting me, and went into the red. The French banking system did not subscribe to the overdraft culture we were used to: for some weeks Chris had to go into Credit Lyonnais in the mornings to prove he had not skipped the country. We were reduced to buying kebabs with cheques. I took on private students to raise more money. My tutees preferred to learn on credit. We would see them in our favourite bar, the Vol de Nuit, a black-painted box festooned with bright rock posters, wincing at the sight of me and sidling off.

Spring came, running across the south like a haphazard clown, dropping dollops of buds and blossom like cream on the trees and hedgerows. I found another job, working on luxury tourist barges on the Rhône. Separated from the dealer, busy from dawn until the late evening, I was happy and clean. The slow unrolling of new worlds around every bend seemed to supply all the novelty and beauty that I had sought in dope.

The *Napoléon* was a double-decker barge, marketed as the most luxurious river cruiser in France. The crew quarters were tiny cabins at the back, leaving most of the space for the guest rooms, which had marble baths and four-poster beds. Our clients ranged from Mexican millionaires, so accustomed to servants that they could not see us, to American millionaires who worried about the exact temperature of the hot tub on the top deck and dispensed wise advice. 'Find out about computers,' one man said. 'You're a bright boy but if you want to make money you need to know about things like modems.'

'Right,' I said, my head full of Joni Mitchell and the wonderful string of sense impressions which every day presented. At dawn I opened the curtains of my box above the engine room and saw Provence stretching away to baked stone hills. At six the river villages were blue-shaded and silent; I pedalled through the alleys following my nose to buy the breakfast. In Arles the cypresses were twisted by the heat exactly as Van Gogh painted them. The river widened and the locks were enormous. In the evening I briefed the captain on the wine selection and manned the sinks, scrubbing pots and waiting for the leftovers to come back from the dining room. I washed dishes while bolting an entire quail, swilled down with Châteauneuf du Pape. Late at night the thunder came: we smoked in the galley door, watching the sky flash coloured coats of lightning and the rain tearing the river into a mass of jumping pinnacles.

I made enough money to pay Chris back and returned to the flat for a weekend between charters. Chris was in bed with the pretty girl who lived on the other side of the courtyard. He emerged triumphantly and foolishly accepted a dare from Robert and me, drinking half a bottle of gin in a couple of minutes. First he danced wildly to the radio, then fell over, crawled into the bathroom and began to be sick, then more sick, vomiting like a bilge pump.

'Call me an ambulance,' he groaned.

'You are definitely an ambulance.'

'Chris is an ambulance! Hey Wilson, we're going to McDonald's, wanna come?'

'Uu-uurghh . . .'

'OK. Stay here then and keep an eye on things.'

'Dear Mr Wilson, you cunt' (Robert had adopted this phrase with relish), 'can you lend us some francs?'

'Hu-hurghh . . .'

'Good man! They're probably in his pocket . . .'

We rifled his clothes for the change and set off, laughing. We had not got far before we were struck by remorse. We ran to McDonald's, purchased and ran back. We stripped him and sprayed him with the shower, avoiding his attempts to punch us, and hauled him to his bed.

'It's a very silly drug,' I admonished him. 'You would be much better off getting stoned.'

*

When the summer comes I leave for New York again, to see Wangechi, my long-distance love, and to stay with Ben and Jen, his sister.

'WPLJ 95.5 and it's 89 degrees in Madison Square Garden . . .' crows the radio.

'Sheesh. It must be over a hundred in here.'

Jen's flat on the Upper East Side has no air conditioning. Ben is bussing tables at the Royalton; he is generally free during the day. We sprawl and sweat, drinking beer and awaiting the coming of Ras Mark. Ras Mark is thin and mercurial. He is contactable by pager and carries his dope stashed in his sock. When he arrives he says 'Bless dis house!' When he produces the drugs he says 'Bless dis weed!'

'I don't think I've ever made a joint with weed before . . .'

'Well. This is your chance to learn. Seize the day.'

Wangechi, Ben and I play Dyslexic Scrabble, a game which Theo claims is all the rage at York. I pass on the rules. 'What you do is, you use any letters you like and as long as you can convince one other player that what you've got sounds like a word or phrase, you get the points.'

We roll, smoke and go at it. Carefully expressionless, Ben puts down his letters and sits back.

UMEIBUGN

'Um ee bug na? What planet are you on, Hardiman, for Christ's sake? That's gibberish.'

'Look again.'

'You me I bugun?'

'Benjamin's dear little brain has blown,' Wangechi concludes. She is being very patient with me. I had promised a romantic and intimate time, in my letters, but now I am mostly interested in getting very stoned with Ben.

Ben looks confident. 'You may begin,' he said, patiently.

'You may begin again, mate, but you're not having that.'

'Say it quickly. Youmaybug-in. Gechi, say it quickly. Youmaybegin!'

'So sweet, Benjamin, but so hopeless!'

'Jwanagitoojerassicprk?'

'Excuse me?'

'Do you want to go to *Jurassic Park*? If so – skin up. I'm not facing those mothers remotely straight.'

America is in a lather about this film. In order to derive maximum benefit from the vaunted special effects we resolve to go higher than any kites. We had seen Sylvester Stallone's climbing blockbuster *Cliffhanger* so stoned we could barely squeak, and it had helped, though when the dope began to wear off after the first hour it had still been a long way down to the end. We make no mistake with *Jurassic Park*.

The helicopter flight to the island, with full orchestral back-up, is outstanding. The first dinosaurs to appear are rather lame but by the time the T-Rex begins his assault on the jeep convoy we are entranced. The thing is about twenty yards long: the screen is huge and we are only five rows away. The audience is definitely on the dinosaur's side. The T-Rex has received the best of the pre-publicity and he is living up to it superbly. 'Eat that sucker an' shit!' yells someone. 'Bite dat bitch!'

It is a commonplace among stoners that the original *Star Wars* trilogy is a pot parable: Han Solo and Chewbacca are 'spice' smugglers, the latter is obviously caned, the Dark Side of the Force is paranoia, Jabba the Hut is a dealer who has overdone it on the munchies, Yoda's supreme wisdom and long green ears are the fruits of a millennium of smoking – yadda yadda yadda. But as the cinema cracked and popped with the crunch of tyrannosaurus-sized buckets of popcorn and gurgled with the multiple suckle of fizzy drinks it seemed that *Jurassic Park* was a more perfect illustration of the marijuana parabola. The skittish happiness and swooping dopamine ride of the first hits are a psychological helicopter ride. Suddenly you want to talk about Chaos Theory and speculate about the possibility of dinosaur DNA surviving in the innards of mosquitoes sealed in phials of amber. You arrive on the sunlit uplands and marvel as outlandish and exaggerated theories lumber past you like gentle Diplodocuses. Then the monsters of the mind emerge, and chase you through the jungle of your own fears – it is half hilarious, half terrifying. At first these monsters are very small, mere chameleons and iguanas: they are sudden flashes of fear that you are an idiot, that you are not funny, that you look weird, that you are weird . . . The tyrannosaurs do not emerge in the first act. The story ends in numbed gluttony, as you stuff yourself on sweets and ice cream like Dickie Attenborough's mad scientist character, feasting away the monsters and placidly expecting that your lucidity and intelligence, like Attenborough's niece and nephew, will return unharmed. In the first instalments they always do.

We do not just sit at home and get caned: we go out to do things caned, because it makes them funnier and more difficult. We go boating on the lake in Central Park and forget how to row halfway across. We rollerblade around its avenues. My only way of stopping is to fall over or aim at a fixed object, but neither hurts. We twice try to go to the beach at Coney Island but abandon both missions at Penn Station: the crowds are too intense, it is too complicated and we are too stoned. We attend a rooftop party in lower Manhattan held by friends of a friend of Ben's. Wangechi and I are early so we sit on a step on the other side of the street and watch the partygoers go in. They are rich. A beggar hovers near the door and asks each for change. Every one of them says no until Ben appears, the only busboy among them, and immediately reaches for his pocket.

The Twin Towers loom over the rooftop where the party clusters around a beer keg. I accidentally knock a drink over a girl who has been telling me about her excellent job at Columbia Pictures. She looks as though she will never, ever forgive me.

'Some of these people are awfully uptight,' I mutter.

'Dude, you'd barely finished insulting her before you threw her drink over her. I can kinda see her angle there.'

'I wasn't insulting her, I was just saying I had heard studio executives were the curse of the industry.'

'She is a studio executive.'

'She can't be! She's not much older than us!'

'Uh-huh.'

'Shit!'

At the end of the week I say goodbye to Wangechi again. We are always saying goodbye. It is four in the morning and the tops of the skyscrapers are lost in river mist. Ben and I part with a joint.'

'Look after yourself.'

'You too.'

We are both off to university; Ben to Georgetown, me to York. We are looking forward to it.

'I will.'

4

Red Brick, Red Seal

1993–6

'WOW, LOOK AT this!'
    There was a huge, angular building squatting over a lake, a tall fountain, an embattled feather of water in the wind, and every-where ducks, geese and students. It was all happening. I was caned. Rupert glanced at me.

'It's Central Hall, you fool, you haven't even seen it before? You've been here a week.'

'No!'

'Christ, that's *pathetic*.'

'Impressive . . . Of course I haven't seen it, I've been in my room with you and Theo.'

That was true. Theo had found my room before I did and left his train ticket on the door as a cryptic message. Rupert turned up shortly afterwards. So two of my best friends were here, and also Christian, whom I knew little but knew I was going to like: another German, who had been some sort of a punk at our international school. The first night turned into a party, followed by the second, and so on. While downstairs the rest of the college rang with the excited hubbub of students drinking and the bathrooms reeked with the smell of fresh vomit, we skinned up and laughed. I decided to skive Freshers' Week.

The problem with the International School, many of us felt in ret-rospect, was that whatever came next was an anticlimax. I did not feel the liberation of leaving home for the first time, which many of the other students were now experiencing. I did not feel any sense of pride or achievement in getting to university: compared to being accepted into the castle by the sea it seemed easy. I did not have any particular allegiance or admiration for the institution, as I had had for the college. And among hundreds of fellow Brits I was much less at home than I had been amid the international students. My accent and my pretentious name labelled me again, in a way they had not for years. I was least confident among my own kind.

'Treading water,' my father once said of my plan to do an English degree. I secretly agreed. The International School had given us a sense of purpose and a mission beyond ourselves. Robin and I had been in the lifeboat station one afternoon when an ex-student appeared, someone who had been at the school decades before. We talked.

'So,' he said. 'Do you think you can save the world then?' It was an old college saw, but not a complete joke. We all believed in inter-national understanding. We were all idealistic.

'Probably,' I replied, cheerfully.

'Arrogant bastard,' he laughed.

Now I was just another student and my former feelings of urgency and expectation seemed like a silly and innocent dream.

'We thought you were a vampire in first term,' Mickey told me. Mickey was a chirpy boy from Hounslow, one of the few who did as little work as me. 'You only came out at night, with red eyes, and hung around the coffee machine.' His room, like mine, was a stoner colony. Our corridors reeked of weed. My cleaning lady took to raking the debris of dope flakes and spilled tobacco on my desk into neat brown dunes, ready for use.

'You just laughed and laughed and laughed!' said Jan, who lived across the corridor. 'For hours, all of you.'

'And then you came out and nicked our food from the fridge,' added Victoria. She lived in the room next to mine. I often set my alarm clock with the intention of making it to the first lecture, then awakened to Victoria smashing her hockey stick against our dividing wall.

'How come I can hear it and you bloody can't?'

'I said to my friend in one of the first lectures, we might be really tired, but at least we're not as tired as that guy,' Joanna laughed. Jo was the daughter of a rogue clergyman from Dublin. She never smoked, took no drugs but St John's Wort and barely drank. She did not recognize a stupendous dope hangover, but neither did I, at first. I thought I was just very tired.

Stoned, caned, blasted, mothered, pickled (Theo's phrase), wasted, wankered, fucked, boxed: all much more accurate descriptions of the effect of the heavy 'red seal' hash we smoked than the old-fashioned sixties term, high.

'Believe me,' growled the Head of the English department, another ferocious-eyed Frenchman, 'you will never be so immortal as you feel now.'

I was on a grant from my local authority. On top of which my father had given me a living allowance. 'English isn't obviously for anything,' he said, 'but it's supposed to make you a better human being.'

'Whatever you do, if you are not reading for yourselves, outside the course, you are missing the point of the degree,' said the French professor.

With this in mind I lay on my bed with a huge spliff and lost myself lazily in books which I felt spoke to my condition: Kerouac's *Big Sur*, Kesey's *One Flew Over the Cuckoo's Nest* and *The Electric Kool-Aid Acid Test* by Tom Wolfe, the last two courtesy of Richard, a third year who also lived across the corridor. Richard was going to be an actor. He had huge hair, a torn jumper and thick socks and he took the business of making tea very seriously. 'You have to let it mash, mun,' he said, in a deep voice. He never missed *Neighbours*.

'What degree are you doing, Rich?'

'Politics,' he said with a smile, as though this was a cause for merriment.

'But shouldn't you be going to lectures?'

'No. I should be watching *Neighbours*,' he said, sonorously.

'But you'll get a third! And you could get a first.'

'Exactly. I'll have to be an actor. That *is* politics, mun.'

He was formidably well read, an adept cyclist, had won a gardening trophy, knew a lot about music, dressed, when he dressed, beautifully and was a connoisseur of great films and performances. While writing his girlfriend's essay on Verdi, Richard, who was smoking quite a lot of dope at the time, reported that he had felt Verdi's spirit alongside him.

'I know that! I get that with Shelley!'

'Shelley? "Look on my works, ye mighty, and despair." You have seen *Withnail and I*, haven't you, Horace?' he said, with a significant look over the top of his glasses.

I heard of it first as a rumour, then from Robin. 'Have you seen – ' message lost, garbled – something – '. . . and I?' And then he was off, laughing loudly, reciting lines, 'I *demand* to Have Some Booze! . . . Monty, you *terrible cunt!*'

'What? What's that? What's it called?'

'*Withnail* and *I*. You have to see it. You'll love it. You practically are Withnail, you maniac.'

It is a cause of some pain and some pride that several friends made this comparison over the years. Nothing speaks more clearly of the difference between our generation and the one before than our different responses to this film. When it came out, in the 1980s, it sank unremarked. This gorgeous meditation on failure and the woeful hilarity of the contrast between what is valuable in people and what is valued by the world had nothing to offer Thatcher's youth. It took the recession, and we who hit the age of irresponsibility in John Major's Britain, with our spiralling drug use (consumption and convictions rocketed throughout the 1990s) and our baseless but unshakeable faith in our own judgement (no one was going to tell us about drugs – we were going to tell them, if we could be bothered) and our amused scepticism towards the idols we were supposed to worship – money, power, big cars – to provide Withnail with the audience he deserved.

'What's it about?'

'Two actors in Camden Town at the end of the sixties. They go for a weekend in the country. It is ab-so-lutely *brilliant.*' When Robin is emphatic he enunciates adamantly, like Withnail.

We discovered it on video, its palette of muddy and nauseous colours crammed into the small screen. This meant that almost every fresh viewing revealed new details. I only realized quite recently that the rich and eccentric Uncle Monty wears a radish on his lapel, making sense of 'I's' line 'Suits me, he can eat his fucking radish', which I had thought another of the script's rich and eccentric non-sequiturs.

It is full of truth. And full of the way truth is uttered by fools in an instant, and lost and forgotten.

'I mean *free* to those that can afford it,' Withnail grins, brandishing the key to Monty's house in the country. '*Very* expensive to those that can't.'

If there is a more concise critique of capitalism I have not heard it, but the script does not trouble itself with the big isms. Instead it lavishes loving attention on the gunge between their teeth: us.

The unnamed 'I' of the film is called Marwood by the script, in which the entire ground floor of humanity, among whom Withnail and Marwood spend their time, are 'wankers'. Withnail and Marwood are certainly wankers too, but they alone are fully conscious of their fate, and fully horrified by it.

As the saxophone of 'A Whiter Shade of Pale' wraps itself around the titles rolling over shots of the ghastly interior of their flat, we who have already seen it a dozen times relax into a profound feeling of happiness and security. Here, in the story of an arch-bullshitter, there is no bullshit. It does not contain a single note that is false or contrived and is therefore entirely comforting.

The opening summarizes the argument: to be powerless in Britain is to be smeared between the newspapers and the fish and chips. We flinch under the assault of raised voices: the weasely, insinuating, angst-inducing bray and rumble of 'public opinion' fabricated in the press; we are tormented by the hectoring snobbery and reverse-snobbery of the imaginary 'right-thinking' people who ride on all our backs. We run faster and faster, trying to catch up with spectral versions of ourselves, us with a little more, us doing a little better, us, but quicker and cleverer and better connected; us but more efficient and working harder; us with our doubts lopped off. Those who refuse to run are 'eccentrics' or 'drop-outs': Withnail disdains the race, demanding a winner's medal in return for his existence and gazes around with magnificent, appalled horror. 'I' has paused beside him, and we watch as Withnail makes his hopeless last stand, and is overrun and deserted by his friend.

A folklore sprang up around it. 'Richard E. Grant is allergic to alcohol,' we told each other. 'But Bruce Robinson [the film's writer and director] made him drink just so he knew what it would feel like.'

'They had been awake for days before they shot the first scenes.'

'Who would you rather be, Withnail or I?'

'Have you played the Withnail drinking game?'

A very simple game. You watch the film and match them drink for drink, omitting the lighter fluid Withnail downs in scene 11. I do not know anyone who completed the course, but we did try the equivalent with cannabis. Rupert and I, finding ourselves in possession of a lot of hashish and no particular place to go, resolved one night to take the mission to its conclusion: what would happen if you smoked it all the way to the end? Was there a limit? How much could we take? Theo was there when we started. After a couple of hours he went green, said, 'Guys, is anyone else here really fucking stoned?' and slumped to the floor. Then he shook himself, got up and staggered back to his room, his eyes rolling in different directions. Rupert and I giggled and made another one. It was light and we were still going. It turned into mid morning and we were still going. It was opening time and we were still going.

'Pub.'

I could not sit upright in the bar. I kept slumping down the bench, a jelly sliding down a window. We were collecting resentful looks from the regulars. We trooped back to Rupert's room. We had been awake over thirty hours and smoked sixty joints in the last twelve. I fell over and found I could not get up. I lay on my back, my arms waving feebly above me, and groaned helplessly, 'This is it! This is what happens. It turns you into a fucking *beetle*.'

Which seemed funny at the time.

The university film club showed *Withnail and I* one Saturday night, one of the only times I saw all my friends at once. The reeking dope-holes emptied, the dealers turned up, parties of red-eyed potheads came trailing in. Everyone had prepared for it in the predictable way. There was a lot of shuffling, giggling and wincing at the bright light of the lecture theatre. Then the lights went down and the trailers began. We were all familiar with the rum advert which showed a party of the rich and beautiful taking a speedboat across a lagoon to drink at a glamorous-yet-authentic bar before swishing off, at closing time, back to their perfect lives, and no doubt perfect sex, under a tropical moon. The voice-over talked about Peckham on a rainy Saturday, having a couple at the Dog and Duck and catching the last bus home – parrots flapped and coconuts bounced – 'If . . . you're drinking Bacardi.' Only this time, as if the magic of Withnail had sent bullshit-busting imps into the projection room, the pictures play backwards. Stoned gales of laughter erupt as a speedboat approaches in reverse and the beautiful people run backwards into the bar to spit in their drinks.

'Woah!' we cry. Split coconuts heal and fly up into palms to gasps of mock wonder.

'Far *out*!'

'This is the coolest thing I've ever *seen*,' someone exclaims, as a parrot flaps overhead, backwards.

Withnail staggers to a wall and shouts at five miles of lake.
    Bastards Bastards Bastards.
Nobody to reply except an echo. As loud and drunk as he is.
    You'll all suffer. (Suffer. Suffer. Suffer.) I'll show the lot of you. (You. You. You.) I'm gonna be a star. (Star. Star. Star. Star.)

It is as near as he or the film comes to expressing an aspiration or an ideal. The actor's dilemma is the dilemma of our time as it appears to us. Either you 'make it', or you are a Withnailian wanker. The irony of Withnail is that his calling is as noble as any; we need and love our stars. And Withnail is a star, unquestionably. Withnail is clever and funny, classy and original but, as he points out, he is thirty in a month and he has a sole flapping off his shoe. He does not have a chance. The film offers the comfort of his unimpeachable brilliance at being what he is but as the rain falls and he totters away to oblivion, alone, we know it is no redemption. In our hearts we are stars, but in our heads, wankers: this was the mirror in which we saw ourselves.

'You're a bloody bohemian!' Christian cackled. 'That's what you are, in this ridiculous blue shirt.'

He seemed to find this very funny. He sat in my chair, in leather trousers, with an upside-down cross around his neck, silver skulls on his fingers and black varnish on his nails, and laughed.

'Yes, I am. Have some more water.'

'Why do you keep trying to make me drink focking water?'

Christian had a scholarship from the German government which allowed him to study anything anywhere, all expenses paid – all he had to do was write them a letter occasionally telling them he was doing fine, as far as I could tell. He was, apparently, the most exciting New Hegelian the philosophy department had seen for years.

'What's a New Hegelian, Christian?'

'I don't fockin know, do I?'

On special occasions he would empty two foot-long canisters of spray on to his central fin of black hair and turn it into a Mohican. During the course of whatever came next – he was an excellent drummer, and an enthusiastic if light-headed drinker – his Mohican would flop gently sideways. He was a hopeless smoker, sucking and wincing and complaining vehemently about the construction of my joints: he was keen to smoke but not to roll.

'Water is the way forward. Have some more.'

'Shit. I have to piss again.'

The God he professed to despise had given Christian a peculiarly small bladder, perhaps as a pre-emptive strike against the slights Christian would pile upon him in the name of freedom, which was Christian's big thing.

'It's ten to five!' I cried, and pulled the curtains back. 'Yes, look, there! It's getting light. It's the dawn. I love the dawn.'

'Ugh, light. Shut it out,' Christian urged. 'Horrible stuff.'

'Did you know, Edinburgh University are talking about renaming their student union. It's called Mandela Hall, and now they want to call it River Phoenix hall.'

'Tossers. Why?'

'Because he's dead!'

'Who is?'

'River Phoenix, you idiot.'

'Is he?'

'Yeah, he had an overdose. Horrible.'

'Oh. Right. Who is this person?'

'Actor.'

'Oh. How sad.' We looked at each other for a moment. 'Actors!' Christian cried. 'Focking hippies!'

I went to the loo. The idea of Christian calling anyone else a hippy struck me suddenly as terribly funny, and I laughed and laughed in the lavatory like a woodpecker in a cupboard, trying not to let it affect my aim. There is something desperate and frightening in the sight of someone laughing at nothing. I suddenly remembered watching the television with my mother and seeing a report on drug use in which the camera settled on a young man wearing a tatty jacket, hovering in a dingy public park, not far from the toilets, laughing and laughing in the grey afternoon, his head nodding rapidly as the waves of silent giggles racked him, his teary eyes, unfocused, staring at the dirty grass.

My mother looked up at me, her expression crumpled with distress. 'Oh poor boy!' she cried. 'The poor, poor boy . . .'

The death of River Phoenix was in the tragic tradition of the premature extinction of the talented and beautiful, like Marilyn and James Dean, Hendrix and Jim Morrison, the newspapers said. In their reports no blame is attached to him. He was too sensitive, too lauded and not robust enough to survive, was the line. He died a victim: the connection Edinburgh students made between him and Mandela was extraordinary. Mandela, unjustly imprisoned, eventually released in 1990, was a hero, freeing a country, inheriting the earth. The injustice of his ordeal was plain, but what was the injustice in the death of River Phoenix? Mandela was the symbol of the torture and eventual liberation of an entire nation; Phoenix, like Kurt Cobain who died the following year, stood for nothing more than our condition: psychological frailty, the anguish of the blessed. In naming a building after Mandela the students said we feel for you, we support you. In proposing to rename it in honour of River they said we mourn us, we feel for us. Was this to be our Che Guevara? A victim of indulgence, of surfeit, a victim of success, killed by drugs, killed by a highball – a combination of heroin and cocaine.

'Oh the poor, poor boy . . .' my mother would have said.

I thought of River Phoenix and I thought of that addict, laughing in the park, and I thought of my mother. Suddenly she was every addict's mother and the addict was every son. I felt terrible guilt. That was me, the me I hid from her. In the loo, laughing at Christian, I said silently, 'It's all right, Mum. It's fun really . . .' but I knew I did not quite believe myself: the tiniest touch of The Fear.

'Look at my thumbs, my thumbs have gone weird, I think I'm getting the Fear!' Marwood cries. The Fear is a phrase which has left common parlance but it was everywhere then. 'You're giving me the Fear!' Mickey would cry, with a burst of laughter. We laughed at it a lot: 'Help! I've got the fucking Fear!'

The Fear is the sound of your own voice ringing hollow. The Fear is the sudden conviction that everything is wrong, every decision a mistake, every joke a dreadful revelation of your idiocy, every view an expression of your ignorance. The Fear is the gut-deep certainty of your doom, the down side of the expansion of consciousness granted by drugs. In that first year it was a joke, a one-liner, a great shadow-monster. We teased it, laughed at it, danced out of its reach.

Lara, my girlfriend from school, came to visit one weekend. There was no hope for our relationship, though a new invention, email, had allowed us to keep in touch. But we were loving and familiar old friends. She laughed at what she found of me, in disbelief.

'I can't believe you're a stoner!' she said. 'A stoner' to me was a woolly figure from the fringes of a mainstream American film; a comic turn, a grungy joker. Her judgement made me laugh; it seemed sweet and rather quaint. If I was, then everyone I knew was a stoner, to some extent. We could not all be minor characters: we were the spirited, the playful, the fun. Lara made it sound as though I had joined some sort of campus clique.

'Neither can I! At least I'm not a Tory.'

There were about six of them, ludicrous and rather wonderful in their tweeds and brogues and obvious pleasure at being smart and isolated among five thousand scruffy left-wingers. They appeared outside my window with a croquet set in the first of the fine weather: Rupert and I blasted them with Jimi Hendrix, waved spliffs out of the window and hooted. The Tories curled their pale lips in good-humoured disgust. Then there were the Thesps, the boaters, the rugby lot, the intellectuals and the various colonies which formed in all the different departments. I made friends in many of these groups and almost everybody I liked I came to know, or to know better, through dope.

'You, a stoner!' Lara exclaimed. 'It's so weird!'

I laughed. I quite liked the idea. I had never been labelled before. It seemed like fancy dress costume: I was happy to put it on if it would make someone laugh. The dope was so ubiquitous it hardly seemed to merit an identity. When in new company, or at parties, rolling and smoking and passing it back and forth seemed a lovely way to interact with people. A stoner! How funny.

Almost as funny as the Tories.

John Major moaned about yob culture and talked about 'Back to Basics'. He and his Home Secretary, Michael Howard, were clear about the way forward: 'Just as Conservatives stuck to basic maxims in economic policy in the 1980s so they should with social policy in the 1990s,' Howard said. 'We should have no truck with trendy theories that try to explain away crime by blaming socio-economic factors. Criminals should be held accountable for their actions and punished accordingly.' Teachers and bishops disagreed with him. My old public school Headmaster appeared in the papers. 'There is a gaping moral vacuum in society,' he said. 'There are no role models for young people, there is no leadership. Back to basics has failed.'

'Bloody hell,' I marvelled at the paper. 'Even the old boy can see it.'

At the same time, a think tank questioned two and a half thousand 18 to 34 year olds and found our dislikes included rigid moral codes, Puritanism, pessimism, authoritarianism and family values: everything society stood for, if our government was our measure. We sought, we told the researchers, excitement, hedonism and risk.

Lara, Theo and I took acid together. We set out from my room as it began to bite. Theo paused as we made our way along a covered walkway, struck by a sudden thought. 'Hey . . .' he said, and flowed up a wall, extended one outlandishly long arm, deftly removed a light bulb, and dropped back down to earth, clutching his prize. 'Look!' he said, delighted. It was as though the fabric of the world was merely screwed in: if you were a little taller than usual, and tripping, you could take it apart on a whim.

'Well done, Theo. What do you want for that, a biscuit?' Lara drawled.

'Hey look, East Germany!' I cried. In the dark, the low concrete blocks of the colleges hunched over their reflections in the lake looked exactly as I imagined the former GDR. 'Lucky you're with us, in case we get asked for our papers.'

'What? Why?'

'You speak German.'

We walked around the lake. A skein of geese passed low above us and I craned, staring up to watch one breasting the evening light, the air carrying it, buoying the bird up, cupping it like an invisible hand. 'I see!' I say. 'That's how it's done . . .' We pause in front of a bush. I have never seen a bush like this. It glistens and pulses with life: every stalk, leaf and blossom thrusting, appealing, almost screaming its existence.

We found a coffee machine at the end of a deserted corridor. I pulled out some change but could not make any sense of it. I could not make the coins mean anything beyond themselves. I stared at them, examining them closely.

'Funny things, aren't they? I've never really looked at them before.'

Theo was studying the coffee machine as though he had never seen one of them before either.

'That's interesting,' he said. 'It's a very simple code . . .'

'What?'

'143,' he said, punching it in.

The machine made grating noises and produced a cup of liquid.

'What's this?'

'Try it.'

'Eugh! What is that, Schmidt?'

'Coffee with tomato soup.'

I went into a long, deserted washroom. Under the strip lights, in the sinister not-quite silence of the room, I had a sudden intimation of horror. Imagine severed arms and hands in the basins. It is not that I see them: it is that I could see them. Something about the way the illumination from the strip lights coats the porcelain makes me think of blood; the light is not right, not natural, it is suddenly terrifying. 'Don't anyone go into the bathroom,' I said tersely. 'It's not good in there.'

Lara and Theo are lying on their backs on the floor, staring at the little holes in the ceiling tiles and marvelling. 'Have a drink, and come and look at this,' Theo says.

'What are we drinking?'

'Tea and chocolate soup, I think.'

It was not very strong acid but it hung around. The night ended and the day came up. Lara and I lay in bed together, holding each other.

'I want it to stop now,' she said, quietly.

'Me too. It is, it will. But we mustn't fight it. Just let it go easy . . .'

One of my new friends was Jamie, a very bright second year, a boy who spoke like a machine gun, perhaps because he had taken too much speed when younger; he told me about taking too much acid. 'I lay in a bath and felt all the physical pain I had ever had, every knock and cut and bruise – I could remember all of them! It was like I was running through them all and undoing them. But then I undid too much! It was like I was disappearing, first my feet and hands, then my legs and arms, so I got hold of it and started to put myself back together but the thing was I had this feeling the disappearance was going to reach my chest and I suddenly thought, Shit I've forgotten how to breathe! So I just lay there and concentrated on that. Breathe, breathe! It was really, really close, I tell you . . .'

Jamie told this story with bright eyes and wildly waving hands, with laughter and amazement. It was as though he was telling a war story, a daring exploit in the face of the enemy and a narrow escape. I laughed too and shook my head. It was how we all told our tales: see how far we had been, look how close we had come.

Christian came to stay at my mother's house at the beginning of the spring holiday. We had a lot of hash which we decided should be eaten on the train. It was a very long journey and we fell asleep. When we woke up we were in Wales, it was dark and raining outside and we both felt peculiar. The taxi driver took one look at

Christian's Mohican, black nail varnish and upside-down crucifix, and obviously felt peculiar too. There was little conversation in the cab, which was lucky, as the hash began to come on very strong.

We stopped in Abergavenny so that I could get some money out. The driver has given me many lifts, over the years.

'Hmm,' he says thoughtfully, watching me yaw towards the cash point. 'Horatio. His parents must have been watching *Mutiny on the Bounty* when they had him.'

The taxi soared up the valleys like a jet fighter. I felt myself grinning in terror. I wanted to scream. We arrived at the yard gate and got out. Lark, my old dog, came padding out to greet us.

'Hello, Larky,' I said, my voice wavering weakly. It sounded scared, giggly and hopeless. Lark could tell something was up.

Christian stumbled after me through the mud. It is very dark outside my mother's house. I could hear Christian cursing speculatively. I had a sudden conviction that this was suicidal folly. If I could not handle Lark there was no way we could face my mother.

'Christian!'

'Wot?'

'Drop your bags.'

'OK. Now what?'

'Run!'

I turned and fled for my life. Christian charged after me. We sprinted up the lane, pell-mell into the blackness, Christian's head floating alongside me, shaven sides gleaming, like a levitating skull.

'Mate, wot the fock are we doing?'

'We're running away!'

'I can see that,' he panted. 'But why?'

'So that we don't have to face Mum. We can't let her see us like this. We can't carry this off!'

'Of course we can, what do you mean?'

'You know what I mean. We're off our tits. I'm tripping.'

'Yes, but we can't just run around in this focking rain, can we? Let's go and see your mother.'

'Oh hell. You think we can handle it?'

'Of course.'

'Oh God. OK. Come on.'

We knocked on the door, which was bolted as usual from the inside. My mother let us in. The kitchen was dimly lit by one small light above the stove, and I could see my mother looking closely at us.

'Are you all right?' she said.

She looked like a small red gnome. Behind her, the lines of the tiled floor did not run parallel as they used to but converged somehow, so that the floor sloped violently down into the middle of the room, then climbed up sharply to the opposite wall.

'We had a few drinks on the train,' I said, lamely. 'That's all.'

'I see,' she said, bristling with suspicion. She began telling a story about a fox she was having trouble with, a story I struggled to follow as I battled to make Christian tea. As I made repeated inconclusive trips across the kitchen, trying not to look down at the extraordinary tiled trench in the middle of the floor, and Christian sat at the table, apparently holding his head on with his hands, the story became more emphatic.

'It's biting their heads off,' my mother cried. 'The fox is biting their heads off!'

I saw teeth and severed necks and blood. Christian's eyes were dark holes of horror. It was like an insane conference between a vampire, a gnome and whatever the hell I was.

'Please, Mum,' I moaned weakly. 'Don't!'

Christian and I went to bed early, but not before I had helped her make Christian's bed and straighten up the spare room, during which she talked about someone whom I realized, after saying 'yes' and 'uh-huh' for a while, was dead. She was talking in the present tense.

'But surely,' I said, 'she's dead?'

My mother started laughing. 'Honestly,' she said, 'you're both out of your tiny minds. Christian looks extraordinary, which is fine, of course, but he seems to be falling asleep.'

'We're both very tired,' I repeated, lamer than ever. Christian had in fact gone to sleep at the table.

The next day my mother and I talked as we did so many times over the years. Was I taking drugs? Was I on drugs?

Sometimes I said no. Sometimes I said, with defiance, yes, I was smoking marijuana. Often I lied and said I was only smoking it sometimes, and then defended that. No one would have minded if I had been drinking – well, I argued, this was not as bad as drinking. Was I taking heroin? she often asked. No, I cried, of course not.

'But I found a burned teaspoon in your room.'

It was for hash, I explained; when you only have a tiny bit left you heat it on the spoon because it is too small to hold.

My mother remembered smoking cannabis in the sixties. She said she had not seen the point of it – it made people silly, she said. Why were we doing so much of it? Because it was fun, I said, feeling stupid. My friends had varying approaches to their parents and their drugs. One or two parents were said to be 'cool' with it, but the majority terribly feared drugs, so their children lied to them. Rather than be lied to many parents watched, hoped and simply did not ask. If we were doing well and seemed happy they did not worry, or did not show their worry. My mother took me as she found me. When I was dirty, unshaven and stoned she was angry and sad. I fought off visions of her lying awake at night, worrying in the dark, as I rolled and smoked upstairs in the attic, lost in my own dreams. When I was moody and withdrawn she was sometimes furious, sometimes agonized.

'The one thing I can't stand,' she warned me, 'is lies. I can't stand liars.'

'But everybody lies!' I cried. 'We all lie, all the time. It's what we *do*.'

She was horrified but it was true for me. I was rarely straight with her about what I was doing, where, with whom, or when I would be back. I had always hated to worry her, ever since my childhood on the mountain when I had seen the agonies she suffered from worry, and now I could not, would not, admit or justify my doings. So I lied.

Years later she talked about how miserable I made her in these years.

'I thought you used to be such a happy, delightful little boy, and now you were so angry, and so evasive, and you lied all the time. But I thought well, he's clever enough to know what he's doing, and if this is what he wants there's nothing I can do. I thought you were choosing it. I never thought you were an addict or that you could not help yourself.'

I never thought that either.

★

'Horatio!' she shouted up the stairs one afternoon. 'Are you there? Come quickly!'

'What is it?'

'Something amazing – something absolutely incredible!'

'What?'

'It's unbelievable – you're fashionable!'

'WHAT?'

'It's true!' She was waving a magazine from one of the Sunday papers. 'You're fashionable! You've been fashionable for years, it turns out. Look! It's called Grunge!'

One day she asked me about acid – LSD, as she called it. I explained in great detail what it was like, how it made the world unfamiliar and miraculous, alien and essential, as if I had never seen it before.

She listened carefully. When I had finished she said, 'I see. But that is exactly how I feel on a beautiful morning here when I go out in the frost to feed the sheep.'

'Yes, Mum, but most people can't do that, can't feel that . . .'

I thought at the time that this said more about her than it did about acid.

I began the new term, as every term, with a host of resolutions, none of which included stopping drugs. I went out before dawn on the first of May and walked across the fields beyond the town. Blossom lay under the hawthorns and the white cherries, scatterings of light which floated on the dark grass as if on water. The day broke in sprays of colour across a reef of sky and the dawn chorus burst from every hedge, every bush and tree, so loud, so excited and ebullient, the birds seemed to greet the whole summer. I sat on a green and watched it all and counted uncountable blessings. My course this term was the seventeenth century: Milton, the Metaphysical Poets, Marvell, George Herbert, Henry Vaughan. I loved it and everything seemed to speak to me, and – and! – I had met someone.

Maria's laugh was a bubbling, tinkling thing, which tailed down to a naughty, throaty sound; it had a sorcerer's quality: you wanted to hear it again and again. Her hair was blue-black and her skin brown as an Indian summer; her eyes were quick and full of questions.

When challenged she flared her nostrils as if scenting battle. A singer, a cellist, slender and quiet in herself, loud and striking in her presence, she was gentle, and bright, and she was so beautiful. Theo, Rupert and I lost our heads to her, one by one.

She knew a lot about music. Rupert and I sat in her room like two courtly lovers, listening to her CDs and smoking the tight joints she rolled neatly, effortlessly, with long thin fingers. While I had been shielded from it at college, Maria had been smoking, like almost everyone else in her sixth form, for the last two years.

'This is Galliano,' she said.

'Mmm,' we said, nodding to the music, 'funky.' We would both buy copies within a week.

Theo was the first; they slept together, she ended it. Then Rupert came to my room, giving me strange, querying looks. 'I've gone into bat!' he said, swinging at an imaginary ball. He looked awkward and embarrassed. I felt sick. Couldn't he see I loved her? It had happened with Thea, my first love, and now it was happening again. I did not say much; I got stoned, ate baked potatoes, watched *Baywatch* and the news.

On the last day, when I had half packed up my room, there was a knock at my door. It was Maria.

'Come in.'

We sat and looked at each other.

'I made a mistake,' she said.

'How's it going with Rupert?'

She shook her head. She seemed deeply embarrassed. 'How's it going with you?'

I stared down at my Doc Martens, and thought hell with it, tell the truth.

'I'm sorry. I think I've fallen in love with you, Maria, but . . . you're going out with Rupert.'

'No. I've ended it. I should never have done it. I wanted to be with you.'

'But Theo – Rupert –'

'I know. I'm so sorry.'

That first night we went to sleep with our noses touching, ever so gently, and when we woke they still were. The bed was full of blood.

It was her time, but it seemed like an omen. I knew I had come to a mortal line, but I did not hesitate to cross it.

We swung out across Europe on trains: we could not afford it and we did not care. We went to Amsterdam ('to see the Van Goghs,' I told my father again: the number of times I have gone to see the Van Goghs, and I still haven't seen them). Not long after we arrived I got the Fear, properly, for the first time. Here in a room in a summer city with the girl I loved I felt a traitor, a thief, a madman. What on earth was I doing? The usual remedy did not work: the dope was much too strong. I looked in the little mirror above the basin and saw the equivocal stare of someone lost, someone bluffing, scared. In a hotel with Maria, in Amsterdam with all the dope legal, all the sex we could ever want available, subject to no governance or restriction but our own whims: it should have been a nirvana but we fluttered around despair, our responsibilities shirked, mooring lines untied, anchors lost.

The next day I moved through a daze; Maria had to keep grabbing my arm, pulling me out of the path of trams and bicycles and cars. A terrible unhappiness, guilt, walked beside us. I was stalked by the thought of Rupert, like Banquo's ghost. We talked about going back but there was no way back. We kept touching each other, for reassurance. We kissed on street corners, as if physical sensation could ward off all the worry. We went on. To a Paris which was emptying for the summer, to the bay of Lerici in Italy, to see where Shelley died, and to Elba, where we could not afford dinner, so ate ice cream. The water was so clear you could see the bottom in the moonlight. We sat on a diving platform, a little way off shore, and kissed. We arrived in Nice, funds almost gone.

'What are we going to do?' Maria worried.

'Something will happen,' I replied. The doubt had fallen away: we were lovers in love, and we had each other.

At the station we met a girl who had a cheap room to let. There: everything was going to be all right. Even the autumn would be all right, one way or another. It was insane, but Rupert and Maria and I were supposed to be living together.

*

The house stood at a road junction just outside York's city wall. It was next door to a chip shop, opposite another chip shop and permanently rattled by traffic. I moved in before term began, needing to work to make back the money we had spent in Europe: I became a glass collector at a nightclub. In the staffroom there was a photograph of a woman having intercourse with a pig, beside which someone had written in a neat and plaintive hand 'Is that the best you can do?' It seemed desperate and telling that this was the extent of the glass collectors' rebellion. I tore the picture down and was sentenced to hours of mopping up puke in return.

Then Rupert arrived. He wore a straggly beard and was full of stories of India. He had been smoking a potent Indian marijuana, charis, lots of charis, and he was beside himself. Gurdjieff, the unseen world beyond, the writings of Ursula K. Le Guin – it was all true, he said. He talked in archetypes and parables. His dark eyes were full of piercing suspicions and unbalanced certainties. 'You have created me,' he said. 'I was a king, and the king must die, and you killed me.'

'No, no, Rupert, I didn't kill you. I just did what you did, I started going out with Maria, and we're still going out, that's all.'

I heard him screaming in the bathroom one morning. 'Come on, motherfuckers!' he shouted. 'Bring it on!'

Then Maria arrived. I went out to do a shift at the nightclub. When I came back Rupert was looking defiant and Maria was in tears. He explained it to me: 'We started talking, then we started kissing, and then she got upset.'

'I didn't want to,' she said.

'She did,' he said.

We tried to carry on. 'My dad says it's an old story, don't let it spoil your friendship,' Rupert reported. It was an old story but the poisonous trauma of those weeks, which destroyed our friendship for ever, was intensified by dope. We both carried on smoking. We began our sessions in the old way but we slipped in and out of a fog, clouds of paranoia and patches of empathy, moments of sympathy and sudden accusations. We sat cross-legged, failing to keep the conversation away from our dispute. I could see the hurt in him, the offended affection, the recrimination. We passed the joints between us with wincing distaste, self-loathing deflected into derision at the other's dependency: now we scorned each new betrayal of weakness instead of laughing at our shared delinquency. And I could see the twitch of his aggression, his bitterness, the threads of his hatred as clearly as he could see my fear, my guilt, selfishness and my venal indignation, all at once, in a horrible mix of lucid perception and stunted articulation.

Now an unwashed plate was an intentional slight, the freesheet dropping through the front door further confirmation of the tawdry swamp in which we daily wrestled. His loud music was aimed at me. My meetings with Maria were spittle on our friendship.

'She's mad,' he said once, 'and you're evil.' I argued that we had all ill-treated each other. I did not blame any of us but I would not take his side against her. I stood by her, and in so doing betrayed my oldest friend. Maria took a room in another student house. I moved in with Theo and Christian. Rupert and I tried to make it up, but it was as if we had seen the other sides of each other and we could never forget them.

Theo and Christian are living in a house in one of York's poorer suburbs. On the way there is a bridge with white graffiti: 'Work, eat, consume, die. We have been conned!' Above it is a poster for the new National Lottery, a hand of mammon pointing down at a corner shop – 'It could be you!' Beyond it there is a view of the Minster, a great stone ship, riding out of time above the trees and rooftops. It is like living in a long-dead country, a world of Sundays. John Mills on the television, bowling on the green, *Gardeners' Question Time* on the radio (topical tips for composting) and always the weekend news. A light plane has come down in Lincolnshire, three fishermen are missing off the coast. Women and children have been mortared in Sarajevo and three thousand bird watchers have gone to see a Siberian Red-flanked Blue Tail at Worth Matravers in Dorset . . .

Robin sent me a photocopy of his face, eyes closed, apparently asleep. 'Sunday Country', he wrote on it. Sunday Country is our shorthand for all this, for daylight leaking into a dim morning after, for a taut absence of urgency, for days of rhythms which all suggest spliffs.

★

We do not have a television so we make our entertainment ourselves. Theo memorizes an entire pack of Trivial Pursuit cards: he can do it backwards, shouting the question and the category in response to half the answer and crowing in triumph. Christian devotes himself to *Civilization* – a world-builder game on his computer – and to *Dungeons and Dragons*.

The *Dungeons and Dragons* group assemble in our living room. They draw the curtains, light candles and roll joints. As I pass through the living room I pick up snatches of the game: all goes well at first, they are elves and clerics and dwarves and thieves, equipping themselves and setting out on their adventure, but then the fighting starts and the dope kicks in. One of the cardinal rules of *Dungeons and Dragons*, as far as I can tell, is that anything which befalls the Elf or the Wizard you are playing befalls 'your character', not you. Unfortunately, dope dissolves that distinction. One of the players is Skinhead Bob. Bob was a SHARP skin, a Skin Head Against Racial Prejudice – he is anti-violence unless someone starts on him, or unless it is deployed against evildoers: racist skins. But as Bob becomes more stoned his character becomes stoned too; when Bob becomes paranoid, his character follows suit.

'Bob, your move,' says Christian, the Dungeon Master. 'There are four Orcs somewhere to your left.'

Bob looks at him with dark, suspicious eyes. Then he nods slowly, with a cunning smile. 'Ah draw my sword, and stab it in fooking Kieran's face.'

Cries of alarm and distress. 'No! Bob! Why are you doing that?'

Kieran, Bob's best friend, is baffled and offended. 'You're joking?'

'No, I'm not joking. Ah don't trust yer fancy little Elf. Ah reckon you're in league with Zuman. Ah saw you and Christian whispering and ah know what you're up to. Plotting. So 'ave some of *that*, you treacherous, plotting *coont!*'

'I'm not in league with anyone! We're on the same side, you idiot.'

'Yeah, *right*. You better roll that dice, sunshine, cos ah'm gonna cut you up.'

'Whoa, whoa,' cries Christian, who has spent the last two weeks designing this adventure. 'Time out!'

They sort it out but when I pass through again, two hours later, Bob's character has acquired a broadsword and is swinging it at Kieran's head.

Robin is studying architecture in London, living in a more sophisticated world: his friends argue about mass culture, Baudrillard, Brit Art and post-modernism. When I visit him the music is better and the students and parties more international, but the ubiquity of dope is identical. He pays a return visit to York.

Robin lies on a mattress on the floor of my room, Maria and I on the bed. We have smoked a lot and been to see *Interview with the Vampire*. Now we are all stoned and sleepy, but not quite done.

'It's terrible,' he rumbles from the floor.

'What?'

'I know we don't need it, I'm so stoned, but some part of my mind is going, Go on . . . go on!'

'What?'

'Have another one!'

'You *dog*.'

'I know, it's terrible.'

'Come on then, one more . . .'

'Yeah!'

Robin and I were always terrible like that. When we ran out of cigarettes we would smoke butts, or empty them out into Rizlas to make disgusting salvage fags. We cackled with delight over chippers – long stubs – and relit them, less for the nicotine than for the shared folly, which amused us, and because if one did, the other had to. At primary school the teacher always said, 'Why did you do that?' and if you answered, 'Because so-and-so did,' she would always say, 'What? Haven't you got a mind of your own? If so-and-so jumped out of a window, does that mean you would too?' To which the true answer, the one you never gave, was yes, definitely, I'd have to! In Robin's case, in fact, I did. For no reason we can remember we did once leap up in the middle of a lesson and jump out of the first floor window.

He was amazed by the activity in the living room the next morning. I walked him to the station.

'Your house is unbelievable.'

'Why?'

'Well, you come down the stairs, there are about twenty people there, everyone fucking stoned, at eleven in the morning. Theo is mad, Christian in his cape, and who is that terrifying fucking skinhead?'

'Bob! Bob's great.'

'Christ, I was scared to speak.'

I waved him off and walked home, puffing another joint.

'Blur or Oasis?'

'I don't give a shit. Got any Rizlas?'

Theo pinned a pair of purple underpants on the wall above the gas fire.

'A statement?'

'Yes.'

'Of what?'

'Pants!'

'How's the work?'

'Good! Economics. Japan. Britain's fucked. Give it twenty years you'll all be shitting in the streets.' He had shaved exactly half his beard off and was wearing a head torch, but he seemed serious.

'Come on, Schmidt, let's go to the Railway Museum.'

The head torch went down well.

'Look, he can see right into the engine there!'

Disappointingly, no one noticed the half beard. We all did things to be noticed. Christian took part in a protest against the introduction of student loans which involved occupying Central Hall. He and twenty others sat around in the foyer giggling until the university authorities charged one of them with breaking and entering and the protest, with one martyr, collapsed. I put on a play, *The Addicts' Opera*, partly as an open letter to Maria: she said she had tried heroin, which made me frantic with worry. The story follows an English student, David, who sits in his college room getting wasted with a university porter, Quentin, and railing about getting wasted.

'That *is* a good time these days,' he moans, 'even if we hate it.'

We have to have a bigger spliff than Withnail's Camberwell Carrot: my dealer makes a gigantic thing, stuffed with hay up to the tip, which is tobacco. Its entrance draws a sigh of admiration from the audience.

The cast are drawn from outside the university drama clique: most have never acted before. The first night is not a disaster. The next night the leading man, Michael, suffering an attack of nerves, ignores my instruction, goes to the bar, and fortifies himself with two large vodkas. He turns in an amazing, hilarious performance.

The word goes around the campus and the third and final night sells out. We pack them in, right up to the performers' feet. The first line is 'Fuck me, I'm bored.' The audience laugh. In another contemporary survey eighty per cent of young people tell researchers that they believe boredom is the principal reason for juvenile crime. The criminal craze of the year is ram raiding: driving a car through the shutters of a shop, often an off-licence, grabbing anything in reach and tearing off. The conviction rate for it is very high but that does not deter the raiders. It is as though the excitement of the act, the business of smashing a stolen car through someone else's window, is as big a draw as the haul.

The Addicts' Opera has David drop out of university, conceal his addiction from his mother, fail to persuade his girlfriend to stop heroin, take it with her and end up in Amsterdam, a world of addicts, where he encounters Quentin, who has won the lottery and is determinedly drugging himself to death. Our boredom is the ennui of spoiled children, overlapping something deeper and timeless, youth's existential love-sickness for something it cannot quite define. Coddled in a luxury of leisure, supplied with all the time and rope we could ask for, we are listless, uneasy with unearned privilege, spear-carriers in an uncertain tribe, expertly hanging ourselves because it is fun and, we believe, we can take it. We sit in our jeans from America, listening to music from Bristol on a stereo from Japan, smoking hash from Morocco, as if globalization is a giant, faulty cash machine, spewing plastic pleasure over our laps.

I watch *The Word*, a late-night Channel 4 programme which revels in cynicism, narcissism, swearing and naked flesh, the beginning of the 'They'll do anything to get on TV' format, in which freaks behave freakishly, licking cack, eating cack, being buried up to the neck in cack, to the marvelling disgust of the presenters and the studio audience. It is knowingly slutty, sullying television. Slumped in my chair, rolling and smoking, I laugh disgustedly at it and myself.

'I want – tits. So you give me – tits.'

One of *The Word*'s guest presenters signs off the last of his slots saying: 'Goodbye and thanks for watching. I've done this for me, but if you've enjoyed it that's a bonus. Goodbye!'

It is not pleasant but it is the truth – all presenters do it for themselves. But the self-regard, chutzpah, one-upmanship and defensiveness all seem horribly typical of us.

While we present ourselves as self-contained and confident, our internal worlds are described in the music we love best. It is there in the longing, keening chants of Portishead. *Please could you stay awhile to share my grief, For it's such a lovely day to have to always feel this way . . .* The sound is dopey and urgent at the same time, redolent of neon light on the fringes of midnight towns, the dirty romance in rumours of warehouse parties and illegal raves. It is the sound of loss, of aftermath. We love Massive Attack and Underworld, their beats driving across words used only for their sounds, against sense, music experienced as incoherent suggestion, like water, roiling tides of sensation. The condition is there too in the lyrics of songs we could sing along to. Radiohead's 'Creep' was a huge favourite long before the band became superstars: *I'm a creep, I'm a weirdo, what the hell am I doing here? I don't belong here . . .*

The audio explosions of the time are wordless dance music, designed for ecstasy users, and hip-hop, the war music of the ghetto, the rhymes and rhythms of a culture that has clear battles to fight, clear injustice to protest at, clear enemies to provoke. We adopt it enthusiastically, parroting its splendid rage and confrontation, though we have nothing in common with it but our ages and a hankering pang for revolt. We are a post-revolutionary generation. *You'll never fail like common people, you'll never watch your life slide out of view, and dance and drink and screw, because there's nothing else to do*, sings Jarvis Cocker, and is amazed, at Glastonbury, when the entire crowd knows every single word and sentiment.

I have a long, stoned argument with Christian about revolution. I argue for a bloodless coup, complete renationalization of infrastructure and radical redistribution of wealth. Christian makes faces and shakes his head. The sixties thing seems quaint and rather naive now: yet we live in the shadow of that legendary decade. The hedonism and freedom and excitement of our parents' time, seen from here, vastly overshadows ours. San Francisco in the mid sixties! Paris in sixty-eight! Chelsea, the Beatles, the Mini! What it would have been to be alive in such times and places, when there was something in the air, when you felt, as Hunter S. Thompson put it, that you could strike sparks anywhere. Even Manchester in the late eighties would have done, when the music was amazing and the ecstasy was pure. But we were just too young. We had heard the sound of it, like children listening to a party downstairs, but we had not been there. All we can do is hanker. Fashions, attitudes and styles are all 'retro'. They have rebuilt the Mini and the VW Beetle and neither look as good as the originals: all style, no personality.

We have retained some sixties vocabulary and attitude. We say 'cool' a lot, it is our highest accolade. When a club night in town goes well, lots of ecstasy, lots of dancing, we exult: 'The vibes were good tonight!' We say 'heavy' when things are not cool. We have the same attitude to sex (with added condoms), and we have drugs. One way we definitely surpass the sixties is in the quantity, variety and availability of our drugs, if not the quality.

We are anti-war, pro-feminist, (theoretically) anti-nuclear, environmentally aware (but inactive: the Germans are amazed by how little recycling we do, compared to what they have been doing for years) and (hypocritically) anti-capitalist. But the idea that we might do anything about these things is laughable. Do what, exactly? The only demonstrations I attend are two anti-fascist, anti-racist marches. There is little feeling, at either, of any urgent peril.

The confrontations of the seventies, viewed from here, had brought us to Thatcher, the eighties and a real revolution, which had crushed the meek and the poor into mulch. Our restlessness differs from preceding generations in that we do not have utopian dreams beyond the borders of the system or the merest grain of political revolutionary zeal. It feels as though we are the first generation which cannot see an alternative to the old ways: the old order is the only order; though we despise it, what is the choice? We look around the world and count ourselves lucky. In Rwanda they are hacking each other to pieces. In Russia the strong are scrambling to join us, mowing down the weak in an orgy of bandit capitalism. South America has been meddled to bits, a maelstrom of feudal regimes, leftist terror and right-wing terror, deforestation and strip mining, a vast beef and drugs allotment for western appetites.

There are no alternatives. Everyone wants to be us. We are living in something called Late Capitalism, at 'the end of history' in post-modernism, as though the necessary breakthroughs have been made, as if it has taken the human race a millennium to reach this adult-hood, this societal maturity in which, thanks to technology, the developed world becomes ever more rich, happy and free.

I am reading Orwell. In 'Writers and Leviathan' in 1948 he wrote: 'This is a political age. War, Fascism, concentration camps, rubber truncheons, atomic bombs, etc. are what we daily think about . . .'

But this is no longer true. Now we think about the killing of Jamie Bulger, and Mad Cow disease, whether there really is hope in Northern Ireland, the new Stone Roses album (which seems to con-firm that the magic times are gone) and Heroin Chic and Safe Havens for the Kurds. Serb massacres and the camps in Srebrenica seem the echo of an anachronistic evil, the dying convulsions of terrible old times, more like the final shot of the Second World War than any-thing that has a place in our time. It does not seem to have anything to do with us but at the same time there is reproach in the way it is reported, and a sense of guilt in watching it. 'How can we allow this to happen?' the pictures ask. 'What are we supposed to do about it?' we counter.

The international news pages of the papers grow thinner as the lifestyle sections fatten. Mind, body, spirit, runs the mantra. In London Robin and his friends are reading a new magazine called *Wallpaper*, slogan: 'It's the stuff that surrounds you.' We are supposed to look ever more closely at our opulent and tiny spheres, to lavish fortunes on our invaluable little portions of space. Style has displaced substance. The must-see films are Tarantino's *Reservoir Dogs* and the record-breaking *Pulp Fiction*, minutely pleasing, stylishly horrifying, lovingly designed productions about nothing at all: riffing, jamming hymns to nihilism, comedy and this thing called cool. Even torture can be cool if it is done to a swinging soundtrack. *Pulp Fiction*'s char-acters are defined not by what they do but by what they like: their tastes in burgers and milkshakes, how they take their coffee, whether or not they eat pork, whether they take coke or heroin.

'It's wank for bad poets,' declares Theo, the night after we watch *Pulp Fiction*. 'It's Jacobean spectacular violence,' says one of my professors, 'like pouring boiling oil on baskets of cats. Anything to keep the mob happy.'

Happiness is presumed to be in the stuff that surrounds us and composes us: our revolutions will be internal, based on consciousness and the self, on learning and connection – physical, psychic, technological or spiritual – with our inner lives and with others. Ecstasy has taught us all what it is to jump up and down in a room with hundreds of others and love each other, across all vagaries of class, occupation and background. All we have to do is survive into the next century, get good jobs (we know it is going to be competitive, the safety nets are melting away with our student grants) and go forward with confidence. Except it does not feel like maturity. It feels like a protracted adolescence. Lad Mags are the latest publishing phenomenon: notions of new, sensitive, 1990s men are swept away in a downpour of tits. At the same time rates of depression and suicide are climbing, particularly among young men. We know there is something wrong, as we turn our protests, our longing for something else, on ourselves.

'What one law would you introduce, Jamie?'

He thought for two seconds. 'No one has the right to alter my consciousness, and no one should have the right to prevent me altering my own.'

'Drugs again then!'

'No! Well, not just drugs.'

Guy, a violinist, took a deep drag on the spliff. 'It's all about release. There is a school of thought which says it's all bound up in the ability to orgasm fully. It's in the Alexander technique . . .'

Jamie and his friends have seen the future. They are going into the internet. They read *Wired*, 'the magazine of the digital revolution', and speculate about the changes to come. Though the possibilities of direct, digitized democracy all seem rather vague, the money angle is very clear.

'Soon,' one explains, 'everybody and every company is going to need a web page. We can do it for them.'

Dope is everywhere now. The press pretend to be shocked when Noel Gallagher of Oasis tells a journalist that for most young people taking drugs is as normal as having a cup of tea. As far as we are concerned he understates it. We have had many more joints than cuppas. At the same time the papers are full of calls for dope's legalization. Everyone is doing it and it is doing no harm, the argument runs, the problem is the state's efforts to control it: the soaring conviction rate for drugs offences and the scores of young people criminalized.

Popular wisdom divides drugs into 'soft' and 'hard': the principal objection to the soft, cannabis, campaigners say, is that its illegality leads users into contact with dealers who introduce them to harder stuff. Let us buy it over the counter and we will all be safer. It will be like Holland: they have lower levels of usage there. The message from us, the generation using it, is unequivocal: we know this drug, we live with it, let us deal with it on our terms. At their 1994 party conference the Liberal Democrats vote to decriminalize it. Channel 4 stages Pot Night, an evening of celebratory programming devoted to cannabis. Short films show policemen sitting down with users, smoking together in harmony. Maria and I get stoned and watch it, then we go to bed. We have hours of slow, stoned, intensely sexy sex.

Sex on dope is like a synthetic version of the best sex without it. The way each second stretches beyond itself, like breathing underwater in a dream. The beauty of her body, the unbelievable perfection of her, like the first time you ever. The wonder in the soft arch, curve and stretch of a leg. The lengthened circle, the little flare and swell of hips, the vanishing of time. The amazement with which you touch warm skin, tiny miracles of sensation, the agonizing pleasure of slowly running fingers. The exchange of touch, like worship and benediction in every moment. The softness and richness of her hair, of her skin, of her, the flow and fall of her, in her eyes, in her expression, in the shape and taste of her mouth, in her breath. Her. And in your mind, below the pant and pulse, is a stillness, a oneness, like a note strengthening, music and silence together at last, at once, like the silence of climax, that only-nowness, like the peace of the midnight all through you. Nothing else, just this, just her, just this.

It was the one thing which dope was practically good for; that, and fixing your bike.

'I love it,' said Theo. 'When there's something wrong with my bike I think great, now I'm going to have a big fat joint and take my time, really slowly, and fix it absolutely perfectly . . .'

Christian and I fell in with Theo's vision of the bachelor pad. Every bottle and can we drained we placed in the back yard, a glass and aluminium army which advanced steadily towards the house and the mythical day when we would march them all to the recycling bins. Whenever we needed to relieve ourselves house tradition required we disdain the scramble up the steep stairs in favour of a plastic dustbin by the back door. The contents went black. Spitting water into the flaming eye of the gas fire was encouraged. Howling matches over the washing up were expected. Showing Christian and me his hoden (testicles, in German) whenever the urge struck him and howling with manic happiness, Theo gave every sign of being a contented head of household, which made Christian an extremely peculiar wife and me, because I had been in the year below them at college, and because they could talk over my head in German, a delinquent son. It was a perfectly happy arrangement which foundered on a fundamental flaw: neither Theo nor I were bachelors.

Theo decided he loathed Maria. Christian followed his lead. Whenever they encountered each other in our dim little living room Theo grimaced, sighed and rolled his eyes. Maria tried to be civil, forcing out pleasantries, at which Theo sneered. I loved both of them and tried, hopelessly, to arbitrate. 'Can't you be nice to her?' I pleaded with him.

'No!'

'Can you be civil, at least?'

'No! I don't know how many ways I can put this – I don't like her, I don't respect her, I don't know what you're doing with her and I'm not going to pretend I do!'

'OK! But for fuck's sake why can't you not be rude to her – for my sake?'

'Because it's dishonest! It's bullshit . . .'

'But it's the way we get on with each other, isn't it?'

'In fucking Britain, yeah . . .'

'So the German way is just to be bloody rude?'

'Well, at least it's honest.'

'If they carry on like this,' Maria grated, 'I'm going to mention the war.'

'Oh God,' I groaned, 'that'll do it.' But she was right. Mentioning and loudly not mentioning the war of loyalties became the culture of the house. Smoking dope in this atmosphere did not help it, though we rolled and smoked and passed joints back and forth in the name of pleasure and relaxation. The intimacy, the deflation of your ability to conceal things, the enhancement of your perceptions, your sensitivity to all the myriad signals on the faces and in the eyes and gestures of your companions make loud unspoken conflicts and write your feelings, bright and dark, in the air between you. Our relationship with the drug was shifting. It was no longer something we did for fun, in celebration. Now it was a stave to push away the grey afternoons, the lines of little houses in the rain, the dripping concrete, the dank, dinge and squabble of the sitting room and the settled hunch of the winter.

When I got a bad mark for an essay I should have done well I decided the time had come to make a stand against the drug, and I stopped. Almost immediately the walls began to close in.

'Christian,' I yelped, 'something's not right! I can't remember anything. I can't think!'

'So? You've been smoking loads of dope, haven't you? Well, this is probably the consequence.'

'Yes, but so have you and Theo. You're not suffering. But I have become thick!'

'Ah, but we haven't stopped!' He laughed. 'And we probably didn't smoke as much as you.'

'Oh God . . .'

I had never had depression before: I did not know what it was. Every time someone asked me how I was I answered with a litany of complaint. My own voice bored me, my problems made me despise myself. I was a disgusting waster. All that time I had spent by myself or with friends stoned I should have been learning and growing up. So now I was ignorant and immature, and it was all my own fault. It was if I had locked myself in a narcotic amber: the world had moved and I had fallen behind. How would I ever catch up?

I sat by the river with Maria and looked at the warehouses on the other side which had been converted into flats. How would I ever afford one of them? How would anybody? How did people make so much money? What did you have to do to earn enough to buy a Mercedes? How on earth did anybody afford a Mercedes? Was that the point? To make enough money for a Mercedes and a house, and have kids, and still have enough money to educate them so that they could afford a Mercedes and a house, and still have enough money to educate their kids . . .? I was appalled by what my culture seemed to regard as fulfilment and terrified that I would fail to find it.

I did not realize that many of the cars belonged to companies, not to the people who drove them, and that many were hire-purchased. If I had not smoked dope I could almost have afforded one myself. But the only person I knew who drove a Mercedes was a dope dealer. Neither did I see that many of the flats were empty, or that most belonged to banks. I did not understand that all around me home owners were floundering with repayments and negative equity, that so much which looked monolithic, achieved and paid for was in fact mortgaged, teetering, eroded by recession.

All I knew was that my choices and those of my peers had put us in a vulnerable, quixotic position. We English students sometimes laughed at our subject, but now the question it raised raised unanswerable questions for me. What was an English degree for? How did you do an English degree? I did not know anything. I was desperate.

'Jamie!' I cried. 'It's like I made a movie of my life, and now I hate it! It's all going wrong. I can't work, I can't write, I can't make Maria happy . . .'

'You hate the movie of your life! Good line, Horace. Well, it's a mind–body thing, isn't it?' he said. He was cutting up vegetables for soup for his girlfriend's lunch. What a pleasant, sensible thing to be doing. Why did I never cut up vegetables for soup for my girlfriend's lunch?

'You're miserable, you've got no serotonin. You need to do something to get it back. Go for a walk in the country – you know, Wordsworth! Take an E with Maria. You'll remember how much you love each other.'

I took plenty of walks but I rejected the ecstasy plan out of hand. I turned away from Maria. An unceasing panic produced a grinding pessimism. I did not believe in me, I did not believe in us, I did not think she could help me and I did not let her try.

'Go and see someone,' people said. I made an appointment with a doctor.

He listened to me. 'I see,' he said. 'You have been addicted to cannabis and now you want me to prescribe Prozac, and no doubt you'd become addicted to that. That does not strike me as a good idea at all.'

He had a thin blond beard which pincushioned his jowls like the hair you sometimes see on bacon. My eyes were fascinated by it, my gaze returned to it. 'Please!' I begged the beard. 'Just something to get the serotonin going again. So that I can work and function.'

'No,' it said. 'No.'

I telephoned my half-sister.

'Look,' she said, 'you won't believe me, but it will end. It will, it just does.'

My father reacted to a phone conversation by leaving work and taking a train to York. I was hugely touched: it was not out of character for him to be concerned and attentive from a distance, but the action, actually coming to see me, was unprecedented.

'You don't look as bad as you feel,' he said. 'It'll pick up, you'll see.' He was very kind and gentle. We talked about what I might do after the degree.

'I'm interested in the edges of things,' I said. 'I'd like to write about it.'

'The edges of things,' he said, thoughtfully. 'I'm not sure there's much money to be made in the mainstream, writing about them.'

It was an understandable, sensible judgement. I could not properly explain myself, could not describe the way I saw people revealed in that instant after laughter when the face recomposes itself; the things I loved about the edges of towns, where they dropped into the countryside over a cliff of rubble, building sites and uncertain space;

the lives which spoke to me, halfway lives, stranded between dreams and reality. I could not explain anything to anyone, but I could describe the inability.

I went to see my tutor and poured out my troubles. She looked at me carefully through thick glasses.

'When I first met you at the beginning of the year you seemed a very happy, confident, well-adjusted young man,' she said, after a pause. 'I do not know what has happened to you, but whatever it is, it will keep happening until you find the cause of the problem and address it.'

The judgement had the ring of truth about it, but I had no idea then how prophetic it would prove to be. I accepted that something was 'happening to me', but I was reluctant to look the obvious in the eye.

Second year ended and I went to stay in my father's flat in London while he was away. It was a hot summer; I sat in my boxer shorts and sweated and tried to stick one word to another: I had essays to do about Proust and Rochester. I went to the shops for whisky and paracetamol, imagining this was the end, but I was being pathetic and I knew it. I drank the whisky. I was digging into a student loan now: more weight and responsibility shifted into the future, in the name of a present which made no sense, which seemed worthless. But my sister was right: slowly, slowly, the words came creeping back. By the time third year began I could think again.

I went back to York and the fallout from the previous year. Rupert was not talking to me. Maria was with someone else. Richard had got into the Bristol Old Vic and Theo had received the results of his degree: not as good as they should have been. It was tempting to put it down to the drugs, but then Jamie, wild Jamie, had landed a double first. Theo was doing a Master's, but I barely saw him. I began to work, full of good intentions, until someone offered me a line of speed.

'What's it like?' Mickey asked. He drew a line between dope and everything else.

'Well,' I say, 'it's like dope is a hat, a hard, heavy hat cramming down on your head and then you take speed and it's like someone comes along and whips it off and throws it away! The guy who gave it to me has been out with seven girls called Katherine, one after another, don't you think that's mad? Have you seen those Magritte paintings with those spheres in them, those spheres with a slit that look like pills? He puts them everywhere, as if he can see them in everyday life, like Blake looking at his angels. They could be atoms or gods. They're the Heebie-Jeebies! And I was looking through Clueless's microscope the other day [Clueless, aka Steve, was studying chemical engineering or something, and was not in the least clueless] and he's doing this thing on polymer films and he showed me in his microscope this amazing world, deep red canyons and mountain ranges and deserts, this whole vast planet and do you know what it was? A teaspoon! It was a polymer film over a bit of a teaspoon! So the Heebie-Jeebies live there, I reckon. In fact, all this bullshit would be a lot better if we somehow precipitated the reign of the Heebie-Jeebies. You know the mushroom [a concrete water tower which dominated the campus], well, they say it was what the Quakers [Rowntree money had been instrumental in starting the University] put there instead of a swimming pool because they didn't want us getting laid – as if a swimming pool ever got anyone laid! How's that for a karmic nightmare? I think we should blow up the bloody mushroom as a signal to the Heebie-Jeebies that we're ready for them and in fact I'm going to go and see Clueless and talk to him about explosives. What's that on your neck?'

'It's a birthmark,' said Mickey. 'And look, see my neck's got a sort of crick in it? And the birthmark looks just like a rope burn? Well, I reckon I was hung in a previous life.'

'Wow!'

'You're not really going to blow up the mushroom, are you?'

'Don't you think it would be a good idea?'

'No!'

'But we've got to do *something*!'

'We need to blow it up so it comes straight down,' I announce a few days later, having studied the problem.

'What?' Mickey is drying glasses and arranging them neatly. He runs his room like a pub.

'We can't have it falling on any of the other buildings – it's got to come straight down, like an umbrella. And we need to do it when no one is around, at five in the morning.'

'Shut up! Stop! You are not to blow up the mushroom – I forbid you.'

'But it's so ugly and pointless. It reeks of bad vibes. Just imagine it! *Come, Heebie-Jeebies – the time of the mushroom is passed – the way is prepared!*'

'Listen, the Heebie-Jeebies do not want you to blow up the mushroom, OK?'

'But even without them, wouldn't it be wonderful! Student pranks taken to a whole new level. *York Students Redesign Campus.* No one would ever beat that.'

The door opens.

'Clueless!'

'All right, boys. What's this about you blowing up the mushroom?'

'Oh no!' Mickey cries. 'See what you've done? If anything happens to that fucking mushroom I am going to tell the police on you, OK?'

A heavy snow swept in, from Siberia they said, and a big cat had been seen on the moors: there was speculation that it would head for York. I went out to meet them both one night, scrambling across shrunken fences and jumping over the skeletons of streams, flashes of black water glittering between snow-fattened banks. The front loped in from the north-east, giant white paws padding over the outlying houses, extinguishing their candle-yellow windows and smothering the street lights. The power of it, the majesty – oh God, look! Look at the world! Who is to say there are not spirits in the air and songs in the storm, eternities in every snowflake? When all this is gone, will not the snows still fall, as they fell before fire, as they fell before man and his light? Were not there ever beasts out there, imagined or glimpsed, driven in by the cold and night? And have not watchers always looked on like this, shuddering, tiny, marvelling at the clouds, awed by their silence and might? Is not this forever, is not this what is? Miraculous and immeasurable, momentary and permanent? Is this not the world beyond?

One night I saw a hand in the air, a hand holding a pen, a perfect sculpture in cigarette smoke. I walked the walls looking for ghosts, waiting for the supernatural freeze within the cold, watching for spectral Roman Legionaries. There was one window in the town where the light stayed on all night, in the ground floor of a council block. Peering in I saw an old man sitting in a corner, his back to the room, holding a cigarette. I wondered about him, this other watcher, always there, always waiting for something. Once I saw him half-turn his head. He was smiling. I wondered how many of us there were, lookouts on a ship aground, keeping lights burning for none to see, doing a duty no one required, taking the late watch and the early, captains to our imagined crew. Sometimes my body carried me home with my brain all but shut down. I let my eyes close and navigated through a thin strip of vision. And many times, home at last, I could not sleep, but watched, raw-eyed, as another day came on.

I had lost my lover and my friends and the degree was in pieces but the wild highs of amphetamine and its psychotic blasts of dopamine had spun threads of ghostly, suggestive sense through the tapestries of my perceptions. Rupert had been right: it was all true. Everything was founded and connected in dreams.

Sometimes it was extraordinarily thrilling: I sat upright in bed at 4 a.m. struck suddenly, inspired, as if the night had whispered a great secret to me. Of course, it's in the letters! A, B, C – they all have an emotional charge, a hinterland of associated qualities so ancient, fundamental and evolved that we overlook them. And their forms reflect and echo these qualities. Take the way we align ourselves with our initials, the way our lovers and friends sometimes reduce us to them – what's in a name? It's all in a name! It's in the letters, stupid. God is the Alpha and the Omega. Alph, the sacred river. Look at drugs, how much everyone loves E, and fears H, and wants Charlie, C, and respects and fears K – special K, ketamin. There is something funny about K. Kubla Khan. It's the key, the k, the key . . . How can I not have seen it before? Quick, I must get up, I must walk and think . . . Think of Derrida – I is not I . . . I is another. Now, where's that speed? Damn. Spilled on the carpet. Oh well, I'll hoover it out of the fibres with my nose . . .

★

Those who know and meet me now have one of two reactions: some are horrified, repelled and disgusted, but others are amused, excited, even fascinated. The excitement and strangeness that I detect in the world I reflect out, like the flickering and temporary light of burning paper. There is a twinge here of something powerful, like the sacred and peculiar position of the court fool, the wise loon, with a manic chatter offering intimations of truth. I gorge on it. I hurtle around campus and town. It is as though I can see people for the first time. I can look unblinking into their eyes and really see them.

'You have to be careful with that,' Jamie warns me over the phone (he is starting a magazine in London). 'People don't want to be seen like that, it's an invasion.'

Desperate to do something with an excess of manic energy, and in the hope of making money while having fun, I staged two more theatrical events. The first, *The Porter's Revue*, a follow-up to *The Addicts' Opera*, was entirely surreal. An unrehearsed cast wandered on and off the stage, fluffing lines they had not had time to learn. Whenever anyone stumbled the prompter threw a lemon at them from the wings. Having cast non-thesps before I now cast non-students from among my friends in town, which was fine, except one of them, a young man who claimed he had been a getaway driver, absconded with the takings.

My brother came up for the performance: I had persuaded him to take a small part. He was appalled. 'What are you doing?' he shouted at me, desperately, afterwards. 'What are you doing? This isn't you. This is shit.'

'At least I'm trying,' I cried, 'I'm trying things, aren't I?'

'But why this? That was bloody embarrassing.'

He was right. I had no defence.

With no warning, alerted by reports from Theo, Robin comes to see me. He finds me in the communal area of the college, rolling a spliff. I am delighted to see him: he is upset and angry.

'This is not you,' he keeps saying. 'Look at you, what are you doing?'

'I'm just trying things! I'm bored, I'm putting on plays. What's wrong with that?'

'You're not right. You're really intense, you're acting mad, and you're not doing any work.'

'How do you know?'

'I know you're not working. Look at you. What's happened to you?'

'Nothing's happened to me! I'm having fun.'

'I used to admire you so much at college. You were good at everything – you played hard, but you worked hard. You were really organized.'

'I'm not doing anything that you're not doing.'

'You are. I'm not behaving like this. You have to stop smoking dope.'

'It's just dope! Everybody smokes dope . . .'

'But you have to stop,' he cries angrily. 'It is not good for anyone but it's particularly not good for you. It makes you loop-de-loop.'

I know he is right. I can see the worry, the fear and frustration in his eyes. My heart aches for the upset I am causing him, and my brother, and anyone who cares for me. I burst into tears. I slow down for a day, for two days, but the heat will not abate. The thoughts will not slow. The ideas will not stop coming. I know I am a loon. I know everything is slipping. But if only something will work, if only I could do something good, to show that these inspirations can succeed: I am desperate to give pleasure and amusement, I am desperate to entertain. It is as though, unable to calm down, I want to ratchet everyone else up. It is as though I am hollering at the world – come over here! Look at it from here, like this! Isn't it beautiful, isn't it mad? Isn't it wonderful fun? Theo and Christian have had enough of my bullshit. I do not see them much any more.

The next piece of theatre is *The Glowing Chicken*. My actor friend Michael and I plan to perform sketches in the middle of a club night. I hire a chicken suit. I am late getting to the venue so run through town, the costume in a sack, except for the head, which I wear. Muffled inside it, I can see the streets bobbing crazily through the eyeholes and hear my breath panting furiously in the beak. This must look great on the CCTV! I arrive laughing to find Michael backstage with a large spliff and an attack of nerves.

'Let's do it!'

'No, I don't think we should.'

'Come on! We can't disappoint them!'

'Not seeing you dancing around me in a chicken suit is not going to disappoint them.'

'On the contrary, Michael! Even if it's shit it will be funny.'

'No. Too shit and not funny enough.'

'Oh, come on! What are you afraid of?'

'Looking like a tit!'

Fair enough, in hindsight, but the wrong thing to say to a maniac in a chicken suit. I threw a pint of water over him. Michael rolled his eyes. We performed the sketch. He looked pained and I looked a tit. At the end of the night we found that we had not made enough money to cover the hire of the bouncers, who refused to let me leave without payment. I had bet my last pound on the enterprise. The conversation with my bank manager the next morning, on a reverse charge call, was not funny at all.

Completely broke, planning to do a part-time job delivering pizza, trudging past the Ministry of Agriculture, Fisheries and Food, I came upon a murder scene. Six geese, strewn across the inner ring road, slaughtered, apparently, by traffic. They were not long dead and one of them was not mashed up: he had died of a broken neck. I did not hesitate. Giggling light-headedly I crammed him into my bag. Unfortunately he was much too big for it: his head and one wing dangled out. There was no one around but the police and drunks and I did not want to explain him to any of them. Michael lived just around the corner so I knocked on his door.

'Michael!'

'Yes! Hullo, Clare de Loon.'

Michael has a sharp and hawky look. (Years later, in another manic phase, I will become convinced he is a sort of human Marsh Harrier. Michael the Marsh Harrier – it seemed to fit.)

'Michael, I've got this goose.'

'Right . . .'

'Can I stash him in your bath?'

'What?'

'Can I stash him in your bath and come back tomorrow with a bigger bag?'

'Where did you get him?'

'Road kill. Honest! He was outside MAFF. Please! He'll be delicious. I'll clean up after him. You and Emma could come for dinner tomorrow – I'll roast him up.'

'O-K . . .'

'Thanks, mate.'

Michael rang me the next morning.

'Oy, fuckwit!'

'Michael! What?'

'You broke our parrot.'

'Parrot?'

'Yes.'

'It's a goose not a goddamn parrot and it's not yours, it's mine.'

'I was coming to that. Get your goose out of my bath!'

'I'm on the way.'

'Good. Hurry up! Emma had a fit.'

'Oops. Doesn't she like wildfowl?'

'Well, I don't think she has she any particular feelings about them either way until she goes for her shower and there's one bleeding down the plughole.'

'Sorry.'

'And the parrot.'

'Oh, the talking parrot.' It was battery powered. Whatever you said it squawked back at you. This was funny for a while, until I heard 'Shut up, fucker!' one time too many, and head-butted it.

I took the goose down to the river bank and plucked him over the water. Then I took him back to the accommodation block I was sharing with my friend Joanna and several computer science students and set about drawing and cutting him up.

Nathan, an English graduate from Durham who was working as a college porter (he needed to be near the rest of his band, who were studying in York), Joanna, Michael, Emma and I feasted like Viking gods. People kept gobbling and giggling and looking at me as though I was mad.

'What? It's perfectly delicious, isn't it?'

'Yes,' said Nathan, 'very tasty. What's the next course? Rat?'

'Ha ha. The only thing I'm worried about . . .'

'Uh-oh. Oh no! What?'

'Well, don't you think it's a bit suspicious? Six geese outside MAFF? Either someone just drove straight at them deliberately, or . . .'

'Or?'

'Or they were being used for some ghastly experiment with drugs like Jacob's Ladder and the experiment went wrong and they had to get rid of them fast and make it look like an accident!'

'Oh, Christ. Now you tell us.'

'Oh no, Horace!' Joanna clapped her hand over her mouth. 'I can't bear it!'

'What?' Nathan cried. 'You can't bear it, you didn't even eat any goose!'

'OK, so, if we all start hallucinating and talking bollocks you can tell the doctors what happened.'

Nathan nodded. 'How is she going to tell the difference?'

There were no chemical repercussions but the goose did not go quietly. A couple of days later I received notification that the Vice-Chancellor wished to see me. He turned out to be a pleasant man with a stern front.

'I have had a complaint from other people in your accommodation.'

The computer science boys had evidently had enough.

'They say you play music at all hours of the day and night. They say you never sleep. They say you are dealing drugs from your room . . .'

'That is absolutely not true.'

'No?'

'No. I have never, ever dealt drugs.' This was true. I was very grateful to my dealers but I was never going to be one of them. 'It's not something I would ever do. I would rather deliver pizza. In fact, I am delivering pizza.'

'But that still leaves the rest of it.' He looked at me tiredly. 'And what's this about a goose?'

'Ah. Er . . .'

'They say you left the head and feet of a goose in the kitchen and it upset them.'

'I did leave a goose head in the kitchen but I didn't mean it to upset them. I found it dead on the road and I cooked it for a few friends, and . . . I was going to get rid of it. But . . . they get up before me.'

There was a silence. I thought I saw a spark of amusement in his eye but I would not have bet a degree on it.

'All right,' said the Vice-Chancellor, 'I want you to leave this room, and stop alarming the people in your house, and keep regular hours, so that you can apply yourself to your work. I do not want to hear from you again, and I expect you to get a good degree. Is that clear?'

'Yes . . .'

There were two new recruits to the pizza delivery franchise, me and a slow-moving boy the others had christened 'Flash', who was lying about being a student in order to avoid paying tax. The old hands did not have much time for students. 'Sit around smoking drugs – and who pays for them? We do! Our taxes!' They did a sketch about delivering a pizza to a student house.

'Pizza!'

'Er, what?'

'Pizza! Someone ordered pizza!'

'Oh. Woah. Far out. Hey, anyone order pizza?'

'Seven quid, please.'

'Woah. Heavy. Anyone, er, anyone got any – got any, like cash? Er . . .'

They marched Flash and me out the back and presented us with mopeds.

'Here you are. You can have the G-reg. Decent bike, excellent for turning left.'

They stood back as we practised driving up and down and took bets on which of us would be the first to fall off. The G-reg, which had suffered a nasty collision, was indeed excellent for turning left. All it wanted to do was turn left. To go in a straight line you had to aim right.

The aim of pizza delivery was to ship the stuff out as quickly as possible and then race back to the shop for more: not because you were concerned that the customers should get their stodge before it went cold but because it allowed you to do more runs and increased the amount of tips you might gather.

This term was Shakespeare: I raced around York, cooling pizza in the box behind me, *King Lear* in my head. Looking for number 269 but thinking about *Lear*, I glanced left, saw the house flashing by and hauled the G-reg in its preferred direction. We missed the stone gateposts, shot across the lawn and crashed into the garden hedge. I was half-sorry nobody had been looking out of the window to see their pizza come flying in as if delivered on a thunderbolt. I retrieved the G-reg from a bush.

'That was quick,' said the customer.

'We try,' I gasped.

A pound tip. A whole pound! On two fifty an hour a tip like that was amazing. It confounded me that anyone could afford to throw away twenty quid on a large pizza and a tub of ice cream, but they could, so many of them could. I liked the tiny glances of other lives the job afforded: hallways, husbands and wives, children being sent to practise their maths by paying for the food and counting the change. Normality was lovely, I decided, interesting and comforting, like television seen through someone else's window, and impossibly far out of reach.

Everyone else was buying books: I was selling mine in order to afford tobacco. They were working: I had taken a wrong turn on to the outer ring road and was buzzing around the city, passing laughing drivers, trying to find a way back in. 'Harrier pilot!' the drunks shouted, as I cut back through the middle of town. 'Bomb us some pizza over 'ere!'

There was a shortage of manpower in the armed forces and the Navy were running a recruiting advert of a young man on a pizza delivery moped under the caption 'Jump Jet Pilot (if he'd joined the Navy)'. Another English student, Howard, had joined the Navy. He said he had seen the whole world and could not remember any of it, so drunk and drugged had he been whenever they made landfall. 'Minesweepers,' he said. 'The oldest boats in the fleet, with the roughest bastards on 'em.' He had eventually chosen literature over acid – popular, he said, on nuclear submarines – and was now one of the most dedicated in our year. It occurred to me that drugs, glass collecting, the loss of friendship and love, pizza delivery and depression were my minesweepers: it was a great pity I had decided to do my tour of dereliction at the same time as the degree.

And now that I was off the drugs, for the second time, and meaning to work hard and do well, for the second time, the depression appeared, for the second time, and this time it was war. It was as though the speed, the ecstasy and the dope had all been a satanic loan. I had had no come-downs, I had simply got higher and faster. After a plateau of a few weeks, during which I felt quite normal, the devil's bailiffs called.

5

The Malign Comedy

THE FIRST SIGN was sinister. I woke up to laughter, a high, empty sound, alarming, strained and desperate. It was me but it was not my laughter. Then I smelled myself: my skin stank, sour and frightened. I tried to ward it off. I groaned aloud, 'Oh Lord, don't say it's coming back . . .' and carried on, doing the things you are supposed to do – reading, note-taking, seminar, essay – but it is like being a believer who is losing his faith in God. No matter what you tell yourself, no matter what you recite inside, no matter how well you go through the motions of normal life, something cold in the core of you does not believe a word of it; something that once listened does not seem to hear your prayers. In the dialogue with yourself it is as though your heart has shrunk and turned away. No one has described the plunge into depression better than the priest who lost his faith, Gerard Manley Hopkins. 'I wake and feel the fell of dark not day,' he wrote. It should not be able to become much more terrible than that, but it does.

I wake and feel the fell of dark, not day. If you have slept all the way through you are lucky, and wake thankful for that. But there seems so little sleep available; it is eaten at both ends, as though the devil is cutting your ration every night, to see how little you can take. Then he slices lumps out of the middle. You travel through tiredness, through exhaustion, into a kind of dreary haze. However early you go to bed, no matter how late you get up, the tiredness grows. You never really switch off – you can be quite as miserable, quite as worried, quite as terrified asleep as you are awake. Though you are dead to the world you are not dead to depression. It does not leave you alone for a second. You smell strange. There is a reek of fear in your pores, staining out across the rest of your skin. It does not matter how many times you wash; it will not go. Sometimes you can actually smell faeces on yourself, as though you are rotting and leaking. In extremis I asked close friends – can you smell shit? No, they said, mystified. But I could.

You fear your friends. You fear the look in their eyes, the pity and the worry: my God, you think, I must be bad. You fear what they will say to each other – of course they will talk, they will compare notes and try to formulate a way to help you – and it all seems so humiliating. How awful to be gossip, to be worry. And you know that when you do see them you will find it hard to talk to them. You will find it desperately hard to say anything, let alone anything funny or diverting – anything that might brighten the world. You will find it hard to follow what they tell you, hard to remember things, impossible to hold and conceive things, to stitch things together. The momentary snap of judgement, observation or humour, the things that made you you, are all gone. You are a shell, an awful warning. So you stay away from them, knowing that in so doing you are making it worse. In the absence of anyone to talk to, your own sad voice in your head becomes louder, higher, more desperate. Sometimes it breaks through. You hear yourself say something, say half something. 'Oh let me not be mad,' says Lear, 'not mad, sweet heaven . . .' It is hard to get dressed in the morning, very hard. Your decision-making is gone, because your confidence is gone. You stand with a dirty sock in one hand and a crumpled shirt in the other and cannot decide which to put on.

If it is difficult in private it is much, much harder in public. You dither. You change your mind. Just buying food is almost impossible – you pick things up and put them down, pick something else up and change your mind, put it down, go back to the first thing for the second time, for the third time, feel the eyes of a shopkeeper, curious, on your back, choose something just to make a choice, fumble the change, drop something, leave, thanking God for letting you off with another defeat – it could have been worse, after all, you could have started crying or something – and then you look down to see what you have decided to have for supper, and wonder, onions and anchovies? What am I supposed to do with that?

A shadow of your intelligence is still there, but now it is working against you. You cannot remember anything – your mind's drawers are locked or empty or the handles are broken off – except whatever the devil wants you to remember. And, my God, you can remember that perfectly, crisply, sublimely – every bad, sad, dull, dumb, cruel, stupid, thoughtless, selfish, twisted thing you ever did is laid out in front of you like a bazaar of evil treasure. You can wander through at will and pick out whatever you like. You can dwell on this or that for ever, you can cringe and whimper and hate yourself as much as you like: the only thing you cannot do is shut your eyes to it. You cannot turn away. Focus on something else.

Focus! Focus, as your eyes glaze and the parade begins again. Here comes the girl you let down, here comes the friend you betrayed, here comes the thing you said, here comes the way you did it, here comes this and here comes that, here comes what that makes you, here comes who you are. And over there is what you could have been, over there is the road you did not travel, and here is a distance you cannot jump and will not bridge, and here at your feet is a chasm, and here at your hand is a bottle, and here for your neck is a rope. Here is a razor, there is a drop. There are lots of ways out, you know . . .

Kill yourself, you think, first as a morbid sort of joke. It's not as if you're going to kill yourself! A week later, it is the only thing you can think. Well, you could kill yourself, you think. And suddenly the mind has a project to work on, your desperate, dulled, miserable mind has something it can do. The one true and certain solution! The one absolutely definite way out! The one door they can't lock or bar or render inaccessible. (This at the point when making an appointment with a doctor seems impossible – too complicated, too weak, too pointless – too late.) And all your thoughts come back to you, to me, me, me. It becomes terribly, deathly boring. This endless, pointless droning voice! You would kill just to shut it up! I do not think I have ever been truly bored except when subjected to this.

You walk the path to destruction as if just testing the road. I found myself climbing to the top of the Minster one morning, vaguely considering, on the way up, what it would be like to throw oneself off. At the top I found the sky was barred, caged off by an iron grille. There was an attendant in a small hut.

'What's this?' I asked, gesturing at the bars.

'Stops people topping themselves,' he grinned.

'When are they going to take it down?'

'They're not.'

'The bastards.'

He looked surprised.

I researched suicide on the internet. There was a hell of a lot of it about. Take a couple of ounces of tobacco, add some water, boil until reduced to a sludge. Eat. Death by asphyxia in a couple of hours, it said.

They must be bloody joking, I cursed, this is ridiculous. I thought about throwing myself under a train – but what about the poor driver? I thought about jumping off a cliff. But, though skinny, I have always been quite tough. It would be just my luck to get really bashed about on the way down and take an hour to go, smeared across a couple of rocks with an eyeball dangling down my neck and the seagulls circling hungrily. I thought about sticking my head in the gas oven, but, though I disliked the computer scientists, I would have hated to blow any of them up. And there was Joanna to consider. Blowing her up was out of the question. And no way was I going down the pills, throwing up blood and stomach pump route. Drowning was supposed to be quite pleasant, after the lethal lungful, but how the hell did anyone know that? Hypothermia! That was it. But how do you get hypothermia in April? The solution I came to was typically complicated and unlikely: I would buy a ferry ticket to Norway and jump off, in a life jacket, halfway across. The life jacket would stop me drowning and the cold would take me quietly. Except, of course, I would not have the nerve and I was in no state to face the streets of Oslo. Hopeless. Coward. How depressing . . .

I worried about the suicide note: for someone with literary training and pretensions this is a nightmare, and for someone so depressed he cannot write more than a third of a sentence, impossible. Even as poor a critic as I would make mincemeat of it. 'I am very sorry.' Terrible – why do it then? 'I hope you will forgive me.' Ditto – rubbish. 'I can't go on.' Oh grow up – you want to go out on a cliché? And then there is Hamlet. What dreams may come? 'I could be bounded in a nutshell and count myself a king of infinite space, were it not that I had bad dreams . . .' The Almighty, as Hamlet points out, has set his hand against self-slaughter. And though I had only a woolly apprehension of God I was terrified of an eternity in hell.

It was not that I wanted to kill myself – I could hardly bear to think of the consequences for my family – but I was desperate not to exist, longing not to be. The news said a Russian satellite had spun out of control and was due to crash somewhere on earth. Perhaps, I thought, brightening momentarily, it will fall on me. Sometimes the feeling was morbidly flippant, a gloomy dialogue with death, but often it was entirely serious. In a French seminar our tutor handed out a list of the books we would need to read for the rest of term. I drew a line under week six, and looked at the books for week eight with a kind of detached curiosity. I will be long dead by then, I thought.

I hid from everyone except Nathan and Jo. They were gentle, and I felt as though I was made of blown glass. Nathan was planning to move out of portering and into something more substantial.

'I've been looking for jobs,' he said.

'Oh yeah, where?'

'The job centre, the papers.'

'Find any?'

'Yeah. Loads! Jobs you can't do, jobs you'll never get and jobs you wouldn't take even if they were going to shoot you.'

We laughed, then I excused myself and went to the gents. There is a peculiar truth and solitude in the gents. The gents, with its gurgling pipes and peeling plaster, its clinging floors and weeping walls, its graffiti, mould and poisoned damp, its dead time and living draughts. As the door swings behind you it shuts out all the bravado, all the face and front we put on for each other, and leaves nothing but your residue, your animal self, bursting for relief. Daubed with anger and despair, lust, violence and the names of football teams, the gents is a terrible sort of id beneath the ego of the bar. Men fall silent, looking down, heads bowed as if in penitence, or stare ahead at the glistening tiles, paraded, comically exposed.

'Nathan,' I muttered on my return, 'I just had a nightmare.'

'In the gents! What, have you shrunk?'

'I looked at the mirror and I didn't know who it was. There were about ten faces there, fading into each other. I tried to smile but I saw all these faces, sad, scared, tentative, bluffing, and I didn't know which was me.'

'Ugh!'

'It's the Fear.'

'It sounds like it, definitely. Nasty. Avoid mirrors?'

'Yeah, I guess.'

'And garlic, just to be on the safe side.'

I will fight this, I decided. There must be a dozen practical things you can do to give the black dog the slip. Research in the 'Mind Body Spirit' sections of bookshops revealed a new problem: the world is awash with competing solutions to depression. Bewildered fellow sufferers search crowded shelves. Despair is a major industry, fighting dejection a full-time job.

Wake up at the right Feng Shui angle to your crystal. Turn on your wave-wash / bird song / whale wail CD. Dress, not forgetting charm, amulet and wristband. Breakfast according to any one of a dozen diets. Select from a hundred supplements, remedies, pills and potions. Do Yoga, Reiki and Tai Chi. See guru. Drink infusions, smear on balm and pastes. Consult spiritual manual, practise self-help technique, attend class, meditate, take exercise, bathe in special salt, sit under special light, light special candles, read recovery charter, recite mantra, receive massage and acupuncture, eat tofu, attend aromatherapy, have hypnotherapy, consult counsellor, see psychiatrist and psychologist, shoot self in face.

No doubt it would all work, if you could muster the faith for any of it, but I could not. Cursing my cynicism I went to a homoeopath.

'Tell me what the trouble is,' she said. Like a puppeteer with a tired and gloomy travelling show I unpacked my collection of woes and rehearsed them for her. She took neat notes, sucked her pen, poured something that looked like water from a jar into a bottle and gave it to me.

'This should help to begin with,' she said. 'Take three drops a day.'

For three days I followed her instructions: no change. On the fourth I drank the lot. It was water. On the fifth day the telephone went. 'You remember we said it was thirty pounds?' she said. I rather liked her and it was not her fault I was an ass, so instead of screaming 'Quack!' and bashing the phone against the wall I sent her the cheque. Another failure. What a venal ass I was, to think you could avoid the consequences of years of drug abuse with a few drops of water. Depression trawled a squirming haul of shame and wretchedness out of every puddle of perception. I was going to fail everything. Life was going to punish me and I deserved it.

'Horace, stop it!' Joanna cried. 'I can't bear the way you leaf through books like that, looking lost. It's so depressing! Just pick one up and read it.'

'I can't! Nothing sticks. It won't go in at all.'

'Then go and have a shower or something – you stink.'

Nathan and Jo saved me. They sympathized but they laughed, refusing to indulge my morbid, inverted egomania. Most people fear the desperation of the undone. The line which separates contentment from despair is so thin: we who have stumbled over it are suspect. There but for the grace of God go most of us. No one wants to be reminded how deep and close is the abyss. At the same time, because we are broken and wretched we serve as a reassurance: however you are, you are better off than this. We can see it in the eyes of our interlocutors. In offering help and advice they inadvertently buttress themselves in our eyes and confirm how far we have fallen. Our confessions make a reality of our plight. 'Which way I fly is hell, myself am hell,' says Milton's Satan. It was as though the books were reading me.

'Oh Lord, another one!' cried one of my professors when I offered this as an explanation for a late essay. She was in a hurry. 'The number of times I've heard that! Just write the bloody thing and hand it in.'

As finals approached the library became busier. All the books we had not read queued reproachfully on the shelves. I looked up past papers and convinced myself that I could not answer any of their questions. My dissertation came back, marked. It was worth ten per cent of the degree and I had written it, in the aftermath of *The Porter's Revue*, on drugs. At one stage the words had floated off the paper, kite strings of letters, lifting away from the page. I had, I remembered now, made ill-advised reference to my deconstructionist theories about phonetics. It had ended, I recalled, wincing, with a sort of bravura flourish, something like 'I equals I, I end where I began, and we cannot go further without undoing literature or ourselves.' Which is a hell of a place for an examiner to end up, having been promised 'The Modern Short Story in the Theory and Practice of H. E. Bates'. The mark was 32 out of a hundred, an unconditional fail with no chance of appeal. It caused howls of laughter: no one had ever heard of anyone achieving such a pathetic mark. People begged to read it. I refused. Numerate friends did the maths.

'If you push it you can still get a third!'

'Are you sure?'

'Yes. Maybe even a 2:2 if you're lucky.'

I groaned. The library was full of people groaning. 'I got really stoned last night and for a moment I thought I understood Derrida,' said a girl called Charlie. I was sympathizing with her when Mickey arrived. Mickey in the library! It caused a kind of mass panic. People jumped out of their chairs and rushed up to him. 'What are you doing here?'

'I'm working, what does it look like?' Mickey's Hounslow accent was particularly suited to a kind of comic grievance.

'But you never come here!'

'Well, I'm here now, aren't I?'

'Mickey! What are you doing here?'

'I'm working! I've come – to the library – to get a book! What's so amazing about that?'

'Mickey! Shit! It must be finals, what are you doing here?'

'Faackin' 'ell! I'm *working*!'

Then a librarian approached, identified Mickey as the cause of the disturbance, and banned him for three weeks.

'Three weeks!' Mickey wailed. 'That's no good, is it? My finals are finished in two!'

'Are you coming to graduation?' he asked me.

'Are you kidding? I'm running away to France straight after my last exam.'

6

Fear and Loathing in Mid Devon

1996

THE LETTER SAID the editor would be expecting me in the offices of the *Torpington Gazette*, Torpington, Devon. I had never been to Devon and never heard of Torpington. I did not imagine there would be much in the way of career-making national news down there, but you never know: all the joys and pathos of rural and small town Britain, I imagined, a cross between *The Archers* and *Trainspotting*. I was looking forward to it. I was going to be a trainee (unpaid) reporter on the *Torpington Gazette* and everything was well with me. I had not smoked dope for a year. Over the months in France the depression had lifted. I had been working at an ecological centre in the south-east, recruiting staff and prospecting for the site of an Eco Village. I had telephoned for my results from a phone box in a remote town. The department secretary was a friend.

'Hello, Rose, I'm calling for the bad news.'

'Oh hello! How are you?'

'Dreading it.'

'Well . . . wait a minute . . . here we are. Oh, you can celebrate! You got a 2:1.'

'What?'

'A 2:1!'

'There must be some mistake, Rose, it isn't possible.'

'No, no mistake. A very broad spectrum of marks, but that's what it comes to.'

'Jesus H. *Christ*. Are you absolutely certain?'

It was embarrassing. I did not deserve it. I felt like a universal fraud; nor was I sure I was capable of founding an Eco Village. It was a wonderful idea to which the French authorities were instinctively hostile. They did not want a bunch of international hippies generating their own power and growing their own vegetables. What is this, one mayor asked, some sort of cult? I handed over to another project director and returned to Britain. Before I could help with the alternatives, I felt, I had to cut it in the mainstream. I would go into the family business. I would become a journalist.

I looked up Torpington in a road atlas. It stood alone, surrounded by untroubled space, spotted with patches of green. With what offcuts of news did they fill the *Gazette*, I wondered; what went on down there? The train rolled south from Bristol through a green, undulating land of large fields, apparently peaceful farms and small, almost apologetic hills. Torpington Parkway, the station, stood by a dual carriageway and some sheds. A few fellow travellers headed for the car park. I made for a single white taxi.

The driver was friendly, wry and inquisitive. His taxi smelled of rolling tobacco and he encouraged me to smoke. We interrogated each other in a good-natured way as he twisted the car to Torpington between bushy hedgerows, past hamlets of small houses and neat cottages. There were no people to be seen anywhere and few cars. By the time we reached the outskirts of town he had established that I was Welsh, had come to work on the *Gazette*, had little experience of local journalism, had never been to Torpington before and knew nothing about Devon or Devonians. I had established that the constituency of Torpington and its neighbours all voted Liberal Democrat, and that the taxi driver's name was Wes. He recommended a B & B called The Star.

The owner of the guesthouse welcomed me into his dim, brown-carpeted hall and showed me to a small, dim, brown-carpeted room. There was a low bed, draped in a dun and yellow-checked duvet which felt as though it had not completely dried. There were cheap pillows, cheap sheets, two poor and embarrassed-about-themselves pictures, there was a basin and vague smell, a sort of undertone of nondescript cooking. Was it egg? There was a television, on which there was snooker. I felt a twinge of melancholy but it passed. After all, even great journalists have to start as small fry, I told myself, and we all have to stay in lonely, disheartening and tawdry places now and then. The Star was perfectly acceptable and it was cheap. The view from the window was of an extension, possibly the kitchen, and a car park. I could hear an extractor fan at work somewhere. The Twinge of Melancholy, I thought, would have been a better name for the place than The Star.

I hung up my shirt, jacket and smartish trousers, ready for tomorrow, unpacked my library (*Point of Departure*, by one of the greatest journalists of all, James Cameron, and *The Red and the Black*, by Stendhal) and went out to see the sights.

It was Sunday evening, I reminded myself magnanimously, having ascertained, ten minutes later, that there were no sights. There was a main street, on which there was a Woolworths and the offices of the *Torpington Gazette* and various small shops; there was a road at the bottom on which there was a closed cinema advertising tatty films; and where the town's market should have been, there was a large car park. CCTV cameras kept watch over scenes as devoid of life or interest as anywhere in Britain. I bought chips from a man who looked like a fish who had fallen into his own fryer and took them down to the river to eat. They were as delicious as chips can ever be. The river poured relentlessly by, failing to conceal the shopping trolley which had been thrown in off the bridge. There was still no sign of life, but from the profuse scatterings of polystyrene and greasy paper I deduced that people had been here quite recently, and that they too had eaten chips.

I went back to my room, emptied my change on to the formica top of a bedside cabinet, washed, stripped, climbed into bed and watched snooker until my eyes began to close. I turned off the television and set my alarm. I reckoned it would take three and a half minutes to get to work from The Twinge of Melancholy, as long as there were no riots, bombs, burning barricades or crowd disturbances to negotiate. I slept well.

'Good morning,' said the landlord. 'Tea or coffee?'

'Hello. Coffee, please.'

'Cooked breakfast?'

'Yes, please.'

'Toast?'

'Erm . . . no, thank you.'

'Right.'

I am not fast, fresh or happy in the mornings, as a rule, but I did not fail to notice when this exchange was repeated, word for word, every day for the next three weeks.

There were a couple of men who looked like builders at breakfast. We nodded at each other. I went out, bought two newspapers and at five to nine set course for the office, where I arrived, unscathed, two minutes early.

There were two rafts of tables bearing computers. A cheery woman bustled forward and shook my hand.

'Hello! I'm Pat, I'm the editor. There's no one else in yet, as you can see!'

She laughed happily and l laughed too. She was delightful, warm and – judging by her quick eyes, which seemed to take me in rapidly and thoroughly – she was sharp. Her voice had a soft edge to it, that west country sound so beloved of butter adverts and people pretending to be thick. She pointed at empty chairs one by one.

'We're very small really. There's Nick, who's our chief reporter, he'll be in later. There's Pete, our news editor, and Pete, our subeditor, and Marcus, the photographer and . . .'

The door opened.

'Oh, good. Hello, Tristram. This is Tristram, he's a reporter.'

'Morning, Pat. Hello . . .'

'This is our new trainee, Horatio.'

'Hello.'

The young man who stepped forward and shook my hand had an open, kindly face. You could tell he was funny, and you immediately wanted to see him laugh. He had dark hair and dark eyes; he looked kind and honest. He wore jeans, a woolly jumper with a hole in it and a clean striped shirt. I liked him too, straight away, especially the hole in his jumper, but even as I was shaking his hand and being introduced a voice inside me was shouting 'Run! Run away – now!' and I was fighting to keep from my expression the effects of seething urges which made my legs feel weak and shaky with a need to sprint away, pell-mell, howling, waving my fists at the sky. If Tristram had had any intimation of what was coming he would have kept a firm grip on my right and swung his left into my jaw with all the force he could muster before opening the door and booting me down the stairs and out into the gutter.

As I told myself to stop being silly and began the business of settling into my new office, my first job and the beginning of my working life, I swear I could hear something laughing.

'Have you got anything Horatio can do, Tristram? Blimey, Tristram and Horatio! People are going to think we've gone posh!'

We all laughed.

'I'm sure we can find something, Pat,' said Tristram, brightly.

'You can sit there, that's the reporters' table. Tristram will show you the ropes.'

My desk was at the end of the room, by a window which looked on to the High Street. From my seat I could see over the roofs of the town to a round green hill, tousled with trees and spotted with sheep. The sky behind it was blue, and I felt very lucky. The computers, I was amazed to discover, were not connected to the internet. Pat looked vaguely alarmed by the question. Tristram sat opposite me.

'Nothing doing at court this morning?' Pat asked him.

'No. There's this,' he said to me. 'Someone's appealing to save a wood.'

The press release announced that Rhododendron Wood, much loved by locals, was threatened with destruction. 'You could give them a call, it should make something.'

I called the wood's supporters. They did not answer. The rest of the office arrived for work. There was Nick, a pallid young man who ate bright chemical crisps, chain-smoked and mocked Tristram and Lyn. Lyn, the typist, was a kind, gossipy woman who sat at the reporters' table and teased Tristram. There was Pete the subeditor, an Old Etonian, who had the accent, manner and mockery of his old school, which he soon focused on me, and Pete the news editor, who laughed a lot and gossiped with Pat. John, a man with a bright red nose who said he had led a long and unhappy life in industry, was the business correspondent, and on the wagon. Tristram teased him. Marcus, the photographer, was obsessed by picking up good deals from the For Sale column. Everyone teased him.

Nick explained the job. We dealt, he said, with shitty stories about shitty institutions which periodically staged shitty events. Nick's previous job was with 150 on British Telecom, the number people dialled to report a problem. Dealing with a vast, random and often angry cross-section of the British public had been perfect preparation for journalism, he said. We aimed to pitch our reports somewhere between the levels of the *Sun* and the *Daily Mail*. He advised me to buy these publications and copy them. Before that, though, there was the first job of my first job. Would I like to go to the sawmill and write an ad feature? Yes, I said, I was very keen. Tristram and Nick sniggered. They hated ad features, advertising articles paid for by the subject who has copy approval, or, more likely, copy disapproval. Tristram and Nick regarded them as an irksome waste of their time and talents. The cynicism of old hands, I thought.

Clutching a new notebook and rattling with spare pens I grilled the saw miller in the spirit of James Cameron interviewing Nehru. I prised and wheedled every aspect of his business out of him, recorded everything, missed nothing. By the time I had finished the miller was hoarse and impressed: he called the editor to praise my thoroughness but then I faxed him the copy and he called again, to damn. He had quite a short temper.

'It don't matter that I travel to Russia and speak Latvian!' he shouted, enraged by the emphasis on aspects of saw milling I thought unexpected and noteworthy – 'I just want people to go to Good in Wood!' Good in Wood was his shop, which sold chairs, tables and shelves.

'More advertising, less feature,' Nick explained. 'See?'

And so it began. Cheese contests. Rows about drains. Rhododendron Wood saved – the first tangible impression I made on planet earth. A new organist at the church. Holes repaired in the High School roof. More cheese contests. In the second week I wrote my first front page: 'Torpington's A Dump, Claims Top Author'. A character in Margaret Drabble's new novel thought the town 'hilly and grim'.

'Most of the shops seem to be selling second-rate second-hand clothing in aid of obscure charities. The population looks elderly and grey and idle,' she wrote. The Gazette office cackled with glee as we stoked the controversy. The Tourist Board and the Chamber of Commerce provided a baseline of objection; a tour of the charity shops and a few passers-by stopped on the High Street contributed a melody of complaint. The novelist confirmed that she shared her character's views, while expressing surprise and irritation at the 'stir'.

Torpington was short on stir. A facility for synonyms was the hallmark of a Gazette reporter. Tristram reeled off a list of the essentials. 'Plan, scheme, undertaking, project, proposal,' he said. 'Mission, endeavour, strategy,' Nick muttered, through a Silk Cut. Sometimes it did not matter how assiduous or cunning we were with our subjects – the story refused to ignite.

'Hello, I'm calling from the Gazette. Is that Mrs Sharland?'

'Yes?'

'Hello, Mrs Sharland. I'm bothering you because I hear your son Ben has grown an enormous sunflower – is it true?'

'Oh yes, it is pretty big.'

'How big?'

'Thirteen feet six inches.'

'Vast! May I speak to him? Hello, Ben, sorry to bother you, I'm calling about this gigantic sunflower.'

'Yes.'

'So how did you do it?'

'Muck.'

'Oh really? What kind of muck?'

'Sheep.'

'I see. Any other tricks? Did you sing to it?'

'No. Just muck. And water.'

'How big was it when you planted it?'

'Two inches.'

'And do you think it's going to get bigger?'

'Maybe. Yes. I think it's still growing.'

'And you grew one last year which won second prize in a competition, is that right?'

'Yes.'

'And how big was that?'

'Nine and a half feet.'

'Pretty good! But stunted compared to this monster. So did you do anything different this time?'

'No.'

'Well, it sounds like you're going to win this year, aren't you?'

'I haven't entered.'

'Oh, right. Well, thank you very much. Good luck with it! Can I speak to your mother again. Hello, Mrs Sharland – how come your son is such a wizard with sunflowers? What's his secret?'

'Muck.'

'Right . . . yes.'

After work we went drinking, then to the snooker club, then we ate junk and I went back to the Twinge of Melancholy where the quiet girl who cleaned the room had arranged the change by my bed into a star pattern or a smiley face, depending. Snooker on TV, then sleep, then down to breakfast, coffee yes, toast no, and back to the office.

'So, Mr Gray, I hear you have been sleeping in your turkey shed to beat the turkey rustlers?'

'That's right, yes.'

'What's it like, sleeping with one thousand five hundred birds? Noisy?'

'No, quite quiet really. They cluck a bit.'

'Don't the cluckers stink?'

'I work with them all the time so it doesn't bother me. If they're well cared for it's not too bad. But they are naturally quite strong-smelling.'

'You were married recently, weren't you?'

'That's right.'

'How does your wife feel about losing you to the turkeys?'

'Well, she'll be happy to have me back.'

'Did you eat turkey at your wedding?'

'No.'

'Did you go on honeymoon to Turkey?'

'No! Bulgaria.'

'Oh! Close, though!'

Not quite obscured by turkeys and sunflowers, various symptoms of the age flowed through Torpington. The Ambulance Service complained of chronic underfunding as its workload increased and its budget lagged behind inflation. The town's after-school play scheme failed to secure lottery funding and shut down. Cannier farmers went into organic production as the supermarkets strangled livestock prices. The Post Office was closed, a soldier on leave talked quietly about horrors he had seen in Bosnia, a national campaign against benefit fraud came to town, we argued fiercely over the relative merits of Spice Girls and a parish council bankrupted itself evicting a group of travellers from a disused quarry.

Press protocol demanded that we refer to them as New Age Travellers, though there was something rather timeless about the last to leave, a youth called Wayne, who, the photographer was delighted to find, had a pin through his nose, a goatee, dreadlocks, a baggy jumper and a caravan sprouting spider plants through broken windows. He and his friends had been living peacefully in a damp patch of woodland for four years, to the fear and disgust of householders (according to the parish council) and the ire of the local farmer, who had shot three of their dogs.

'We don't know where we'll go next,' said Wayne. 'We never meant to cause any trouble. We're really very quiet people,' he added, quietly.

I had seldom met a less fearsome or disgusting individual. The idea of riot police and bailiffs, society's answer to Travellers, clearly terrified him. The national press were very excited about confrontations between the law and young environmentally minded alternative types who objected to road-building and wood-flattening schemes. The protestors never won. Personified by a youth known as Swampy, they dug themselves into holes or chained themselves to trees and clung on until they were taken away. There did not seem much to choose between the rat race, the weak sloganeering of Major's tottering country ('If it isn't hurting it isn't working' and 'Britain's Getting Better') and the cowed, dank and harried option represented by Swampy and Wayne.

Something between the two, enabling one to survey the whole, was the solution. I realized journalism suited me perfectly as a huge slice of my generation came to the same conclusion. Applications for media studies courses dwarfed those for engineering. Rather than join the dance, rather than commit to building anything, we would report it. We would damn the bad and praise the good – comment would be our contribution. It would also be a very good way of getting our names in the papers, and, hopefully, our faces on TV: hundreds of thousands of us wanted to be famous, for no other reason than famous people seemed to live exciting and glamorous lives and apparently did not have to worry about money.

There was another less facile reason why so many of us turned towards the media. Having grown up knowing only one-party rule, watching Thatcher's 'individuals' act exactly as they pleased in the name of money, justifying all means and ends by it, and accruing it, at the expense of the poor, in obscene quantities, we had come to feel that nothing could defeat or effectively oppose the expensively suited, infinitely well connected ruling class; that nothing could answer the triumphant assertion with which they greeted the collapse of the Soviet Union ('Capitalism's the only game in town now!'), as if the collapse of one ill meant the absolution of another, and that there was no alternative to their demonstrably false and cynically complacent sop-theory, 'trickle down', which suggested that if the rich got fat enough the poor might benefit, as if we would be nourished by licking the food stains off their waistcoats.

There was no obvious way to confront all this, except through the media. The point of journalism, I believed, was to discover and tell the truth about what was being done to whom, by whom and why. I read *Primary Colours* by 'Anonymous', Joe Klein's barely fictionalized account of Clinton's progress to the Democratic Party's nomination, and was struck that the only thing the masters of the universe seemed to fear, the great threat to the triumph of their power, money and hypocrisy, were 'the scorps' – the scorpions – the press. It did not escape me that the writer was a journalist, and it seemed only vaguely ironic that the only people the public thought worse than journalists were politicians.

After a couple of weeks Pat took me aside and quietly and apologetically offered me a salary – one hundred pounds a week. It was embarrassing all round, as I was now writing news, features, reviews and sports reports and there was no good reason for not paying me a respectable wage, except that they did not have to. There were thousands out there who would do it for nothing: the entire industry was built on exploitation. I accepted gratefully and moved into a small flat.

It was all going beautifully. There was nothing I was not interested in. Town council meetings, disputes over sewers, motorway spot checks, arguments between vicars . . . Tristram and Nick laughed at my enthusiasm, while Pete the subeditor slashed the more exuberant tendencies out of my prose.

'Hor-a-tio,' he drawled from the top table.

Muffled and expectant giggles from all sides.

'Pete?'

'What *is* this . . . self-indulgent . . . *twaddle*?'

Two words too many. When he liked something it felt like a Pulitzer.

'Go with Nick to the game tonight,' instructed Pete the news editor. 'We'll make a football reporter out of you.'

Any enthusiast can read a game on television, played by experts, relayed from multiple cameras with lots of high-angle shots. It is a very different thing to make sense of a bunch of scrappers having it out under weak floodlighting in a patch of mud. We huddled on a freezing bench marked 'press', eating smouldering pies of indeterminate provenance, watching twenty-two puffing and swearing battlers disputing their rankings in the Screwfix Direct League Premier Division.

'See that!' Nick exclaimed. 'See the way he turned? He may be a fat smoker but that was a classy turn. That's how you tell a good striker, he can turn.'

'Christ,' I moaned. 'Don't you think it's weird under the lights? It's like a hallucination. Some of them on that side look closer than the ones over here. It's bizarre. I think I'm getting motion sickness . . .'

'Goal! Did you get his number?'

'Er, eighteen?'

'Bloody useless! Where's your lighter?'

'Here. Hell, look at my notes! I can't read any of this. My hands have gone numb.'

'Ooh, nasty! Surely he's got to get a card for that. Referee!'

'What did he do?'

'Took him out.'

'It's like watching two games superimposed on each other.'

'Bloody hell. You on drugs or something?'

I was not. I was not. I was not until one day my phone went and the receptionist said there was someone downstairs to see me. In the lobby, grinning, was an old friend from college, wearing a white coat.

'Michelle! What are you doing here?'

'What am I doing here? What are you doing here, more like? I work here, I live here! I saw your name in the paper!'

Michelle was from Liverpool. Her white lab coat and dreadlocks made her look like a species of futuristic soul doctor. She was working in a health food shop, she explained. We arranged to meet later.

'I dropped out after college, I've been a traveller for ages,' she said. She was living in a freezing farmhouse on the moors with a parrot called Ernie. Ernie liked the Rolling Stones, whistling and clicking in time. Michelle was living on vegetables, candlelight and dope. She had skunk.

Skunk is well named. A bright, almost luminous bud, sulphurously sweet, its odour is yellow-green, a nauseous, hiccupping stink, not so different from the smell of crack cocaine. A skunk-smoker's face turns sickly pale and the whites of the eyes cloud with blood as the world thickens, slows, closes in. Suddenly you feel the disorientation, narrowed focus, hesitancy and insecurity of one waking up in the dark of evening after a deep sleep through the afternoon. The moods, suggestions and atmospheres which attach themselves naturally to objects and places are hugely intensified. Beauty is sublime; ugliness, desolation and emptiness are fearful. It is much more like taking acid than smoking dope. Everything seems to proclaim itself to you at the same time, the implications and evocations of all the eye or mind lights upon become a kaleidoscope of competing suggestions, muffling and interrupting each other in a confused, barbaric chorus. If you think of some failing now, your laziness, say, your lack of fitness or your bad teeth, the notion will rise and swell and billow through you like smoke filling an oven. Suddenly you are an idle, legless, breathless creature with yellow fangs, a red-eyed haggis, clinging to existence like a tick. Hideous visions and silly inspirations clash and intermingle. It takes real bravery to joke or make an observation as paranoia echoes through you like the tolling of a bell: if you do and you are smoking with someone, they laugh with relief at the release from their own miasma of internal hallucinations. Under fire from your own minds you come together, a tiny stoned unit, allied against the appalling complexity of the world. If mild hashish or gentle home-grown weed is real ale, then skunk is vodka laced with meths. Some kinds of cannabis may be soft drugs, but there is nothing 'soft' about skunk. It had been a rarity in York but it was spreading out across the country, from hubs in Bristol and London. Now its hairy tendrils reached me.

I did not fall straight away. I tried. Every night I lugged the office laptop home to write. Thanks to Nick, my snooker improved. I read *Point of Departure* and lots of Harold Evans on the craft of journalism. I went to municipal meetings. Tristram and I played fives at the local public school. I stood in pubs and the town's only bar, reviewing bands. But as the autumn turned to winter and a colder darkness stole in from the moors, and the town emptied and quietened quickly after the shops shut, as the curtains were drawn earlier and the televisions came on, and Michelle gave me a puff, then a joint, then, at my request, a bag, I began to crave. I craved laughter and company, culture, intimacy, humour, action and sex. I was not the only one. Sometimes someone else exploded: we wrote up the consequences, laughing.

A two-man stag night began with the groom and his best man drinking and playing pool. The next thing they knew, they said, they were hanging upside down in the groom's overturned car in a ditch and the police were there. It emerged that they had become catastrophically drunk, smoked dope and run away from the pub with a selection of pool balls, which, they now recalled with horror, they had thrown through various shop windows, before speeding away pursued by the police to their rendezvous with the ditch. The groom spent his wedding day in the cells. The bride's feelings are easily imagined.

Tristram could not stop laughing as he typed it up. 'Torpington munters,' he sighed, affectionately. 'One minute you're having a drink, the next you've smashed up the High Street and turned your car over. What can you do? Fancy a drink later?'

'Yes, I would, but I'm having supper with Michelle. Could do a quick one . . .?'

Tristram was very sweet to me. I stayed a night at his family's farm to keep him company when they were away. We went to Bristol together to see my friend Richard the actor in a play, and to drink with Tristram's friends and his girlfriend, Jane. We were great new friends. 'Mate!' he would cry, delightedly, at some folly or sally of mine. 'Mate!' We drank a great deal together: one Bristol weekend, after handfuls of whiskies and endless pints, the backs of my hands discoloured. John, the ex-drinker, diagnosed alcoholic poisoning. I thought it hilarious.

I was smoking skunk regularly now, every evening and at weekends. I justified it to myself easily. All my university friends still smoked: they had not become manic or depressed. The problem was not with me but with the substance – I had smoked too much, that was all. I was fine now, doing well, a bit bored. I would be careful, I would have more fun, I would be less bored. I would, in a funny way, be in tune with my generation again. Something for the weekend. No big deal.

One of my heroes, Will Self, is writing restaurant reviews for the *Observer*. I love the way he turns language on the world like a fire hose; the way he looks at things like a horrified alien, vastly sophisticated and disgustedly funny. Like many drug users, I keep a roll-call in my head of all the people who have used drugs and still been successful. Will Self seems to have taken all the stiffs on his terms, on our terms, and they love it. They lap it up. I want to be like him. I will be. I am . . . I must have lost touch with reason fairly quickly, because I thought it would be fun to try stand-up comedy.

The owner of the town's only club had become a friend, thanks to weekly phone calls for the listing section. James was surprised and bemused by the idea of a stand-up set. 'I don't think we've ever had comedy in Torpington,' he said. (Several people made the same remark, subsequently.) 'Have you done it before?'

'No! It'll be hilarious. I'll promote it in the paper. Might review it too . . . go on!'

'OK. Next Thursday then?'

'Excellent. How much do you pay?'

'Er, thirty quid?'

'Fantastic!'

The announcement in the *Gazette* was suitably mysterious and enticing. Boris Filipovich, readers were informed, a well-known stand-up in his home town, Moscow, was passing through Torpington en route from London to New York and would be performing sketches from his comedy routine, *Gangster's Paraglide*, at the club on Thursday night.

When in the office they realized I was serious they gave me one very sincere warning.

'Whatever you do, whatever you say, do not do any jokes about incest.'

'Yes, steer clear of that, if I were you.'

'Why?'

Torpington, they said, had an incest thing. At some point in mid century a Yorkshire mill owner had transplanted his works and entire staff from the dales to Torpington. Locals and incomers had not mixed well, turned to their own communities, and not mixed well. That was the theory, anyway. There was a definite Torpington look, they said, and an understandable sensitivity.

'Right,' I said. Unfortunately when Thursday evening arrived I had not learned the material I had written and some demon in me had composed a comic song, 'Daddy, Daddy, Give Me Your Answer Do', about incest.

I put on a suit and lugged a collection of records down to the club. As it began to fill I withdrew to the DJ booth and put the records on. There was nothing wrong with them, anyway: the atmosphere became excited and happy, people danced and drank and laughed. They were looking forward to the entertainment. I drank a couple of pints and fortified myself with skunk. Not having the jokes off by heart was definitely a problem. I could not remember them clearly enough to wing it: after the skunk I could not remember them at all. I would have to read them. Perhaps it would be fine. Readings could be funny, I reasoned. I drank more. I needed the loo. James appeared.

'Ready?'

'Not quite. Give it a bit . . .'

'OK,' he said, doubtfully.

I had another pint and another joint. It was not going to work. What on earth was I thinking, why had I done this, what the hell was I going to do?

James appeared.

'Ready?'

'Give me five minutes.'

'OK,' he said, more doubtfully.

I was desperate for a pee but there was no way I could emerge from the DJ booth and appear on the floor without James dimming the lights. Actually, making an entrance in order to exit to the gents might be the one funny thing I did all night. I put on another song. The crowd were becoming impatient. They had heard my entire record collection twice and now they wanted comedy. I needed the lavatory terribly. I had an empty pint glass.

James appeared.

'Right. Now. Come – what are you doing?'

'Nothing!'

'Come on.'

'OK. OK . . .'

Stoned, drunk, giggling and terrified, I took the floor. My friends took one look and reversed out of the sight lines. It was an interestingly mixed crowd. Farmers in wellingtons and girls in strappy tops; the town drug dealer in the front row. I assumed a Russian accent and began to read the material. There were one or two titters and some restive stirring.

'Chere in England you call junk food shop bugger outlet. But what is outlet meaning? Shit gap?'

Oh how they did not laugh.

'Incest,' I said, speculatively.

'Don't go there,' said a firm voice, quickly.

'No, do!' shouted someone else.

I sang the song. There was some heckling, led by the dealer, a rough individual who sold heroin from his flat. His basic contention was correct: I was a tosser. But it struck me forcefully that he was too – he would not shut up – and so I offered him a challenge. Could he tell the difference between a pint of lager and a mystery (lager-coloured) pint? He could not. He reached for the wrong one and sipped it. His face wrinkled with revulsion, but when his friends asked him what was wrong he said nothing. The evening began to lose its shape. James stepped in.

'Thank you very much, Boris Filipovich!' he cried. 'And now, Freddy from Steamer!'

A former member of the acclaimed Vibrators and the Toy Dolls, Freddy was now a local hero who would occasionally show up in the Gazette offices demanding coverage, secure it and shake my hand with crippling force. He was even more wrecked than I, but not insensitive to the tension in the room.

'Ey!' he roared, stumbling slightly, wielding his guitar like a pirate threatening a hijacked crew with an assault rifle. 'EY!'

He shot out one hand, grabbed me and hauled me into the lime-light.

'This fella – Horatio – this fella – is – ALL RIGHT! He's a GOOD bloke, ALL RIGHT?'

There was a murmur which might have been assent. Freddy struck up a song but before the second verse he fell over, toppling gently backwards like a cardboard cut-out, causing his guitar to become unplugged from its amplifier. I hauled him back up, plugged him back in and the performance continued sublimely. Freddy had not stopped strumming for a second.

The evening ended with laughing farmers telling us we should do more comedy and a disbelieving James shelling out thirty quid each. Had it not been for Freddy's intervention I would certainly have received a beating in the alley behind the club. It was perhaps unfortunate that I escaped. It might have slowed me down.

The first time I saw Jane, Tristram's girlfriend, after we had hurtled up the M5 in Tristram's sports car and cruised into the city over the suspension bridge, and Bristol suddenly seemed bright and new and thrilling with promise, as she came out of her flat, locked the door, turned around and said hello, something lurched in me. She was lovely, a lovely person – you could see it, obviously, instantly: a beautiful, funny young woman with curling lines from her eyes which made me think of a puffin. We flirted. I did not mean anything to happen, but it carried on happening. We all drank and smoked and drank more and Tristram went out gambling with his friend Paul, and came back later with hundreds of pounds, and without Paul's trousers (torn off in a wrestling match) to find me on the floor of Jane's flat, insensible. He did not know that Jane and I had been kissing before I blacked out, but it was in the air.

I am not making excuses. Clearly, if you are not the sort of person who would ever kiss his friend's girlfriend, then being drunk or high will not change you. I am probably not the sort of person who would do it if he was not drunk and high. I cannot be sure because I have not initiated, done it, committed the initial betrayal from which all the rest flow, when I was not wrecked. There is no defence, morally, or, had it been a crime, legally. I fell for Jane and I treated Tristram abominably. He could have punched me to a pulp, but he turned a blind eye to it as he and Jane broke up.

Fuelled by skunk, my engagement with local journalism became more combative and more vexed. Being sent out into the High Street to do a vox pop on the closure of the Post Office had never been a thrilling assignment, but now it became an opportunity for mischief. I hit the supermarket and purchased handfuls of miniature bottles of spirits which Marcus and I drained discreetly, between ambushing the public with his snaps and my questions. The time passed quickly and amusingly and we returned to the office as soon as we had enough material.

Although it involves intoxication in pursuit of the story this method is not to be confused with Gonzo journalism, which begins with the writer's deranged participation in the story and proceeds to the subordination of its course to his perceptions, smashed. This is Reverse Gonzo, in which the idea is to keep all trace of the experience out of the story while getting as smashed as possible. It may not be as appealing or as popular as the Hunter S. Thompson model but it is certainly more widely practised. Stand outside a supermarket for a while, drinking and daring each other to pop the question to pretty women, and you will soon feel you have done enough. Our jackets clinking with miniatures, and with one eye on side-roads where I could smoke, we filled the newspaper with shots of bemused towns-folk, recoiling from our reeking breath, wondering why two wasters would want to know their opinions on the threatened closure.

Even if people know nothing and care less about the Post Office a couple of cautious questions can lead them to pronounce the firmest views. We laid it on too thick that day: Pete the editor seemed incredulous that our sample of uncertainly smiling blondes con-demning this latest privatization was representative. The miserable fact was, I thought, as I bashed their objections into the computer, it did not matter what they said or thought or what we printed. No one had ever stopped a privatization, and despite the fact that no one could point to a single example of the private sector providing better services or even worse services for less money, no one was ever going to. Although we could stick it to the council when they ripped off their tenants, and scream when valuable services shut down for lack of funds, we made no more difference than a noticeboard. In fact, we were probably regarded by those in power as a useful outlet, a way for the little people to vent their spleen, while progress trampled on, unhindered.

I began to look for opportunities to ambush officialdom. Woe betide the press release which revealed weakness or inconsistency. Officials and vets were considering gassing badgers, because they were blamed for spreading Bovine Tuberculosis. I thought I saw a gap in their argument. I made a call to one of the vets involved.

Me: So, you want to gas badgers?

Vet: Well, we're trying to find ways of stopping the spread of TB in cattle.

Me: And you think the badgers are giving it to the cows?

Vet: We know badgers do contract it, and spread it, yes.

Me: But don't the cows spread it among themselves?

Vet: Oh yes, it's highly infectious.

Me: So perhaps the cows are giving it to the badgers as much as the badgers are giving it to the cows?

Vet: Well, it does cross the species barrier, yes.

Me: So you might as well gas the cows and spare the badgers!

Vet: Well . . . we don't know where it starts . . .

Me: See, look at it that way and it's 'Cows Kill Badgers'! But the thrust of your press release is 'Badgers Kill Cows'. Isn't that speciesist?

Vet: Speciesist?

Me: (Signing off and slamming down the phone) Ha! Got the bastard . . .

The night before Christmas Eve, having narrowly escaped a beating a second time, this time in the flat of the town drug dealer (I do not think he was ever clear about what was in that pint) after an argument with one or two of his other clients turns nasty (I had upbraided them for taking heroin and they had told me where to go), I head back to my flat (which is littered with fag ash and scrawled attempts at a first novel called, for some reason, *The Acid Candles*) laughing and delighted at having not locked myself out, for once. I have locked myself out a lot recently as skunk obliterates my short-term memory and come to rather enjoy climbing up the back of the house and smashing my bathroom window. There is something satisfying about the sound and sensation of breaking glass. I have begged my landlord not to repair it but he ignores me. I am just putting my key into the lock of my front door when something makes me turn around. There, glinting – splendid tiers of bottles glowing pale orange under the street light – unattended, poised and, it seems to me, beckoning, is a pristine and fully loaded milk float.

'Oh ho! *Hello* . . .'

I do not hesitate. I am grinning as I cross the road and giggling as I climb into the cab. I have wanted to do this ever since school: at last, the chance has come. Fate has parked the milk float in exactly the right place at precisely the wrong moment. I have no driving licence and have never operated an electric vehicle but it comes naturally. I stamp down on the pedal and aim up the deserted road. With a gratifying hum the milk float takes off. I head for the housing estate, swooping down a little hill and up around a hard left-hander.

There is a sense of validation in stepping outside the law like this. You stand in opposition to all of 'them', you redraw the code of laws and the map of morals; you are no longer an object, a number, a function of fate and circumstance: you are an author, a protagonist, the subject; the devil may care but you do not. The world is suddenly unfamiliar, it has become the setting for your adventure. It is thrilling and hilarious, as much fun as it is possible to have alone. You do not feel alone. You feel accompanied and egged on by all the friends you would like to have with you, and you cannot wait to tell them about it. And there is going to be recognition in this, you know. Deep down, that is what you really want. Young men like me are desperate for it, it must be hard-wired, a mate-attracting display. Look at me! If we cannot have fame, infamy will do.

'Yeah, baby, fly!' I urge the float. We take a sharp bend. There is a grating sound and a smash behind us. 'Woah, milk overboard! Oh well. Plenty left . . .'

We enter the estate at maximum speed. Not a creature stirs. I am not sure about reversing so when we hit cul-de-sacs we pull wide-angled U-turns, bumping across lawns and flower beds, slaloming between saplings and the more substantial shrubs. I chat happily to the vehicle.

'Look at this place, it looks like a collection of ancient huts. We Brits do love our huts. Look at these juniper bushes! Oof! Hit one. What's that? Christ! The milk. Lost another crate. Lost a couple of crates, in fact. Must be more careful. Whoah, though, you can really turn . . . Flower bed! Too late. Aagh! Another juniper! They use them to hide their septic tanks. Ooh, look, the road to the moors. Up we go. Come on, baby. Punch it! Come on! My friend Nikki lives on the other side of the moors. Let's go there. I'm sure she'd like some milk for Christmas. And orange juice. Or yoghurt . . .'

We yaw through another fast corner and begin to climb the hill towards the moors. The moon is up and there are pale clouds in a starry sky. It is cold in the cab but I do not mind. Everything is quiet beyond the purring motor. A couple of feet above the road, with no bonnet between you and the next bend, you seem to hover: majestic and ludicrous, you trundle along. It is like piloting a magic carpet loaded with dairy products. As the road becomes steeper the float labours and slows. The milkman must have contacted the police. Our trail will not be hard to follow. There is no question of outrunning them, but if we can just keep going for a while, on and up into the dark, we might quietly withdraw from the scene and escape the search. If we can just make it to Nikki, I can present the present and give the dairy an anonymous tip-off. But the float is making heavy weather of it.

'Come on! What's the matter with you? Not built for mountain work?'

The float groans and slows to walking pace.

'This is hopeless. We need to lose weight. I'll see if I can shake off a bit more milk . . .'

Reaching around behind the cab I try to dislodge the stacked crates but the angles make it difficult. I cannot get sufficient purchase. Cursing and struggling I take my eye off the road. Gratefully, gently but quite firmly, the milk float crashes into a hedge.

'Aw, don't be like that! Reverse! . . . No. Forward! No. Rats.'

I light a cigarette and ponder the matter. Weight is the problem. If I can unload enough milk I might be able to back out of the hedge. I jump out and begin to unload, stacking the crates neatly in a gateway. It takes a while. When I have shifted a significant portion I climb back in and begin the manoeuvre. We are just starting to move when I notice that the darkness ahead is lightening. Headlights are approaching up the road behind.

I freeze, undecided. Do you hurl yourself out of the cab and over the hedge and leg it, or sit tight and hope they drive by? I am on the point of the former when the vehicle arrives. It stops. There seems to be some sort of structure on its roof. Oh let it be a taxi, I pray, as two figures emerge. One of them is carrying a torch. They have the unmistakeable bulk and clink of the law. Light flashes into the cab and settles on my face.

'Get out of the vehicle and lie in the road, face down,' says a calm voice.

'Er . . .'

'Lie in the road,' says the voice, more insistently.

'OK.'

I climb out and lower myself to the tarmac. They handcuff me, help me up and escort me to their car. They ease me into the back seat. They climb into the front.

'We're just going to wait for another car,' they explain. They seem very nice. 'What's all that milk doing over there?'

'I got stuck, so I took it off to lighten the load. I'll put it back if you like.'

'No, you stay there.'

We sit in silence.

'What would you have done if I had refused to lie in the road?'

'I would've hit you with this,' says one of the policemen affably, displaying an extendable baton.

Another police car arrives. Two more policemen emerge, accompanied by a very angry milkman. He is shouting something.

'What's he saying?'

'Happy Christmas,' says one of the officers. 'OK, we're off.'

We turn and roll down the road towards the town.

'I'm sorry about this. I do apologize for wasting your time.'

'That's OK.' The officer sounds slightly surprised. 'Makes a change. Better than fighting drunks in Exeter.'

It is warm and comfortable in the back of the car, despite the cuffs. Sliding down the dope and alcohol gradient into the muddy, woozy, drowsy zone, I feel relaxed and wonderfully safe. It is deeply comforting, like being a child again, protected, safely driven, someone else's responsibility. You can now do no harm at all. You are absolved of the cares of life. You do not even have to think about what you are going to do next, or where you are going to go. Anything you should have done you cannot now do: there is no point worrying. I yawn. There is a comfortable, satisfied air emanating from the two officers. We are complete, somehow: arresting officer in the passenger seat, driver at the wheel, culprit in the back. We reach the M5 and set course for Exeter. I fall asleep.

I woke up in a sort of cage. There was a lot of banter in the station. Various policemen paused in front of their incident board and laughed. Grievous bodily harm, assault, road traffic accident, assault with a weapon, runaway milk float . . . They produced a breathalyser and instructed me to blow. We all expected to see it go off the scale. One of the officers whistled.

'Two milligrammes below!' he announced. 'Lucky beggar.'

They emptied my pockets, put my details into the computer, took my picture and my fingerprints. The system is geared to the most violent and the most drunk. You are not allowed to do anything yourself – a strong hand takes your finger, rolls it in the ink, presses it on to the pad. The first stabs of humiliation begin to penetrate. You have proved yourself incapable of being trusted to do the simplest thing. Next they presented a cotton bud.

'DNA swab,' said the officer. 'Just rub it in the inside of your cheek.'

'Do I have to?'

'Yes.'

'This is so you can mix it up with someone else and do me for the Brighton Bomb, right?'

'That's right.'

'There you are, then.'

'Thank you.'

'What now?'

'You can sleep it off while we decide what to do with you.'

The cell was extremely warm. There was a sort of bed, an evil-smelling blanket and a lavatory without paper or a seat. I woke up after a dreamless sleep to find a woman pushing a cooked breakfast through a slot in the door. I had paid for worse.

I sat on the bunk and awaited developments. I was quietly content; even, perversely, proud. All the magazines say it: in one hundred things to do before you die you always have to have spent a night in the cells. I had not committed an ugly sin. In the secret and alternative CV I carried around in my head, and would only ever show to friends, being arrested drunk in charge of a milk float was rather good. Worth a laugh.

After a while I was escorted to an interview room. A tired-looking officer faced me across the desk.

'Ah, the milkman. Why did you do it?'

I told him. 'I see. Christmas high spirits. The milkman was cross but you didn't do much damage. A couple of broken bottles. We're going to let you go with a caution. But here's the point. It might seem like a laugh this time, but someone reads about this is in the paper, thinks it sounds funny, and they go for a joyride in a lorry. Then someone dies. That's the kind of idiots we're dealing with. So don't do it again, right?'

'Right. Sorry. Thank you.'

*

I went home for Christmas and the New Year. Five friends and Jane, my brother and his girlfriend celebrated in the village pub. On the stroke of midnight we were in the graveyard, toasting 1997 with champagne. On the way home Chris, Michael, Robin and I began play-fighting. Wilson was in the middle of an alcohol and Territorial Army phase: he could drink and he could fight. In a knot like an octopus with four heads we inched our way, grunting, wrestling and punching, across my mother's garden.

'I think young men are like mad elephants,' she said the next day, surveying the tracks of the struggle in the flower beds.

We agreed with her. Chris was carrying a stash of pornography, the residue, he claimed, of a TA exercise. 'There's nothing like it in the field,' he boomed. 'When you're all freezing in the rain on the side of some mountain and the platoon are all huddled in shit tents feeling miserable, you dish out the Tactical Porn – morale goes through the roof!'

'Tactical Porn! Ha ha, Wilson. Genius. Pervert!'

He had managed to get himself arrested for being drunk and incapable. He had gone to the Clapham Grand intending to meet two friends. The meeting never happened. Catastrophically drunk, Chris made it to a traffic island where he fell asleep, propped against a lamp post. He woke up surrounded by the police.

'What's your name?' one asked.

In between throwing up on them, Chris, his eyes rolling, limbs flopping, spelled it out in the way we had learned in Lifeboats, the way he had practised in the army.

'Whisky – India – Lima – Sierra – Oscar – November – Sir!'

God knows what his brain was telling him at the time. Engage them on their own level . . . show them you are not to be messed with . . . take the piss. A blend of sentiments I recognized: a tactic I was about to take a disastrous step further.

But Chris was rebelling in a productive way, too. Though we teased him for the TA, it was definitely a more positive use of time than getting stoned. Chris may have been as much a mad elephant as I, but he put it to good use. Fit as a paratrooper, fully trained in combat, command and battlefield medicine, bustling with social con-science and eager as Action Man, he was constantly on the lookout for opportunities to do the right thing. No mugger, pickpocket or yob was safe if Wilson was in the vicinity. He pursued and tackled malefactors, broke up fights, made citizen's arrests, administered first aid, rescued the distressed and stood up to thugs on trains.

On New Year's day we went out into the fields to mend fences. Michael was a natural with a sledgehammer. Strong drink, fighting, eating and manual labour made the perfect party, though the boys were disappointed by the shortage of available women. We would have liked some weed but we did not miss it.

I returned to Torpington on the second of January, an hour or two late, having missed a train connection. I arrived in the office and was sacked. A classic newspaper dismissal: take your pen and jacket and get out. I went on a bender with Chris, who had accompanied me back to Devon. We drank beer and vodka and I smoked dope. Chris crashed out in the early hours, but I was not finished. I went out.

So you think you can just use me until you have had enough, and then kick me out? You pluck me up, take whatever I can give and then throw me back. What about my life? What about the time and the trouble and the care, what about those weeks in the guesthouse, and this flat I have rented? What about what my family will say? What about all the cheese contests, all the football reports, the band reviews, the so-called news? What about the pride and the pleasure this has given my parents, and the disgrace and disappointment now? So I'm not good enough for your crummy little rag? I'm nothing. Some sort of freak: office gossip? Just another loser, another weirdo, a work-experience jerk. Don't you know what you are messing with? Don't you know who I am? You think I'm going to go quietly? You think I'm just going to swallow it, as if I'm some sap? But I'm wild. I'm dangerous, romantic, passionate. I'm mad, haven't you heard? I am the best friend you could ever have, and the worst enemy you could make. Don't you know how proud I was to call myself your reporter? Don't you know you could have been proud of me? Don't you know I cared? I did, I cared. I know I took the piss and laughed, but I cared about the play scheme, and the wood, and the sewers, and the knife amnesty, and South Molton football team. I was useful! You made me useful, damn you. I was going to make it my life, my career. I was going to be good. I was good, wasn't I? Wasn't I good? *Bastards. You'll all suffer. I'm going to be a star . . . star . . . star.*

A fierce wind blew through the streets. The silence of the little town was a further reproach, a further scorn. See how proper we all are, the darkened houses said. With our respectable owners tucked up in respectable beds. We will not be needing anything more from you, and we won't be hearing from you again, either. Rant around as much as you like. We never liked you. Never mind London or New York, you could not even cut it in Torpington. Torpington will be glad to see the back of you. Good riddance, trash.

Oh for a milk float now, I thought. I would give the Gazette a delivery they would not forget. Eighteen crates of milk stacked in front of the door would do it . . . But the milk floats hid. I marched on, dope smoke whipped away behind me by the wind. I felt strong and powerful: I had drunk so much and smoked so much and yet here I was, clear-headed, vigorous, not sleepy in the least, gliding along the streets, my carnival of secret heroes baying like a mob, cheering me on. Do it. Do it. Do what? Do whatever. Make the gesture. Give them two fingers. Keep going. They have asked for it. For what? For something. For something which will suggest itself, for a riposte. Something funny and cutting. Some answer. Some last word.

I circle the whole town and return to where I began, outside the Gazette offices. And there it is. The answer. There are two black rubbish sacks, a couple of metres from the front door. I laugh. Two black rubbish bags now, but not tomorrow. Tomorrow, when they arrive for work, there will be a blown-about pile of ash. And they will have to walk through it to get in, and it will cling to their shoes and follow them across reception and up the stairs. A little bit of shit, from a little shit. And they will not be able to prove it, but I know they will know that it is a message, a jeering two fingers, from me.

I bend down and tear open one of the bags. It is full of newspaper. I strike a match and flick it in. The paper catches straight away. I retreat, well satisfied. All the clamour in my head has stopped. The carnival is quiet, pride salved, anger released. I have given my response. Goodnight, Torpington. Fuck you very much.

★

We rose late the next day.

'Breakfast, Wilson?'

'Yes. What have you got?'

'Nothing much. We'll have to go out.'

We pull on our coats. It is a raw January day. We stroll down the main street. And even fifty metres away I can see something is wrong. The door. There is something wrong with the door. The smart blue paint is scorched. A scrappy piece of chipboard has been nailed across some of the panels. Others are blackened and bubbled. There is ash everywhere and burn marks up one side of the door. My God, it looks as though someone has tried to burn the building down.

Chris looks at me. There is disbelief and dreadful suspicion in his eyes.

'You didn't.'

I try to smile, but I can't. I feel sick.

'Oh no, H, you didn't!'

'I didn't mean it to . . .'

'I don't believe it. I don't believe it! You utter idiot, what have you done?'

We bought two pastries and hurried back to the flat. Chris had to get back to London, to work.

'What are you going to do?'

'I'm getting out.'

'Getting out where?'

'Anywhere. Far away.'

'You're going to have to own up.'

'Well, I'm not going to volunteer it.'

'H, I don't want you to take this wrong, but I can't lie for you.'

'I don't expect you to. It won't come to that. I'd be grateful if you wouldn't drop me in it though . . .'

Eight hours later I am on a plane, chewing hash and tipping down vodka.

7

And Other Clichés

1997

THE NEW YORK night reeks of gasoline and burgers, cinnamon, garbage and sour milk. The sidewalks are crowded with the hurrying living and the loitering dead: everywhere there are spectres, visible only to the drunk and the mad who talk to them ceaselessly, upbraiding vanished women, long-lost employers, disappeared fathers and dead friends. 'Who are you?' the city asks, again and again. Are you soya or beef? American cheese or Swiss? Italian or Indonesian? Dirty tissue or white linen? The Waldorf or a flop house? Silver or chopsticks or fingers? Who are you? I have no idea.

I have woken up in an hotel called the Helmsley Middletowne (*sic*), once run by a woman who said 'only the little people pay taxes'. You could not have built a better set for purgatory. I stumble outside. Walk. Don't Walk. Walk. It is hard to keep up. The night sky glowers with a peculiar light, a dirty chromium wash, trapped between topless towers and sagging clouds. Shop assistants appeal over rising ramparts of food; thousands fight the flood, gulping it down and mopping it up, but the tide cannot be stemmed. Waves of it swell in the alleys, reefs form along the kerbs. Huge garbage trucks join the assault, battleships trailing clouds of putrefaction. It is valiant but they cannot hope to win.

Wangechi is living in Brooklyn. She has a housemate who does not like the look of me, and a boyfriend. 'What's your deal, man?' he asks me quietly. I am drunk, have accidentally peed on the bathroom floor and badly miscooked a chicken which nobody wanted. I am a ranting, jealous, confrontational, friendless nightmare. I believe Wangechi and I have a connection beyond whatever she has with her boyfriend. The fact that I have burst into a random night of her life, even more drugged and unstable than before, appealing to a mythical past which exists, heavily edited, only in my imagination, I ignore. They decide to shake me off in a Brooklyn park: they think I deserve a comeuppance, and the shadow figures in the park should provide it. But it fails, and I trail after them. After another bout of fencing I tell the housemate to fuck off, and Wangechi throws me out.

I join the refugees at the Port Authority bus station, make it on to a Greyhound for Boston and Ben's family home, a beautiful white house, tall and dignified on a river bluff, surrounded by trees whispering in admiration. It feels lowly and humbling to be welcomed to such a place. Ben's father is a dapper man who was European director of a huge car company. He is pictured on the mantelpiece meeting the Pope. How can I, how can we ever compare? We are a sham, a shame. Ben is in the doghouse, having flunked college yet again. For years he went to university and managed a couple of terms, even a year, before being thrown out for not turning up and failing to work. Then he would have some vexed time off before being persuaded to reapply, promising to do better. He is at this stage now, about to go back and, this time, make a go of it.

In bare and snowy woods where Redcoats fought Americans we run, haphazard, with Henry, the family's dog. He is not entirely well. Ben's sister Jen and I go to the vet in her car to pick up some medicine for him. We roll through white streets on a sunny winter day. Ketamin, the pillbox says on the side. I palm a couple.

Ben and his father hold some sort of conference. They emerge, quiet and apparently satisfied. We pack Ben's little car and say our goodbyes. The plan is New York and Washington, but first, Ben said, Rhode Island, to pick up a girl.

'What girl?'

'Georgetown. She's coming back to college too.'

'Who is she?'

'Whadaya mean, who is she? You'll see.'

'Is she . . . dude . . .! Are you . . .?'

'Get in the fuckin' car, *dude*,' he said under his breath, smiling at his family.

★

I wake up in the back seat. The car is flying through flashing layers of motorways, traffic whizzes by both sides of us, above and below. Disoriented, I feel as though I have come to in a Lichtenstein; speed, colour and light cartwheel towards us. In front, slightly hunched over the wheel, Ben looks like a manic pilot, steering us into the heat of all this as if we rode a diving bomb. The girl, Helen, sits next to him and they seem absurdly calm.

I start to laugh. 'Where are we?'

'New York,' he drawls and we swoop down the FDR drive. The night struggles and falls backwards, beaten down by the towers of light. The bars are full of smoke and booze. For some reason I decide I will be staying at the Paramount and invite Ben and Helen to join me. We take a small room. The staff are so eager to please we take a gamble and, when they ask if there is anything further we require, ask if they have any weed.

Amazingly they do. We smoke, drink and consider the Ketamin. Helen shakes her head as Ben examines a little white pill.

'We don't eat it, right?'

'I dunno, people do. My friend Steph at university saw a sheep which wasn't there.'

'You think Henry's seein' sheep that aren't there?'

'Possibly, yes.'

'Nah, if he'd been off his face I'd definitely have known.'

'He was pretty dopey. Maybe you should ring Jen and ask her . . .'

'Oh-ho, ask her *what*? Does Henry look like he's trippin'? Cuz I got some of his stash here . . .'

'No, idiot. You call her for a chat, and then casually ask her how Henry's doing, if his pills are working, are there any side-effects?'

'Fuck off, dude, I am *not* calling my sister. Perhaps we snort it.'

'I'm not sure. That goes wrong and we're in hospital. I think people smoke it.'

'Really? Hmm. Helen, whadaya reckon?'

'What do I reckon? You've got pot and beer – why, like, take the chance at all?'

We look at her, grinning. 'Cuz it might be fun.'

'It might be incredible!'

★

We mash one of the pills into some tobacco and smoke it in the hope that the Ketamin it contains will have a particularly violent effect. We are out for nebbishes, machine elves pulling the levers of the universe, bouncing spheres of light energy like orgasmic basketballs. It seems perfectly obvious to me that if there are machine elves behind the curtains of the visible world, as reported by Timothy Leary and his associates, then any chance to meet them should be seized. The warm little room with its mannered, spiky decor and all of New York freezing beyond the windows seems the perfect point of departure for an expedition to the frontiers of consciousness. If we had had acid we would have dropped it; ecstasy, we would have necked it; smack, we would have chased it; crack, we might well have smoked it. The dog medicine tastes disgusting.

'Ya feel anything?'

'. . . No. You?'

'Nada.'

'Bloody *hell* . . .'

I leave the room to Ben and Helen and withdraw to the lobby with a six-pack. The immaculate designer mouth of the Paramount is wide open and shining, even in the depths of the night. There are the bouncers – porters, as they would have been in an English hotel: glossy hunks in charcoal fashion statements who call you 'sir' in a guarded way until your credit card checks out, ready to put you in an armlock if it does not. There is a young man about my age who says he is making a fortune selling clothes to the Japanese. There is the pop star Beck, gliding shyly into one of the coloured-light lifts. There are the waitresses knocking off from the Whiskey Bar, their anatomically tight catsuits not quite as tight as their smiles. And there is me, with my too-big head and rough-cut hair, my stare and too-eager smile.

People nod uncertainly and hurry by. I sit drinking and scribbling until a receptionist, Abigail, from whom I have borrowed a pen, frowns, leans over me and plucks some mote off my suit. (Ben has requested that I wear the suit at all times, as it amuses him.)

'So what's your story, Abigail?'

'My story? I'm an actress on the brink of the big time! Tra-la!'

'Really? I'm a journalist. Care to do an interview?'

'No! The whole point of being an actress is to hide my true identity!'

Just before dawn Abigail finishes her shift and we go for breakfast, then walk down to the river to watch New York wake. The first signs of day are the helicopters, tracking slaloms up the Hudson. The light widens and the aeroplanes appear. The traffic mumbles and we kiss tentatively. Abigail is in an off-Broadway play. Now she looks like a black-haired Bonnie, in her soft cream beret and her hard red smile. Tomorrow she is being paid to dance the Macarena in the Copacabana, part of some sort of drink promotion. She will give my name to the doormen.

Ben and Helen leave for Georgetown: I will join them in a few days. I drink so much vodka I throw up while walking along Forty-second Street. The fact that I do it without breaking stride seems a sort of triumph. I find a dope dealer in Washington Square, and, weaving now, heavy-legged and sick with sleeplessness, ask for a room at the Chelsea Hotel.

Stanley, a man like an old eagle whose feathers have fallen out, looks me up and down and seems to decide I fit in, apiece with all the mad art, the twisted metal in the corners and the blood-splash paintings on the walls. He charges me almost nothing for a room. Both Dylans were here, Thomas and Bob. Cohen and Joplin, Miller, Kerouac, De Beauvoir, Joni Mitchell, all of them. And I have done nothing to deserve a bed beside theirs except that I feel like them, and for them and through them; except that I believe in them, and that I am here, a pilgrim to their chapel.

They know why I stay awake all night, kiss receptionists, scavenge for drugs and smoke dog anaesthetic, their poems and songs and stories explain it. There is something more than this. There is something more than getting and spending, more than spending certainly, which is all I do now. The modest inheritance which funds all this is running through my fingers. I should save it, of course, invest it. Save it for what, though? Invest it in what, if not this? Experience, experience is what I value, experience is all I want, all the experience money can buy. When it runs out I will worry about it, and then there's the old stoner's adage: times with weed and no money pass easier than times with money and no weed. And I've got weed, and all these ghosts whose gods are mine. Sleep comes down like a cosh.

The Macarena is one of those songs which catches like a fishbone in the throats of all radios, which yak on it and yak on it for months until at last it dislodges, gobbed out for ever. It sounds like 'One-macca-two-macca-three Macarena! Four-macca-five-macca-six Macarena! Seven-macca-eight-macca-nine Marcarena, Ay – Macarena!' Tonight the Copacabana is hosting the finals of a nationwide competition to find the best two Macarena dancers in America. The competition is being run by a new brand of alcopop called Mazoo which looks like semen and tastes like shit. Abigail and three other beauties are the backing dancers, smiling encouragingly at the competitors who are prancing their beating hearts out, desperately trying to grin and shake their way to ten thousand dollars. Ten thousand dollars!

They all dance the Macarena, then some are weeded out, for insufficient displays of skill or joy, and the remainder dance the Macarena again – and again. It is death by Macarena. And as it kills them off, crushing them back down into the human mulch from which this mighty city springs, the Macarena demands their love. It scours their expressions for any hint of pain or desperation or false enthusiasm for their imminent destruction, and at the merest glint of it, down they go.

By the sixth heat I am emitting negative energy like teargas. Were I not with Abigail the bouncers would ask me to leave. We meet during a brief break. Her Mazoo T-shirt clings to her; underneath it her fatless body runs with sweat, still throbbing with the beat.

'Hey!' she pants. 'How ya doin'?'

'Er, fine,' I stumble, thrown by her bright professional smile. 'It's terrible. How are you? How on earth do you keep it up?'

'I'm doin' great! What? So, you having a good time?'

'It's vicious. You're wonderful, though. What a dancer!'

She does not seem to hear the first part, smiles and kisses me. 'It's the final now!' she cries, joining in with the whoops and applause. Even the first beats of the song seem to have to pick themselves off the floor.

'People!' the DJ bellows at last. 'We have our winners!'

'Thank Christ!' I shout, lost in the cheering. The winners are crying, the losers are crying, the branding people are congratulating each other. The winning girl and boy are clinging to each other and jumping up and down, out of sync at last. They have won a free holiday to the Caribbean as well as the money. 'Can't believe it! Can't believe it!' they shriek. But the dreams Mazoo gave them Mazoo has made come true.

We take a taxi down town, bucking and bouncing down the sagging New York streets. We are euphoric, our arms around one another, Abigail high on the dancing, me on the release from it. We tumble out at the Chelsea. A beggar catches sight of us and shouts, 'Whoa, pretty lady, you're beautiful! Lucky man!' Abigail laughs gleefully; she is indeed beautiful and I am lucky.

Later, in the dark, she bursts into tears. 'I knew someone like you once,' she says. 'He was English,' she sobs. 'He was blond. I married him. We had a daughter. Then he found out he was gay!' she wails.

'Look,' I say, firmly, 'I'm Welsh.'

'Oh but I'm going to hurt you!' she cries. 'I just know I am.'

She tells me she was once cursed by a jealous woman. 'But I went to a healer. She put a jar over my stomach and the curse jumped out. It was alive, I saw it. We buried it under a tree.'

I am awake for the morning, watching the sun as it knifes between the giants, dazzles the snow on their foothill roofs, backlights their white steam plumes and falls on Abigail, her hair bright black against the sheets. Whatever it is that I seek I feel it there, in the New York daybreak, as behind the thousand glinting windows people begin to stir.

Abigail invites me to stay with her in Queens. Her flat has Elvis mirrors and Elvis stamps in frames, Elvis mugs and Elvis magnets. An Elvis clock keeps time with swings of its hips.

'I was born to be Elvis's leading lady!' she cries, doing a twirl in the kitchen. 'But I was born too late,' she pouts. She goes to bed with a red ribbon around her neck.

Her play is a sex comedy written and directed by a man called Warren whose card says 'Rabbit Ahead Productions'. 'Giving her the bunny behind' is the trope of his piece. Warren and I loathe each other immediately. Abigail is a snappy actress, by far the star attraction. I attend the dress rehearsal, then the opening night. Abigail steals it. It is now obvious that the men in the cast are with Warren: they all prefer her single. I can only partially understand it: I can get on with almost anybody, what is wrong with them all? She brings me their concerns. What am I doing, what's my deal, what's my damage? I cannot give satisfactory answers. She begins to lean more and more towards them. I do not blame her: who the hell am I, after all? No job, no residence, no place on New York's matrix, a wandering bum.

I resolve to go quietly. I'll take a train to Washington tomorrow. But first there is a party. Abigail wants me to be there. The cast turn their backs pointedly. I try to be friendly, then sit quietly. Finally their combined dislike becomes difficult to ignore and I begin to drink seriously until, blotto and obnoxious, I find myself offering to fight Warren, his mates, the lot of them. At last the suspicion and confusion I have been causing are swept away. Their faces clear. They knew it. Abigail has been dating a psycho. New York is on permanent lookout for psychos: it is almost a relief when it sights one.

Abigail demands her keys back. I return them. We say goodbye. But what about my stuff, I cry suddenly, it's in your flat! Not her problem. Well, I'm going to get it. I set off into a blizzard, snow pouring through the canyons in torrents. It is a long, long walk back to Queens. How many hundreds of miles I have walked through cities at night. Through Paris, my feet hurting so much I talked to them; through London, past the bodies in shop doorways, the silent change of traffic lights; now through New York, where the lights of windows appear momentarily through the snow, so warm, so far away. A figure appears beside me in the blizzard, head bowed like mine against the blasting snow. He is Russian. We grin at the insanity of it.

'Holodna!' I shout.

'Da,' he replies. 'Ocheen holodna!' Very cold.

In Queens I sit in Abigail's hallway and try to sleep. She appears mid-morning accompanied by a huge man who is itching to punch me. She stands, face closed, lips pursed, as the huge man hovers and I pack. It is intensely irritating to be treated like a loon. It makes you want to behave like one. There is a short iron bar behind the door in the bathroom. For a moment I consider wrapping a towel around it and tapping the huge man behind his huge ear. I imagine putting it down carefully, stepping over his prone figure and bidding Abigail a polite goodbye. Instead I stuff my stuff into the bag and slink away, hangdog, to Washington.

Bill Clinton was being sworn in for his second term. Chelsea looked happy, Hillary looked buttoned-up and Washington was awash with the most terrifying kind of policemen – resentful, violent-seeming thugs, bristling with confrontation. We took a wrong turning and were abusively menaced for it. In zero-tolerance New York lingering outside a deli could get you searched; in Washington you felt it could get you shot. The White House seemed to be in a crack park. We listened to Dylan: *Desire* and other albums. We talked about bringing down the government and going to join the Zapatistas. We walked to the Washington Monument, a brutal obelisk ringed with joyful American flags. There were few people around and I was desperate: 'I think I'll just pee behind it.'

'The fuck you will!'

'Oh come on, Hardiman, just quickly! When a man's got to go . . .'

'You are *not* peein' on my monument, dude.'

'Christ! I had no idea you were so patriotic. You can come and pee on Nelson's Column any time you like.'

'I don't wanna pee on your shitty column.'

'So rude! It's an excellent column. You should be honoured. I'll just have to pee behind Lincoln instead . . .'

We walked to the Vietnam memorial. Shabby, privileged and useless, we stood before small-print black columns of dead boys our age and younger. They seemed an indictment of us, and an indictment of them: the invisible fat men all around us in the Capitol, in the banks and the departments of state.

The forty-second president promised to be good and true. His helicopter trailed thick banners of fumes down the Potomac. We partied with Ben's friends, students, a journalist. Ben and I shared a bottle of bourbon for breakfast while watching the Cindy Crawford workout video.

'It can't get much worse then!'

'We're spending – like, a hundred dollars a day on all this shit . . .?
Each?'

'Gotta stop.'

'Sure can't go on much longer.'

'Jesus, Cindy.'

We went back to New York, helping a friend of Ben's move into his
first flat. He was going to be a banker. He had a place in Brooklyn
and a great deal of new furniture in boxes from something called Ikea.
Apparently you assembled it yourself. Awake at dawn again, trying
to be useful, I assembled it wrong. I was stoned all the time now,
rambling and ranting in different voices.

'When I wanted to describe you then,' Ben says, years later, 'I
would say have you seen that Mike Leigh film, *Naked*? You know
Johnny? Well, he thinks he's that guy . . .'

And I did. Johnny, who watches the world throng by and shakes
his head in appalled amazement. Johnny, who believes everything and
nothing, in the end of the world in every moment, into coming into
being and passing away, coming into being and passing away. I can
hear his voice now, the sarcasm in his Manchester accent, the bitterness, the mockery. Money, power, convention: it's all shit it's all shit
it's all shit . . . Not that Johnny would have put it so simply.

'So what happened,' he is asked, 'were you bored in Manchester?'

'Was I bored? No, I wasn't fuckin' bored. I'm never bored. That's
the trouble with everybody – you're all so bored. You've had nature
explained to you and you're bored with it, you've had the living
body explained to you and you're bored with it, you've had the universe explained to you and you're bored with it, so now you want
cheap thrills and, like, plenty of them, and it doesn't matter how
tawdry or vacuous they are as long as it's new as long as it's new as
long as it flashes and fuckin' bleeps in forty fuckin' different colours.
So whatever else you can say about me, I'm not fuckin' bored.'

'Don't waste your life,' says Brian, a middle-aged, crushingly
under-employed security guard, in a tone of urgent, intimate seri-
ousness, momentarily arresting Johnny's desperate flippancy.

'What?'

'Don't – waste – your life.'

But see it with Johnny's eyes, with my eyes, and there is nothing you can do that would waste it and nothing that would not waste it.

'Waste not want not,' says Brian.

'And *other* clichés,' Johnny rejoins, with withering mockery.

'Ah – but a cliché is full of truth or it wouldn't be a cliché.'

'Which is in itself a cliché,' Johnny snaps in exasperation.

It is terrible how much normality can be erased like that, how much comfort obviated, how much of the support of others destroyed. If every time someone says something you have heard before a cackling Mancunian voice inside you replies 'And *other* clichés . . .' it is not long before, freaked and freaking, suspicious and suspecting, you are quite alone.

They had already cleaned up Times Square, a lot of Brooklyn and slices of all five boroughs. Big police in huge cars idled along the blocks and you needed ID for a drink even if you were twenty-four and looked twenty-three, in your own mind.

'If you have a problem, talk to Rudi Giuliani – y'know we hate the bastard too?'

I took to reading my passport to bartenders: 'Her Britannic Majesty's Secretary of State requests and requires in the Name of Her Majesty all those whom it may concern to allow the bearer to pass freely without let or hindrance and to afford the bearer such assistance and protection as may be necessary . . .!'

'Uhrilly. So where does it say you're twenty-one?'

'Fuckin' Inglish bastard,' said a guy by a loo.

'I'm a fuckin' Welsh bastard!' I insisted, like a belligerent ass. Straight, drunk, stoned or high on heroin, I was a wretched ass. Only Ben could pull me up short.

'Fuckin' get a hold of yourself and stop being an ass, or I'll have to . . .'

'. . . what?'

'. . . fuckin' kick your ass, man.'

'Sorry.'

That night we went to an apartment on the Upper East Side, huge and shadowed, tinkling with wealth and bad taste, where Ben's friend's girlfriend's parents were away and Ben's friend and his girl-friend were injecting themselves with heroin. It had given his friend extraordinary eyes, glazed and blazing at once, like fire behind glass, poet's eyes. But no poetry came from him, only monosyllables and that senior addict's aura of expertise and dreadful self-possession. We sat cross-legged before him and refused to inject it, but thought we might smoke it off foil.

The frightening thing was how warm and physical it was. No drug had ever reached beyond my brain to my body, nothing had ever gone so deep so quickly; my bones felt soft, my body swaddled, as though the opiate had wrapped warm arms around me, enfolding me in a comfort and security I had not known since I was a small child snuggled deep in a duvet. One by one they keeled over gently, the boy and girlfriend kissing, Ben slumbering.

I went out at daybreak, wanting to use the drug, to see the world through it. I took a cable car to Roosevelt Island, wandered around and took the cable car back. It was a grey and hesitant morning: the tone of the day, echoed in the glum faces of my fellow travellers, seemed heavy and dragging. I looked at what there was to look at, the East River, the giant-crenellated Manhattan shore and the mighty towers of Harlem, and was unmoved: I sensed only a tiny echo of the resonance of beauty, cruelty and strangeness I would have expected had I been straight. Rather than increasing what I might see in the world, heroin reduced it; rather than exposing things, it seemed to insulate and muffle them.

I sat on the balcony and watched the day begin again. I smoked and drank, laughed to myself, picked up the phone and called Abigail's director, Warren, assuming the kind of Irish accent that would surely get you shot for incompetence in Belfast.

'This is Warren?'

'Ah, Warren. You've been a naughty boy.'

'Excuse me? Who is this?'

'This is Paddy O'Reilly. Warren. Thur's a bam in yer phone. When yer put it down she's gonna go aff, Warren. Bang. No more Warren.'

'What the fuck . . .'

'So you better not put it down, Warren. Good luck, slantcha.'

*

Pushing it and pushing it until the morning after and your body's final refusal to take any more does not necessarily lead you to sensory mummification and acts of random stupidity. Every now and then I did break through the skin of things, with little harm beyond the battering to my health.

There was a bar beneath a certain hotel where if you wanted to take cocaine you needed to use the Ladies. There the principal lady took a few dollars from you and showed you to your stall. There you chopped out your tiny line, ever so huge, suddenly, ever so clumsy, a great crystal-imperilling ogre of enormous fingers and blasting breath, and you nose-sucked it all up, a giant bee greedy for nectar.

It clogs the front of the mind with misfiring fireworks and gently cups the rest of your brain with a warm and fatherly hand. You are another sort of child now. Your notions and insights are as final, precocious and pretentious as a scholar-athlete wunderkind. You are so good you have to hide it, so clever and happy you grin to keep it down. You do not want to embarrass anyone with your supreme perceptions. Certain little children and coke-kites know no doubt. They hold their own strings. Your niceness is amazingly graceful, your modesty quite saintly. You sit at the bar with your friend, and a very handsome pair you make, swilling beer and swallowing fags. Everything tastes of the crystals. Centred, balanced and enlightened, you pose. And you chuckle low, because you both know this is bad, this is silly, this all blow. Eventually, back at some flat, you go to bed and to the torpid half-sleep that coke permits. For a long, long time you half-float in it, a body in a mangrove swamp of half-thoughts, dreams like encrusted roots climbing in and out and over you.

At some point, unable to submerge, you flounder up and out into the early morning. Eighth Street is freaks dormitory and all the freaks are sleeping. You paddle down to the corner. The air is thick with mist, the smell of garbage rises like marsh gas and your pores feel drunk on the soup of it as a cocaine sweat prickles your scalp. Into the bagel buffet for the inevitable coffee, out again for the obvious cigarette, and you stand, swaying, as stuck as if this corner were a fly-paper, and then it happens.

Suddenly, there in front of you, hove-to on the corner like a spaceship, is a New York Fire Department fire truck. Red and white, silver and gold, fat black tyres like oil balloons, ladders to climb the walls of Eden, a horn to drown the bells of Hell, utility, power, beauty and excess, dwarfing the world and ready to save it: nothing can daunt this fire truck, nothing deter and nothing compare to this giant toy which faces down infernos. Peeled to the nerves under your raw skin you see the fire truck as if you had never seen one before, and as you stand and stare at it, for an instant you feel it, you see it, you even, for a moment, understand it: *America*.

Ben's plan was to give college yet another shot. What was mine? Previous generations must have had this discussion in such different ways. Fifty years ago it would have been army, navy or air force? A couple of decades before that it might have been a stroll into the family firm, or an exam for the colonial service or study for one of the professions. We were still the same immensely privileged class, a tiny percentile of the planet, monstrously blessed. Yet we did not regard our futures with excitement or even enthusiasm; the whole business of making our ways seemed a wearying grind, a coercion, a vast formulaic trick practised on our freedoms and the inclinations of our spirits by powers and societies we did not respect.

He spoke to me as though he thought he might not see me again. I was going to go back, sort myself out and get another job, right? I am sure we must have talked about getting help but I do not remember it. We said goodbye. Dead within six months, he bet himself, watching me go. The Chelsea Hotel gave me a last night of something like grace before the airport. One of the city's finest was waiting for me at the boarding gate.

Approaching a document check where the hero will be found out is a familiar and thrilling thing, lived through war movies and spy stories. Shuffling forward in the queue, aware of their eyes on you, handing it over, knowing it's going wrong, seeing the uniforms closing in, craning for a closer look, when you have something to hide, on the other hand, has a terror all of its own. There is no hero. There is only you. All eyes are suddenly on you and the questions come piling in. The stewardess summoned the policeman – a formality, as he was already moving in – and he took me aside.

'Is there a problem?' I said. 'Can I help you with anything?'

The policeman had a photocopy of my passport, passed to him via the Paramount by Abigail. As far as the cop knew I had made some sort of trouble and a hotel had it in for me. I did not know if he knew I had put on an Irish accent while high on heroin and made bomb threats against an American citizen, but I assumed he believed the absolute worst.

'How long have you been here?'

'You're going home today – where?'

'When are you coming back?'

I told them.

The policeman looked blank, hands resting on his cuffs and gun. The check-in woman, who was English, looked very hard and said the airline would take me on the plane, no problem. The policeman looked tempted.

'I'm very happy for you to make a call to the British Consulate if you think . . .' I offered.

'No,' said the cop. 'It's OK.'

Imagine getting away with that now. If they had run a scan, swab or dog anywhere near me there would have been no doubt about the presence of suspicious chemicals: I was sweating THC and alcohol, my blood was specked with heroin and canine anaesthetic.

The great white jet swallowed us all quietly, we took our seats, buckled up, and the captain said we were just waiting for one more passenger, then we would be on our way. After ten minutes a bearded man walked up the aisle, all the way to the back of the plane, which was now starting to move, quietly nodding at people and looking around in a friendly way before hurrying back to first class. We were off. I was not looking forward to the British police but at least they were different, then. I wrote a note to the bearded man requesting an interview and sent it to first class via a stewardess. She brought back a reply.

Dear Horatio,

Thank you for your delightfully written letter. I'm afraid I came over last night – have had a full day's work – and have another full day tomorrow. So I've decided to get as much kip as possible. I am sorry. However you obviously can write and will go far and so don't really need me!

Best of luck to you,

Richard Branson

It was the nearest thing I would have to a reference for a long, long time.

From the airport I went to Brixton, where Theo was living. Robin and his flatmate Toby had bought a PlayStation. They were in another world with Lara Croft: for weeks and weeks they had been jumping, puzzling, climbing, shooting and fighting with her through *Tomb Raider*. I felt a pang of loneliness as they talked and laughed about their adventures. In the world of the computer screen you could do anything: violent, silly or misconceived it did not matter. It was all normal, even admirable, a projection and development of the games my brother and I had played on the mountain when we were young children, with our sticks. *Tomb Raider* was a nationwide, worldwide craze, an acceptable, fashionable way for young men to continue all the wars we had fought as children against invisible foes. Compared to the pixelated adventures of Robin and Toby my actual exploits in New York and elsewhere were freakish, bizarre and dangerous. I kept quiet about them as more and more of us assembled. We bought beer, and someone was sent off, with a handful of our ten pound notes, to buy dope.

'Where has he gone?'

'There's this place down Coldharbour Lane . . .'

When he returned we all got stoned and talked about college. What had happened in Torpington came out. Robin looked at me. He did not say much, but I could see him thinking, *what the fuck?* I could see them all thinking it. I was thinking it. A couple of days later I returned to Torpington, and went to see the police.

8

Crime and Punishment in South Wales &c.

1997

I THOUGHT ABOUT denying it but the officer who interviewed me said he knew I was the one and advised me not to bother. He placed a video cassette on the table between us. It was probably *The Simpsons* but we both knew I could not be sure it did not show me, red handed on the town's CCTV. I confessed.

'So you weren't trying to burn it down?'

'No! It was just a couple of rubbish bags, they were nowhere near the door. I thought there would be a puddle of ash and they would have to walk through it to get to the office. I thought it would be a fair expression of how I felt. They treated me like dirt and – well – you know – have some dirt. I had no idea . . . there was a strong wind – it must have blown it . . .'

'OK. Well, I'm going to charge you with arson . . .'

'Criminal damage, surely!'

'Deliberately starting a fire is arson. Come this way.'

'Where to?'

'The cells, while I do the paperwork.'

Sober, straight and fully conscious this time, I took it all in. Dim light comes from a panel in the ceiling. A shadow of the day fails to penetrate small thick glass squares set in concrete. The cell smells of old dirt rubbed over with detergent so many times that it has taken on a chemical edge, and of sweat, regret and semen. It is a unique and unmistakeable tang: on a train many years later I caught the reek of it and turned to see a young man next to me reading a charge sheet. The cell walls are scored with broken, unreadable scratches and half-erased graffiti: it is too late to make the merest mark now. You feel shame and self-loathing. What are you doing here? How have you managed to do this to yourself? What is wrong with you? Are you really so bad, so stupid and so dangerous that you cannot be trusted to exist in the world? Evidently you are. It is a kind of death: you feel that all the good and all the ill you have done have been weighed and the scales come down to this. You feel fear, too. You can scream in a cell, you can beg and plead in a cell, you can be raped, tortured and killed in a cell and no one will hear or help you. You begin to pace but there is no room; you turn and turn again, going back on yourself faster and faster as the walls press in. Claustrophobia rises in you like a yell and you sit down, quickly, and fight it.

I heard chatting and shouting, children's voices. A school group was being shown around the station. I jumped behind the door and prayed they would not come down here, to the end of the corridor. They went away. Eventually a policeman appeared and let me out, but it was a figurative freedom. Waiting for the court appearance you carry the cell with you.

The case before mine made the bench angry. The chief magistrate looked like a retired army officer. Infuriation lurked in his face. The first defendant was a surreptitious, slightly hunched middle-aged man who confirmed his name softly. He was charged with thirteen counts of stealing and selling E-Type Jaguars. A vague feeling of admiration ran around the court when this was read out. This was crime all right, but it had taste and style. However it was beyond the power of the magistrates to try or sentence, to the chairman's apparent frustration: they referred his case up to the Crown Court. They then listened to my solicitor's detailed plea and retired, the chairman looking furious as he withdrew. They were going to dish it out now, it was certain. Mr Smith, my solicitor, had seemed convinced of the justice and rectitude of our argument, but the chief magistrate had looked angrier and more impatient the longer it went on.

They were gone for a while. Three months, I bet myself, the maximum they can give before they have to refer it up. Three months. I'll have to be a writer now. I'll never get a job with a prison record. Three months. They say ex-public school boys do OK in jail. When you get into your first fight you have to really go for it or they rape you every day. Christ, I wish I'd learned to box. Three months. For that. I wonder if it would be worth running.

They came back in.

'You are very lucky that we are not asking for pre-sentence reports prior to sending you to jail. In view of previous good character, and because we accept that you had no intention of burning the building down . . .'

A fine, compensation and a suspended sentence. 'You will not be so lucky again. We hope you have learned your lesson.'

I had, oh I had! Thank you God, thank you Life, thank you Chairman, thank you Mr Smith, thank you other two Magistrates, thank Christ!

Wes ran me back to the station and waived the fare. We shook hands and I left Torpington, vowing never to return. I was a disgrace, a horrible lunatic, but I was not in jail. I had learned my lesson. This was the first day of the rest of my life, I was not going to go lower than that, it would all be better, I would be better, from now on.

Not so.

I slunk into the next job, more 'work experience' (you experience the work as a reward in itself, as there is no other remuneration) on a daily paper in Cardiff. They must have thought me very quiet. I was quiet. I was sure that they must either know of my madness and my crimes, or must be on the point of finding out.

There are two ways the criminally branded can go: either you assimilate your misdemeanours, take a perverse pride in them and trumpet them as part of your identity, or you lock them away from the sight of the world and carry them gingerly, like a wound, pretending outwardly that they do not exist. I have met men who have taken the first route many times in pubs, where, in a certain sort of bar, they reign. Everyone is careful with them and they seem to revel in it. Their record of going too far becomes a sort of power, a potential – they might at any minute go too far again. At the same time, no one can stand being suspected, being handled, indefinitely. At some point the sore spot is touched, the pressure bursts out, and with a dreadful release, the snap of breaking tension, the damned damns himself again.

An air of villainy is a strange and powerful thing. You can never be the local hero now but people will notice you, they will talk when you go by. Women will notice you. Your official iniquity makes the rest of us, with our secret sins, feel better. Every anti-hero knows something of the hero's resistance, individuality and daring, and knows too that he will never be credited for it. As our hunter's eyes are attracted to movement, so something in our hearts responds to those who cause movement, disturbance, stir. A bad boy does not necessarily lack friends, associates, even good women. There is a blend of resentment and exultation in him, as he barges into the bar: *How dare you label me – make me this?* and *See how bad I am!* Look out, here comes trouble. Anything could happen now. There is dark romance in an outlaw: anyone who has been in trouble at school or dismissed from a job will remember it. People want to know you then, if only because they are ghoulishly curious about how it feels to be you, and because you make good gossip.

No one on the paper could have mistaken me for good gossip. I was ashamed and embarrassed by myself; I could barely speak. I was trying to give up cigarettes too, which was interesting. On the first day I arrived with a packet of nicotine chewing gum, just in case. Called upon to turn a press release into a 'news in brief' I drew a square of gum and bit on it, receiving a charge of nicotine as intense as anything I had known with illegal drugs and a head-rush so violent that I grabbed the desk in order not to fall off the chair. No one noticed. There was a General Election taking place: everyone was busy.

At the weekends I lay in bed and swore at the Tories on the television. I had never known them lose an election: they surely could not win this time, but I was certain that Labour were going to drop the ball again, somehow. Bloody Tories. I talked to Jane on the phone. I could not understand why she was still interested in me, but she was.

'Are you coming to Bristol then?' she asked.

'I'd love to but . . .'

'Oh, but what?'

'My arms seem to have packed in. I think I sprained my shoulder.'

'Oh dear,' she purred, with immaculate sarcasm, 'how have you managed that?'

'Well, I saw my left arm in the mirror and it looked like a piece of chicken so I thought I'd start building it up so I brushed my teeth using my left and – I think it's sprained.'

'Ha ha! Come on!'

'And I need to shave.'

'Shave then!'

'I can't face myself in the mirror.'

'Don't shave then!'

'And I need a shower but showering in the middle of the afternoon . . .'

'What?'

'It's a concession to uselessness I am unwilling to make.'

'Come and bloody stink here then.'

'OK. But I'm no fun – it's the fags.'

She picked me up at the station, piloting her car like a missile, kissed me and refused to countenance any moaning, complaint or mood swings.

'When people give up smoking they think they can get away with it: well, not with me, buster. You can bloody well suffer if you want to, but as far as I'm concerned it's no excuse, all right? Just be nice. It's not difficult.'

We zipped back to her flat. She drove beautifully and fast. She was a scenic artist working in south Wales, commuting across the channel. A tag on her car meant she could pass the Severn Bridge tolls with only the briefest pause for the machine to register her and raise the barrier. Every time we did it she seemed to decelerate faster and accelerate again quicker – the barrier leaping out of the way always with less and less time to spare. At home she read and watched television. 'I'm a simple girl really,' she said. She loved Salinger's short stories. I read her 'A Perfect Day for Banana Fish' while she had a bath. Giving up smoking swings you wildly from euphoria to despair. It was a good reading, she said, a really good reading. I was as happy and proud as I have ever been. Half an hour later, watching television, I wanted to pull my eyes out, or eat glass, as Jane would say.

'I can't believe you like this bloody *Friends* thing! It's dreadful.'

'No it isn't!' she cried. 'They're really nice and really funny and you're only saying you don't like them because you're a miserable git. I bet you can't watch it without laughing.'

'Huh! Done. Bet you.'

'There! You're laughing.'

'Well, that was quite funny. But it's still rubbish.'
'Oh cock off.'

I did not contribute much to the paper, beyond press releases turned into notes from around Wales, but I saw a lot. While the *Torpington Gazette* did not have the internet, this one did not even have the mouse. The computers were ancient things standing on gunmetal stalks. It did not hold anyone back. I sat opposite their chief reporter, who was widely admired.

'And how is the finest policeman in south Wales this morning?' the chief reporter would say suddenly, into his phone. It never failed. They sent him out searching for the Beast of Borth – he hung a sheep's skeleton on a fence, got the photographer to snap it, then speculated that it had been a victim of the mystery cat. In the evening he went to Boxercise, then drinking with the police, the councillors, the quango members, anyone who could be useful. When they lied to him on the phone he knew it.

'It doesn't add up, somehow, there's something I don't . . . Ah, right . . . OK. Yes, same as always, of course. "A source confirmed," no names.'

He is very personable, very pushy. There is something endearing about his unconcealed ambition and drive: I can easily imagine the men who run this town laughing at his cheeky sallies, he is one of the boys. I cannot imagine the same men wanting anything to do with me: without cigarettes or weed I had no confidence, no volume, few ideas. Every sentence, written or spoken, was a struggle.

Cardiff was an idiosyncratic town, from the bright seagulls paddling about on the station roof to the biblical darkness of the pub humour. Two women discussed match day tactics. 'Puke at three, you'll be ready to go again by five!' A group of girls, miles under age, screamed for more drink. 'Mad as fishes,' said a young man with a withered arm and a gift for summing people up. 'My brother's got a great job with Tarmac up in Merthyr. Lovely car, lovely wife, strong bloke, you know, have anybody, not a muppet like us . . .'

They were tearing down the old Arms Park and selling it off, everything from the pitch to the pot plants in the bar. There was general scepticism that the new stadium would be ready for the World Cup in 1999, and a kind of phlegmatic curiosity about the new city being developed in Cardiff Bay. The townspeople came down to the bay to eat pricey fish and chips and stare at the construction, wondering whether it would really be as glittering as it promised, and if it would have any place for them.

On the first of May, having stayed up all night, we all knew the first promise of the millennium had come true. A new government, a new leader, a new Britain. The morning broke in gold and blue and fresh summer green, it seemed the fairest Mayday the country had ever seen. We all watched as our new leader arrived in Downing Street to the delirious greeting of a crowd of people waving flags and cheering: people who looked like us, happy voters, but who turned out to be a stage-managed band of his supporters masquerading as members of the general public.

The next work experience placement is with a paper which does not do bylines, promises or payment. A local weekly modelled on *The Times* of the 1950s, it is owned by a wealthy family and runs to several editions every press day, covering a swathe of the suburbs from its headquarters in Richmond on Thames. The office near the village green is quietly plush downstairs: upstairs cramped and dull, a coop where strained young men struggle to fill endless columns of small print. They made me court reporter. A famous inventor charged with speeding was the best of it in news terms and we had him on the first day. The rest of the weeks I sat there, as the summer of 1997 passed outside, engrossed, as a stream of defendants were fed through the mechanisms of British justice.

Mr Water and his wife are out for a drink. While parking their car they become involved in an altercation with some youths in a white convertible, the youths having driven it too close to Mrs Water for Mr Water's liking, and not in his view safely, and said crude things. Mr and Mrs Water then happen to walk by the youths' car, now parked on an incline in River Street. To his great regret Mr Water, in a moment of frustration – and, he now admits, stupidity – lets the handbrake off and watches the car roll down the short incline into the river and disappear. Many customers at an adjacent pub witness the incident and cheer.

Mr Water felt great horror and dismay. He had no idea the car, value approximately £20,000, would vanish – he had hardly meant to get the wheels wet. He intended a small gesture of defiance, a nothing: he had been sure it would stop. He was not to know the river was so deep just there.

Mr Shave is caught stealing a packet of razors from Boots in the High Street, value around £3. He has been here before, recently: he is well and truly in the mechanism. Mr Shave is on conditional discharge for several similar offences. He has a drug problem, a probation officer, welfare problems, medical problems. He has entered programmes to help him pay fines before and defaulted. The extent of the unpaid fines, let alone the continuing thefts and drug abuse, suggest jail. The court hears that jail will not help Mr Shave, who requires urgent and costly help with his drug addiction.

What would a reasonable person do with Mr Water? The court gives Water a small fine – on top of the bill for rescuing and repairing the car – and sends him on his way. What would the same reasonable person do in Mr Shave's case? The court asks for some further reports and actions from various parties, but decides it has little choice: Mr Shave will have to return soon for a prison sentence.

My criminal career was broadly similar to Mr Shave's, in that it was directly linked to drug addiction, but in its actions it was much more like those of Mr Water, and treated accordingly. Had its Shave-type been more apparent, it may not have led to Water-type sentences. In none of its major events was my drug addiction apparent or ever brought to the court's attention. Had Mr Shave also behaved like Mr Water, while high, as I was to do, he would have definitely gone down straight away.

I came 'home' from the office one summer evening; to my father's house, which he shared with his wife, where I was a guest. I was happy enough, after a day of following court proceedings and Tim Henman's progress through Wimbledon (and moreover through our local property market), thoroughly sick of all things Henman, and there in the house was my father and a message from the North. 'We are delighted to be able to offer you a place on the editorial training scheme at the *Northern Chronicle*, Newcastle upon Tyne. Delegates are invited to join us in the offices . . . Reception . . . Course weekdays Sept–Dec 1997 . . .'

I punched the air, below the belt, hard. Perhaps Tim Henman's celebrations had affected me. Back to the North, it meant, though I had vowed never to stay there again after York, especially not in winter. But this was a superb course, one of the best in the country. My father had not been with me when I received good news for a long time, if ever, though he had been there when Oxford told me to bugger off, the same day my nice French teacher's report said he thought I was asleep in lessons: my father left that morning, Christmas eve, with a parting note demanding to know what the hell I had been doing when I should have been sleeping, among other things. But this was a very happy evening for us both. We drank wine, he smoked his pipe, we talked about Newcastle. 'It's a young man's city,' he said, fondly, remembering the kind of place it had been when he had known it, in the 1960s.

The train came in over the Tyne, arriving in Newcastle Central in the middle of Saturday afternoon. Everyone was watching the football; the airy streets were empty. I was on a budget which would allow me to survive as long as I continued not to smoke cigarettes and economized on food and booze. I would get a part-time job in a bookshop or something. I took the Metro to the address my new landlady had given me. She was a senior journalist on the paper. A tall blonde woman on crutches opened the door, smiled a pretty smile and said hello! Yes, I'm Tanya, come in . . . With two friends, she was screwing on new doors to the bedrooms, ready for her new tenants, me and two other trainees.

We went to bed early. I awoke to voices in the hall and the murmur of the television. I stumbled out. 'Di and Dodi . . .' they said.

'It's 'orrible to say it, but it's like – that was the biggest story ever. Nothing really comes close. I can't imagine a bigger one in my lifetime. And since then it all feels a bit flat really . . .'

Six weeks later the latest in our line of afternoon sessions is a talk from the head of a wire service, the man who pressed the button which told the world she was not just injured. Timed, dated and on screen in every newspaper, TV and radio station in the world, with two little letters, PA, beside it, and only one thing mattered then, would ever matter. They were first.

The expression on his face was distant for a moment, then he refocused.

Seagulls cry from the roof of an old building, a tower with a cabin perched at the top. The grey northern sky dims . . . Body counts, round up at first, later take the nearest convenient number. Corpses, divide into ours and theirs. The good-looking are always at the front, likewise the truly grotesque, the freaks, marvels and anything involving dogs or children. Follow power and soaps. Your best background you get from each other, maybe an academic. Birthday cards and presents encouraged: keep them sweet, you'll be all over your best sources when the good stuff comes out. Eavesdrop, everywhere. A kerb-crawling judge, a drunken bishop, a mouse in a can of beans − as long as you have the picture − are gold dust.

Fair play to them though, they did say right at the beginning that they did not do ethics, just 'news'. And what's the essence of 'news'? We are. We the tabloids. Ours are the values, ours the audience, ours the art. Your old grey ladies, your thunderers, your pinks, supplements, inserts, hats and high debates − froth and lace! Long dogs and burning bitches all, ravening to feed you what you want, hot for scandal, under the fur.

Some of the best trainees are going straight to the *Daily Mirror*. I had no paper, no employer. I tilt things at the *Independent*. The *Telegraph* follows up a story of mine about arson busting. I am encouraged to apply for a job on the *Western Mail*. I am unsure. I can see the fun in this business, but do I really want to give it my life? I dither. I drink and smoke and start a novel.

Jane comes to see me one weekend. We go to Whitley Bay and walk along the cliffs. It is October but it is wonderfully warm, almost an Indian summer. We sit on a rock, lapped by the tide, and drink champagne. All seems well.

★

Robin and his architecture class go on a unit trip to what is left of Yugoslavia. He sends me a photograph in an envelope: a building which has been half torn away by shelling. It is a dreadful thing. The floors and walls are smashed and hanging, as if civilization itself has been bitten off, chewed and spat out as rubble. He has enclosed a note: 'This is what they did to newspaper offices in Sarajevo.' I cannot work out if it is a joke or a terrible reproach. Is he drawing a parallel between me and the Serb gunners? Or is he just teasing? Doesn't he believe that I had no intention of burning it down? Or maybe he is just warning me. Stay straight. That is probably it.

Unfortunately, the warning comes too late.

Return to house. Have been with a friend, new friend of old friend from York, now living with parents in Newcastle, and his friends. Watching football, smoking dope, drinking. Stumble, slur. So much drinking. Much, much more than before. Imagine the rivers of livers which have flowed through Newcastle's hospitals. Tanya is in the kitchen. Bang on the music. Smoke dope with one of her mates. Later, alone –

'Sho, sex or drugs, Tanya?'

'Ooh. I dunno,' smiling. 'Which would you like, Horatio?'

'Drugs!'

Return to house another night, not drunk this time. Tanya has a brand new car for the weekend: she is reviewing the Nissan Terrano II for the paper. She takes me for a spin to the sea at North Shields. The sand is side-lit from the land, the sea black. We run on the beach and go home. Tanya is not to know she has the psychological equivalent of a firework bouncing around in her hall, its paper smoking. I had recently interviewed the detective in charge of Intelligence-Led Policing in a part of the west end of Newcastle. It made a good feature. I had secured a trip on a fishing boat with two phone calls. Newcastle and the world seemed full of possibility, though I had been drinking and smoking copiously in my off-duty hours and was not as happy as I appeared.

I was worried about Jane who was now living in London; she was fed up with me: I was never there. For years of my life I have been in a different place or country from my girlfriend. Being routinely separated from your beloved is an old story, but the normality of the distances involved was new. In 1993 in York, we first took to the internet and to email. Schools and universities were taking in foreign students at a higher rate than ever and we had all started to travel younger. Now Jane is in London and I am on Tyneside. The old story: the longing, the worry, the dreaming. Listening to bloody Dylan and the Violent Femmes and barely managing to get up in time for class and work at nine, never mind a fishing boat at four.

That night Jane telephones. She says I am fucking around and says it is over and that she is going to New York tomorrow. I say I will come to see her now, in London.

'I'm not in London,' she says. 'I'm in Skegness tonight.'

'Why?'

'I'm photographing birds in marshes early tomorrow morning.'

'OK. I'll come to Skegness.'

'Don't be stupid.'

'I'm not being stupid, I'm coming to Skegness.'

I call National Rail Enquiries. The last train to Skegness, or anywhere near, has gone. Would I like to go to Grantham and change tomorrow morning?

No, that will be too late.

Standing in a hall in a little terraced house in Newcastle I see myself suddenly, a stupid, unreliable, peculiar figure, another idiot losing the woman he loves, and think no. There is my little room with its pile of clothes, newspapers, notes and books and my so-called novel, and there is the front door, with everything else beyond it, and somewhere beyond it, Jane.

The hall carpet is bright red and the Nissan's key is lying there, where Tanya left it. With no hesitation I scoop it up. It seems the obvious thing. I can drive: I just do not have a licence or insurance. I leave Tanya a scrawled note. The car stands at the kerb, lumpy and strident with overstated power, the kind of thing you would expect a slum landlord to drive. You really have to climb up into those four-by-fours like mounting a horse, but you get a great view. It is all over in the first forty seconds: if you get off OK, out of the parking space and a few metres down the road, then you are good to go. If I nudge something or stall in this first minute I might stop, but I do not. I do not.

It is serious this time. Footling a milk float around a deserted housing estate in the middle of the night on the edge of an isolated country town is one thing: this is quite another. Make a mistake now and people will die.

Deep breaths. No mistakes. Relax into it. Think of Danny the Champion of the World. Think of Jane. I am going to Skegness to tell the girl I love that I love her. I am going to show her that I love her. What did the Highwayman say? I'll come to you by moonlight, though hell should bar the way. They shot him, come to think of it, shot him down like a dog in the roadway, but this is not going to come to that. The vehicle is austere and new-smelling, a giant ugly duckling, bullish as a bouncer, but it certainly goes: should hell bar the way I am confident that we will barge through it. Remember your driving lessons. Mirror, signal, manoeuvre. Watch your speed.

The instruments glow green with that luminous wash I used to love as a child. We slide down a tunnel under the Tyne and emerge on the other side as the roads open up. The brute swishes along, slurping diesel. The motorway lights splash rapid orange bars over the bonnet. I am buzzing with cigarettes, cola and adrenalin. At service stations I ask – is this the way to Skegness? Pulling in and out of them, manoeuvring the monster in tight spaces, is slightly nervy. The machine is worth £32,000, according to Tanya. Enjoy it, you'll drive better. I would never want one. Go easy, imagine you own it. I cannot believe I will ever earn enough to buy one. I cannot believe that no one at these service stations telephones the police. Perhaps 24-year-olds driving monstrous cars are not a suspicious sight. Perhaps the freak climbing out of the Terrano II is a sacked stockbroker, fired for the non-haircut. And the grubby jeans. Or perhaps that is the grunge look again. Perhaps the idiot thinks he is fashionable. One young man behind a counter knows there is something not right, but he grins. 'Good luck, mate!'

How many other people on this motorway are beyond the law? How many in the aeroplanes above are carrying secrets, hiding things, pretending to be other than they are? How many others tense slightly when they see a police car in the mirror? How many of us, out there in the dark, are throwing ourselves like dice after some half-lost chance?

I switch on Radio 4 but the respectful voices with their mature and civilized tones seem to clash with the enterprise. Car thieves probably prefer Radio 1. Not that I'm stealing anything. Borrowing. I hear Radio Five Live is popular in prisons . . . Don't think about prisons. Drive the thing safely, talk to Jane, call Tanya when she wakes up and tell her not to worry, drive the thing safely back, finish the course, get a job on a paper, write the book in the evenings: it will all be fine.

Not so: I am hiding behind this formulation even as I think it and accepting its falsehood again now, in recollection. Because I can feel and remember something else there, too. An impish, errant part of me exulting, as I roll down the motorway – take *this!* Take this, you Gods of dull normality, of trains which arrive too late and aeroplanes which leave too soon. Have a bit of *this*, you who say I cannot drive without a piece of paper, cannot be free without a car, cannot have a car without a job. Screw you all. Licences, timetables, norms, regulations, established patterns, rules, what are these compared to love? Compared to life? Paper and platitudes. What will rule me but my conscience? The 'real world'? 'Society'? I thought we said there was no such thing. 'Them' – as in 'they'll lock you up'? Let them try: 'They'll have to catch me first!' cries the bandit, betraying his existence in a line: we bandits need laws to break and pursuers to flee.

What would Byron have done? What would Shelley do? What would any hero do, if his life were an adventure? It always enraged me, that moment in the story when fate pulls two lovers apart. To hell with warring clans, invading armies, antagonistic religions, duty, structure – fuck it all if it is not love. Should love be thwarted now, by a mere three hundred miles of dark and sodden England?

And there is something else, too. Some part of me knows that this is an irrevocable step. I know that you do not behave like this and walk away smiling. It is as though some part of me wants to destroy everything I have been painstakingly building, as though some part of me always wants to. I scraped a degree, worked for nothing for months, landed a break, threw myself at it . . . and here I am, humming quietly, tearing away from it all at seventy miles an hour. Part of me is burning everything – for fun? Is there something addictive in this, a brighter and darker reality in the test of a genuine adventure (with no guide, instructor or safety line, in which you alone can save or destroy yourself) that you come to crave? Is that why a policeman's first question is always 'Have you been in trouble with the police before?' (You know you are in trouble then. Say yes and you might as well admit guilt for whatever they have stopped you for, say no and you have just committed another offence.) Is that why a criminal record carries such a weight of shame and fear? Not because of the record. Because of the prediction.

I arrive in Skegness around breakfast time. It is a grey, drizzly morning. The rain feels warm and kind after the plastic smell of the car. I park outside the station and call Jane. She pulls up in the same way she always does, quickly, smoothly. Suddenly I wish to God I had come on the train, in the same old way.

'All right,' she says, her face a blend of affection and suspicion.

'All right, darling,' I reply.

'How did you get here?'

'I came in that.'

'What?'

'I borrowed that thing.'

'What?'

'It's a Nissan Terrano II.'

'No!' she cries. 'No, you didn't! Tell me you didn't!'

'I'm afraid I did.'

'Oh God.'

'It's all right, I didn't steal it, I borrowed it from Tanya.'

'Does she know you can't drive?'

'I have to call her . . .' Suddenly I am exhausted, sick from the drive and the sleepless night. Everything that seemed brave and romantic in the dark a few hours ago seems ludicrous now. I must be mad. Looking at the way Jane is looking at me I know there is no doubt: I am. Perhaps I can still stick it back together. 'May I borrow your phone?'

Jane is shaking her head. She looks disgusted and incredulous. 'Sure.'

'Hi, Tanya.'

'Horatio. Where are you?'

'Skegness. I'm fine, the car's fine, I just needed to see Jane. I'll bring it back when I've slept.'

'So you are going to bring it back?'

'Of course! Of course, don't worry about anything.'

'I've called the police.'

'Well, can you call them again and say it's OK, you know where it is, it's all fine?'

'Just bring it back.'

'I will!'

We eat breakfast in a supermarket café, because it is the closest place serving coffee. I am shattered now. I keep trying to put a brave face on things, because I have come all this way to try to win Jane back and I do not want it to end here, like this, surrounded by pensioners who give us long unblinking looks and mothers with little children, who steer them around us, not quite oblivious to the disaster in their midst.

We go out to the marshes in Jane's car. She sets off to photograph birds. I go to sleep – I must sleep, if I am to drive back. The rain falls steadily on the windscreen and the reed beds gush and sway in the wind. I am cold and sticky and in trouble. Sleep comes and goes like patches of mist. Jane returns in the early afternoon. She is going to London now, to catch her plane.

I have failed to win her back. 'Yes!' she cries. 'Maybe it is the most romantic thing that anyone has ever done for me, but it's ridiculous. It's incredibly fucking stupid! Just take it back safely, will you?'

She drives away. It is all over. Now I can only hope to get away with it. I climb back into the monster and set off. Mark and Lard are on Radio 1. They gabble away. They play the Stone Roses, the inevitably disappointing second album. How strange to hear them now. It seems like an omen, a reproach, a hint or a sign of something: *Ten storey love song, I wrote this song for you* . . . I set off up the A1 and reach Newcastle after dark. I park outside the house and get out. Thank goodness. Car unscratched, no damage done. But my key will not fit the front door. I do not understand it. It is definitely the right house. Then the door opens.

'Hi, Tanya.'

Tanya looks like an undertaker who has finished for the day and is rather surprised to find the corpse in her garden.

'My key's not working.'

'I changed the locks,' she said. 'I want you to leave now.' She is dragging a black bin bag, half full of my things.

'OK.'

After a quarter of an hour there is a knock on the front door. I ignore it and carry on packing. I hear Tanya go down the hall and open up. There is a murmur of voices, then I hear a man's voice say, 'He's in here, is he?'

I turn around slowly. Through the door jamb I can see a bulky black jacket with silver insignia. There is a knock on the bedroom door as it is pushed open. He looks calm and quite gentle, but he is definitely a policeman.

'Oh no,' I cry. 'Oh fucking hell.'

He is a pleasant policeman. He goes out to check on the car, then comes back in and arrests me. 'You do not have to say anything but it may harm your defence if you fail to say anything when questioned which you later rely on in court . . .'

He drives me to the station and puts me in a cell. He goes to do the paperwork and locks the door.

Here we are again, in a cell. There must be something terribly wrong with me. I must be mad or damned.

They throw me off the course, two weeks shy of becoming a qualified journalist. At least I am fully trained, I comfort myself. I tell my parents what has happened. They are incredulous. They seem numbed by my delinquency. My cousin, a solicitor, predicts I will get jail this time.

I have very little money and cannot face going home. Awaiting trial is bad enough: I do not want to put my mother through it too. Nathan, my erstwhile university porter friend, offers me his sofa in York.

He is now working for the Ministry of Agriculture, Fisheries and Food. He says it is deadly, apart from the abusive letters he occasionally receives from farmers, one of whom signs himself Alan H. Wanker. Also resident are Graham, another English graduate with too much dope in his past who has moved into university portering, and Simon, who is into computers and martial arts. It is a dismal little house smelling of onions and deodorant, strained by underlying unhappiness and overbearing poverty, with computer games a poor substitute for female company, except on Friday nights, when friends and their girlfriends assemble in the living room to drink. The house has honed cheap drunkenness to an expertise. A quarter bottle of gut-rot vodka, four litres of bargain cider and a few cans of basement lager yield euphoria for a tenner. There is a choice between eating well and smoking: I live on bread, noodles, cigarettes and Nathan's generosity. For three young men who love music they seem very quiet, but one of their neighbours hates them.

'I can hear everything that goes on in your bathroom,' she hisses at Nathan. 'Everything!'

'But why is she listening?' he cries. 'What's she doing, standing in her bath with a wineglass on the wall?' Whenever anyone goes to the bathroom we shout, 'She can hear everything!'

One night, with great ceremony, Nathan unveils the remains of his treasured marijuana plant. Eighteen inches high, it looks as though it had been attacked by a crazed caterpillar which has scoured the stalk from the bottom up, collapsing in a stupor two leaves short of a clean sweep. I yelp with laughter.

'What the hell are we supposed to do with that?'

'What do you think?'

We smoke it. Two leaves do not take you far.

'What about this?' I demand, flicking the stalk.

'I wonder. What do you reckon?'

We smoke some of it. No high. We fry it in a saucepan and smoke it: no high. We pound it up, bake it in the oven with biscuit crumbs and eat it. The fact that it is a complete failure does not detract from the fun: there is a lot of fun to be had with drug substitutes. Since the age of sixteen I had tried banana skin (scraped and smoked), nutmeg (grated and smoked), Tippex thinner (sniffed off a sleeve), hyperventilation, massive and deliberate coffee overdoses, sniffing vodka (an appalling idea, even by these standards), Pro Plus overdoses (we took it at public school in handfuls), poppy sap from my mother's garden (wrong kind of poppy), absinthe, amyl nitrate and various misadventures with aerosols, all in pursuit of that famous mirage, the legal high. There were a range of consequences, none of them best described as a high, except perhaps for the absinthe. Nathan had had great success with a mail-order substance called Salvia Divinorum: so much so that he was loath ever to go near it again.

During the days I read *Giovanni's Room* by James Baldwin and make plans to turn it into a film. It would make a wonderful, low-budget, hand-held feature. The script is practically written: the book is already cinematic – all I have to do is find some actors and hire a camera. I will be a film-maker. It does not matter if a film-maker has been to jail: they are judged on their work. That is the solution. It is just a case of surviving the trial and whatever comes with it. I while away a great deal of time playing *Grand Theft Auto* on the house PlayStation. The first version of this game uses deliberately retro graphics: you look down on peaceful city streets as if from a helicopter. Your character's powers include stealing cars and firing weapons. A series of instructions orders you to pick up drug packages and take bombs to the headquarters of rival drug dealers. I was not interested in these or any other instructions, besides which we did not have the full version of the game: we had a seven and a half minute demonstration version. The challenge therefore is to create as much mayhem as possible in 450 seconds. I discover a real talent for this.

Simon and Nathan have a healthier release in Tae Kwon Do.

'Simon's amazing at it,' Nathan reports. 'He could kill.'

Simon is very tall and very gentle. I cannot imagine him ever being faced with a killing situation.

'Simon, if I do go to prison, and I have to fight, what should I do?'

Simon looks at me over the top of his glasses. 'You should bend over, Horace.'

'And pull your cheeks open and smile,' Nathan adds.

'Piss off!'

'You don't want to be saying that to Mr Big.'

'So what do I do, kick him in the nuts, if he has any nuts?'

Simon shakes his head. 'Try punching him in the throat and goug-ing his eyes.'

I thought about prison, at night, on the sofa, in the stale smoke smell of the sleeping bag, with a backyard light bleeding through the cur-tains. I could not believe that what I had done would merit it but my cousin seemed convinced, and they were coming down hard on car crime at the moment, and the right sort of magistrate might easily conclude it was exactly the sort of 'short sharp shock' I needed. Perhaps it was. But what a stupid, stupid thing. Where are the vic-tims of my crimes? Apart from me and that milkman, who has suffered? What am I to be punished for, actually? Exuberance? Madness? A refusal to *take this shit*?

The court date approached. I found a solicitor, Mr Grant, a man entirely unimpressed by the charges.

'You don't need to worry about this too much,' he said.

I did not think he understood. 'If I could just explain it to them,' I said, 'I'm sure I can make them understand.'

'No, no,' he said, firmly. 'They don't want to hear from the defend-ant. They don't want to hear it from you. Don't worry. I'll tell them.'

I put on my suit and went to court. It was a windy January day. A reporter and two young men in fleeces carrying big cameras hung around in the foyer. We had been warned on the course. 'If any of your own gets done for something, you go big on them in the paper,' said one of our instructors. 'It's a way of showing that you're not biased, that you can be trusted to tell the story, even if it's your editor. Especially if it's your editor! And if anyone tries to keep you quiet, you know, offers you something not to run a piece, you make sure you make a fuss about it. Then the readers know they can trust you.'

The case was called. I went in and pleaded guilty. The prosecu-tion described the events. The bench, a woman chief magistrate and two men, looked thoughtful. Mr Grant stood up. His manner was respectful but not over-formal. It was obvious that the magistrates liked him: they looked at him expectantly. Mr Grant's tone was a combination of weariness and private wonder at the folly of the world. He seemed so unimpressed with the prosecution, with the charges, with the fact that any of us were here at all, that you felt yourself begin to wonder what the fuss was about. I thought there was the ghost of a smile about the chief.

They set me free, with a conditional discharge, eight penalty points on my provisional licence and forty pounds costs. I wanted to hug Mr Grant but he was for shaking hands. I walked out of the building into a cold sunlight which seemed to glitter with joy and reprieve. I looked right and one of the young men in a fleece took my picture. I looked the other way quickly, straight at the other man, who did the same. Then the reporter appeared.

'Have you got any comment to make?' he asked, with an ingratiating smile.

'What?'

'Have you got any comment?'

'Who are you?'

'News North.'

'What's that?'

'An agency. So how do you feel, mate?'

'No comment, *mate*.'

He stopped following me. I went to a phone box and rang my parents. My mother said, 'Thank God.' My father said, 'I see.'

I told him the agency might report it. We both knew that when they did it would appear on a screen in front of his colleagues. 'What are you going to do now?' he asked.

'I'm going to make a film,' I said.

My mother's local paper in Wales ran the story under the headline 'Horatio Loses All'. The article ended with Mr Grant's summary:

There were problems with the relationship, Mr Grant said, and the defendant foolishly decided the only way to see his girlfriend quickly was to drive to Skegness. This has cost him a lot. He funded the course through an inheritance but has lost the course place, his reputation, his inheritance; his talks with his girlfriend failed, and he has now lost her and has no income.

★

My father lived in a house in Teddington with his wife. I asked them if I could stay with them while I looked for a job and a room. They said yes, though they were not happy to see me. After we had eaten, my father's wife withdrew to her study. My father packed his pipe and began to ask about what I was doing, what I thought I was doing, and about what I had done. He looked at me as if from a great distance, as if I were a total stranger, someone suspicious and bizarre. His voice was quiet, very measured and very cold.

'I can't help taking this personally,' he said. 'It's a sort of fuck you, journalism, fuck you, father, isn't it?'

'No!' I cried. 'That's nothing to do with it.'

'And you're still using drugs?'

'Well, sometimes I have a joint, yes.'

'And you still haven't understood that you aren't using them so much as they are using you.'

'Nothing's using me,' I said, anger and distress rising. 'Is it true you asked Mum if she had seen a copy of my degree, because you didn't believe me?'

'Oh yes,' he said soberly. 'Absolutely. I don't know what to believe any more.'

I went out to look for jobs and rooms. January had turned icy, the streets were brutally bleak. The traffic puffed exhaust like clouds of beasts' breath and I walked for miles and miles. I found a room in Hammersmith which had everything, the bare bulbs, the grime, the darkness, the insects, the traffic noise – everything except the chalk outline of a body on the floor. 'If you'll take my advice you won't move in here,' whispered a cowed and ill-looking tenant. 'Seriously, it's terrible. Don't.'

I went to temping agencies and called telesales recruiters: all said my CV showed too much and too little. Too many changes of job, said one.

'It's the nature of journalism,' I explained. 'When you're starting out you take work experience wherever you can get it.'

'Our clients are looking for rather more stability,' the recruiter replied.

'Do what everyone does when they come to London,' Robin said. 'If he can afford it, ask your dad for a month's rent and a month's deposit.'

I asked. My father refused. 'Absolutely not. I'm not going to fund your drug habit. You're twenty-four. It is time you supported yourself and took responsibility for your own problems.'

'But I'm only asking for one month, so that I can get a room.'

'No.'

I hated him then. I hated him for leaving my mother, for leaving my brother and me, for the impeccable cleanliness, comfort and rectitude of his life, for his success, for his marriages, for his professionalism, for his selfishness and his refusal to offer the one thing, now, I had thought I could always count on: unconditional love. I hated him for the shame I caused him. I hated him because I wanted him to be proud of me, because, deep down, I thought since I was a child that making him proud of me would draw him back to us, to me. I hated him because although he had been an absent father he had been a good one: generous, kind and understanding, writing sweet letters, loving, supportive and patient – and it had not been enough. I hated him because I had something to pin on him, at last.

I had seen the lock-jawed, incoherent rage of other young men at their fathers. I had seen it in Robin, whose dad I thought perfect, and Chris, and Ben. And the reasons we gave for our anger never seemed sufficient. Ben, furious with his father's fury when he was in trouble at school. Robin, unreasonable with anger at his father's reasonable worry. Chris, the most grown up of us, swinging his juvenile horns at his father, like a bull looking for a matador and finding only a cape and no blow behind it: just injunctions, advice, anxiety and love. And not the all-embracing love we had once known, but love attached to expectation, to vanity: make me proud of you. Be my equal.

But we cannot, we cannot! we roared, silently. We cannot equal the men you are or even the men you were when you were our age. You grew up faster than us. You surpassed your own fathers. You knew what you wanted to be and we still do not. You knew and you got on with it. You married young, chose careers young, had children young. But we are stuck at the beginning. We barely know who we are, never mind what we want to be. It was as if we wanted them to personify all the opposition of the world, all its difficulty and disappointment, as if, as their heroism faded with our childhoods, we tried to make them the villains of our youth, and they refused us that. I left the next morning.

'You can stay on our sofa,' said Robin.

He was living with Toby, who I had not known well at International School, though I had often seen him, in a T-shirt in all weathers, kicking or throwing or catching balls. I thought Toby looked rather like Tintin. He had studied philosophy at university, to which I ascribed his gently smiling air of detachment. They had rented a huge, empty warehouse in the East End, in De Beauvoir Town. They were sharing it with a student who had fenced his floor space off with bookshelves: Robin and Toby had bought greenhouses and were living in them. Their sofa cushions were quite luxurious.

I had less than eighty pounds remaining in my overdraft. Robin and Toby shared their food and asked for nothing. Robin was still studying architecture and Toby was working in betting shops. Neither was well-off. They did have a PlayStation and the full version of *Grand Theft Auto*, though.

Making a film would be a struggle on seventy quid but I clung to the idea and kept calling the answer phone of the New York copyright holders of James Baldwin's estate, just in case. I door-stepped the editor of *Sight and Sound*, a film review magazine, in her office, and persuaded her to glance at my cuttings book.

'Go and review *Titanic*,' she said. 'If we like it we might give you more.'

I thought *Titanic* terrible. Neither the public nor *Sight and Sound* agreed.

Robin and Toby insisted that I should stay as long as I needed to, but as two weeks turned to three, and to four, I felt I had to leave. No one wants a body on their sofa for long. Michelle had a place at Goldsmiths and a room in a student hall. She put me up for three nights while my overdraft bottomed out. I became adept at travelling into central London without paying the train fare. Wherever I went I kept my eyes on the gutters and the pavements, alert for dropped money. I never passed a phone box without checking the coins returned tray.

Finally, unwilling to impose on Michelle again, and unable to face the risk of being caught without a ticket (a conditional discharge means if you are arrested for anything within the specified period you will be punished for the previous misdemeanour too), a night fell in which I had nowhere to go. I could have walked to De Beauvoir Town and asked for the sofa again but I could not face the embarrassment. I could have gone to Paddington, hidden in a train toilet all the way to Wales and walked to my mother's house, but I could not face that either. There were one or two doors I could have knocked on in London, old friends of the family, but the idea of explaining myself and begging for refuge and whoever it was taking me in, dishevelled and hopeless, was appalling. Even if I could have countenanced ringing my mother and begging for money in an envelope, I did not have an address she could send it to. It would have taken a lump sum I could not ask for just to get my bank account into the permissible red. Nothing on earth would have made me go back to my father's house, so I settled for spending a first night on the street, though I would never have chosen it.

It began in Covent Garden. I watched men in dinner jackets and women wearing thick coats ducking in or out of taxis, bustling into restaurants, clubs and the opera. The smells from those restaurants were amazing. I had not eaten since the night before. The cruelty of hunger in a city is the extraordinary variety, proximity and aroma of food. Everywhere there were plates, dishes, bowls and trays of food. So much of it, and so beautiful. Even the great plastic-looking pizzas in the stalls around Leicester Square were gorgeous, jewel-red salami set in discs of molten cheese. I could distinguish all the different ingredients of a hundred meals. My nose had never been so sensitive. I could smell duck roasting streets away in China Town. I could smell Italian restaurants, thyme and oregano and bubbling tomato sauce. The air was full of roasting lamb, baking pastry, coffee and hot chocolate.

Then there were the pubs, filled with smoky light and laughter. If you had two pounds in your pocket and you were cold you would not hesitate to stand quietly in one of them; you could pick up a newspaper and nurse a half pint, even a glass of water for hours. But

I did not have two pounds. I had coppers. Outside certain offices in Mayfair there were half-smoked cigarettes sticking out of sand-filled trays. I harvested them. Then there were the doors. Everywhere, people with keys were coming and going through doors. The city is a mosaic of locks: without a key you are as alien to it, as separated from it, as if you are a ghost.

I kept walking. The parks were locked and it was too cold to sit or lie on benches. The pubs emptied and soon everyone was either drunk and weaving or hurrying home. I kept walking. By the time I thought of the stations the last trains had gone and they were locking up. The night workers appeared, men in luminous jackets went down to repair the Tube. I found a burst rubbish sack of sandwiches outside a café but I had walked through hunger. My stomach was knotted, I felt sick with nicotine and fatigue. I kept walking, the strap of my bag rubbing my shoulder raw. Now there were only hopeful taxis with their lights on skimming down deserted streets.

In St James's I stood outside a shop selling treasure. Antique mirrors, statues, vases, and above them, vast and glittering chandeliers, crystal miracles filled with light, fit for heaven itself. Imagine the kind of person who might one day decide he or she would like to live under a chandelier like that, go in, buy it, hang it and switch it off before going to bed. People much cleverer than me, not much better educated but much less mad and stupid were doing so, probably within a hundred yards of where I stood. If I met them I could probably talk to such people, get on with them, even make friends. Yet we might as well have been different species; different orders of being.

I stared at the chandelier and imagined the ceiling it would hang from, the great house it would grace, and the family which would possess it. Surely they would have to be beautiful, brilliant, sensible, wealthy, happy, beloved and loving people to have a chandelier like this! And so lucky. All my life, from my childhood when we had been poor, to the schools of the rich, to university and subsequently, right up to and almost including now, I had been lucky, incredibly lucky, and thought myself aware of my luck. How rich, how blessed we were, how blessed I was, compared to the scared, the hungry and desperate: it was a commonplace, a pat little comfort, a sop against numerous normal misfortunes. We're incredibly lucky really, everyone I knew could always say. For the first time, looking at that chandelier, I had an inkling of how the less fortunate, the starving or just-surviving millions I had half-imagined, or rather had not bothered to imagine – had barely been able to imagine even when I saw them on the news – might imagine me.

I found myself near Victoria. There was a kiosk selling tea with people milling around it. I passed by as if I had somewhere to go. When I saw other figures in the empty streets I shied away from them. I had never felt vulnerable before, even in the meanest parts of town: money cannot protect you from violence but its absence makes you feel more exposed. I wanted to be near people, for comfort, without being seen by them. I wanted to be a ghost.

I found a rhythm: stopping to rest until I became cold, then walking again until I became too tired. I was hungry again. Around half past four I was drifting down a street somewhere near Millbank when I came upon an amazing thing. In the doorway of an office block there was a pint of milk and a loaf of bread, wrapped in plastic and neatly tucked into a small cardboard box. I stared in wonder. What on earth were people doing, leaving milk and bread for office blocks in the middle of the night? I had thought all that sort of thing was long done with, if it ever existed, killed by tramps and thieves. It was a delightful and comforting thing to see, a relic of an older England, the sort of place John Major would have liked, where people did not pinch the milkman's deliveries. And it made me feel terrible too, because as soon as I saw it I knew I was going to steal it, and finally kill off that country.

I gulped the milk and wolfed the bread, chewing too fast, furtive, suddenly convinced that the police would appear. Then I felt sleepy and sat on a bench in a little triangle of garden near Scotland Yard. After a while more traffic appeared, speeding suddenly, intent, not last night's remnants now, but today's vanguard. In the east, over the city, it began to get light.

9

A Voyage Down the King's Road

1998

IT WAS RAINING on the King's Road, an afternoon of slushing tyres and the beat of windscreen wipers. I had done my second night on the streets and was wet from socks to shoulders, tired of the strip between the gutter and the shop fronts which is all the city gives free. About halfway down there was a pub I remembered, a once legendary establishment long deserted by its sixties clientele but still clinging to its post. I was penniless but not quite beyond spending: in my wallet was an exhausted debit card. Any electronic reader would reject it and probably ask the merchant to cut it up but there were still some places which used the old plastic imprinters, which were not connected to anything, which would generate a receipt which my bank would be forced to honour. The money would be added to my overdraft, along with a fine, but the vendors would get their cash and I would get a meal. The pub looked like the sort of place which might not have gone electronic. I went in. A spiky-haired girl with hooded eyes gave me the once-over as I approached the bar.

'Can I help you?' she said, as I glanced around, pretending to choose, and spied the plastic card-swipe.

'Yes, please!' I ordered a pint and bangers and mash. I made myself take a long time over them. A man who looked like a superannuated rock star played air guitar to the jukebox. 'Mick Jagger!' he cried. 'Now there's a man!' He made overtures to a laughing woman. He was so familiar with her and she so amused that I assumed they were old friends until she left, whereupon they bid goodbye with the formality of strangers who would never meet again.

The pub's ceiling was a sort of red scab from which dirty lights dangled like drips of pus. The bar was divided into short sections by wooden posts which supported a shelf on which there were books which had never been dusted. Surveying the floor from behind it, the spiky-haired girl had been joined by a woman in a tracksuit who did not look a friend to exercise. She passed quiet comments to the girl, eyeing the customers with a wary disfavour. But the girl's friendliness, the rock star's antics, the hot food, the fatiguing, warming effect of the pint, and something else in the air made me approach the bar once more.

'Yes?'

'I was just wondering – you wouldn't have any jobs, would you?'

The girl looked at me again. 'One minute.'

She approached the lady. The lady gave me the swiftest glance, then summoned me with a tilt of her chin.

'Vat sort of vork are you looking for, sveetie?'

'Full time.'

'You want to live in?'

'Yes, definitely.'

'Have you done bar before?'

'Oh yes . . .'

The lady was looking over my shoulder now, away down the road. 'You may be lucky. Someone is leaving. Come back on Sunday night and do a trial.'

The lady's name was Wanda. She was the licensee and the manager: the pub was owned by a chain, but it was her fiefdom, run according to her whims. I never saw Wanda take more than a second to appraise anyone, nor did I ever see her make a mistake. She had the surest, most instinctive grasp of human nature of anyone I have known. This is not to suggest that she looked at me and saw a good person, but she saw something.

There was no spiky-haired girl on Sunday night and no Wanda. There was a laid-back young Canadian called Wade and a skinhead Geordie called Phil.

'Phil's the assistant manager,' Wade confided, as though this was salacious gossip. He was very likeable and camp. His idea of speaking quietly was certainly loud enough for Phil to hear. 'I have *no idea* what he's saying most of the time, but if it ends in "cool" it's good, and if it ends in "fook" it's bad. I think.'

'Wade, d'ye fancy doin' some fookin' work, aye?'

'Bad,' Wade translated. 'See?'

'Ye've done this before then?' Phil asked at the end of the night.

'I worked in a cocktail place, in York. The Old Orleans. Dreadful . . .'

'Cocktails? *Shite*. So ye know it's fookin' terrible and ye still wanna do it, eh?'

'Better than being on the street.'

'Oh, I don't know about that like, wait till you see yer room!'

'Am I in then?'

'Oh aye. Be nice to have someone who knows what they're doing. Make a change anyway.'

'Brilliant!'

'Ah'm not sure ah'd go that far, mate.'

We went up a flight of dark stairs and through a locked door. Another flight led up to a landing, half filled by a huge fridge.

'Kitchen,' said Phil, pointing straight ahead. He nodded at another locked door. 'That's Wanda's flat there but she's not in much. Up here.'

Once you had squeezed past the fridge, another flight of steps led upwards, narrower and darker than the first. We arrived at the summit, the third floor. To the right was the fire door to the roof, entirely blocked by a huge mound of newspaper and empty cans. Tucked between it and the stairwell was a narrow space which had once been a lavatory, which now held junk and a mattress jammed into a long cubbyhole in the wall.

'That's the Loveshack. Scott's living there at the moment. Aussie bloke,' said Phil, as if this explained it.

To the left was a corridor, which undulated drunkenly underfoot. We passed two doors on the right.

'Kattia and Lucia are in there – Italians . . . nootas . . . Kelly's in there . . . another assistant manager . . . and here's you and Wade.'

The door had a ragged hole punched through it above the handle: someone strong had evidently forgotten his key once upon a time, and ensured that no one would need to remember theirs again. I thought of Torpington and smiled. The room was a bohemian nightmare. The floor sloped and dipped in two planes so everything tilted diagonally. The walls were a dirty shade of lavender, stained by the hands, heads, emissions and feet of a hundred previous barmen and their conquests. There was a broken, leaning wardrobe and a desk but because there was no room for the latter it stood on one end, empty drawer sockets gaping, festooned with bits of clothing, books, ashtrays and candles. My mattress lay on the floor by the window; under the opposite wall was the mattress which belonged to Wade.

A bare bulb dangling from the ceiling revealed the multiple stains in the carpet, the gunge in the corners and a universe of dust and dirt. Beyond the window rain fell steadily on the King's Road.

'Sure?' said Phil, grinning.

'Absolutely!'

'On yer own head be it then. Here's yer front door key. Don't walk between the pillars and the bar or you'll set off the alarms. Enjoy.'

'Do you live here too?'

'Aye. I'm next door. A room of me own and a TV – play yer cards right, son, and in a few years . . . it could be you!'

I unpacked my few things and made a rough bed. Wade appeared and we talked for a little while. Suddenly Wade convulsed violently, smashing a shoe against the floor.

'Ugh!' he shuddered. 'Roaches! I hate roaches. I hate bugs.'

'Are there a lot of them?'

'Yeah, but not in here usually. Rob says there's only one and he keeps coming back from the dead like Elvis. He calls him Colin.'

'Who's Rob?'

'He's another bartender,' said Wade. Then, slowly, 'Now he *is* insane.'

He turned the light out and we said goodnight. I listened to the rain falling and the taxis outside. I had a key, a roof, a bed and the prospect of food tomorrow. I felt a surge of joy: warmth, amusement and happiness combined. I have never been so grateful to be anywhere.

The rock star was back the next day, strutting, posing, shaking his long grey locks to the Stones. He was on form again. 'Tell Kelly I can't stop falling in love with her,' he announced, grandly overlooking Kelly's preference for her own sex. 'Why is she so damn beautiful?' His voice was a whole bass section, his laugh an ovation. His eyes were bright beneath the beery, bleary blue.

'Made five hundred quid today,' he confided.

'Oh really, how?'

'Rare books.' (Celebratory strum on the air guitar.) 'Spotted a couple of beauties, took 'em to my man in Covent Garden. He's the best, the very best in town. You could get into it, you know. It's just a question of knowing what to look for. I'll give you the name of my man.'

Then there was a cockney jockey who looked as though he might be too old for the races. 'Up at six I was this morning, hexercising 'em – 'is Lordship's 'orses. Out in the rain I was, same as every morning, an 'orses don't like it wet. Gor, 'orses. 'Ard work I can tell you.'

'But you do like doing it?'

'Well, 'aven't got qualifications for anything else. 'Orses was all I was interested in when I was a boy, mad on 'em I was, so 'ere I am.'

'What are you doing in Chelsea?'

'Come up to buy me old lady a saucepan, 'aven't I? See, got it 'ere!'

I was entranced. You never knew what or who was going to turn up next. Some perfect combination of the pub's position, its history and its management (Wanda knew the magic secret of the industry, and she taught it to us) drew in a sparkling harvest of stories, lives and characters, and we stood there, serving them all a substance which made them talk. Phil hated it.

'Hoy them fookin' stools away from the bar!'

'Why, Phil?'

'Cos some fookin' noota will come in and sit there and we'll have to talk to the bastard.'

'I like the nootas!'

'Aye, well, yer new to it. Wait till ye've been doing it a while.'

Across the road was a mental health and detox clinic. Patients frequently broke out and came hurrying into the bar.

'I've just had a vision and I think I'm going to die,' said a wavering-faced woman. My instinct was to recommend the house double but Phil's policy was to show the door.

'Oh come on, Phil, let me give her a gin, for Christ's sake.'

'Horatio, the noota's friend!' Phil mocked, as men in white coats appeared and ushered her away. 'Ye can take this one too! No serving nootas on my shift, mate. Ye can do what you like when I'm off. How do ye know she's not trying to come off the sauce, anyway?'

Suddenly there came a piercing scream from the road.

'H! Get out there and check that!' Phil ordered, as if dispatching a combat mission.

'I can't see anything, Phil.'

'Aye,' he said, as if this confirmed his bleakest suspicions. 'Any one of a thousand nootbats . . .'

'The druggies were so much more fun,' Wanda sighed. 'They could drink.'

Brewery policy demanded that we should all be fully trained.

'Yer going to get an NVQ today, mate. Feeling lucky?'

'What do I have to do?'

'Well, it's a testing experience right enough. Here's yer little booklet with all the questions. And here's another little booklet with all the questions – *and* the answers. Copy the lot and don't let anyone see you. Think ye can manage that? Concentrate now . . .'

'. . . Finished!'

'Well done. There's no stopping you, is there? Sky's the limit now, mate.'

'I like the bit about the people we can't serve.'

'Oh aye?'

'Underage, policemen on duty, soliciting prostitutes and drunks.'

'Aye, doesn't leave us much, does it?'

'Just your nutbats!'

'And yer *not* serving *them*.'

Phil is an alcoholic, a full-blown, tremens-tormented soak. Wanda tries not to rota him in the mornings when the shakes are worst. She had saved him, he said. Found him dying in a dump, took it over, took him over, rescued them both and brought him with her when she moved on. His best time was the half an hour before last orders, when the day's demons had worn off and the night's were yet to descend. He is not much older than thirty. In an old photograph of him he appears gentle and happy, a laughing, handsome face framed and almost curtained by a huge headdress of dreadlocks. Phil is a veteran of the battlefield of Newcastle's Bigg Market, where he had manned one of its permanently besieged bars. There was a secret to it: 'Ye neverlookedup, mate. Just kept yer head doon and kept filling pints.'

'Why was that, Phil?'

'Because if ye looked up there were ten million of the bastards screaming at ye, waving tennas.'

He had not escaped unscathed. He had worked in a few rough London pubs, one of which was completely lawless (they kept a pistol behind the bar), and now he was a skinhead, with a gleaming white dome he shaved diligently, which made him look like a vicious killer, rather than the violence-fearing angel that he was.

Phil's best friend is Mark, another Geordie, with no fear of violence at all. He ran a pub in Hammersmith, a nicer place than his last. 'We used to hire people there on size and fighting ability,' he said. 'We went through that many pool cues.' On Phil's night off they would go up to the West End, drinking. Phil would lose his memory after a while, urinate on people, be thrown out, lose fights with bouncers, other punters and Mark. They left a trail of clothing, urine and offence. One morning Phil woke up on beautiful cushions, surrounded by a curious Indian family. He had no idea how he came to be in their house. They regarded the dazed skinhead with more amazement than alarm. He left quietly. Later he and Mark would ring each other up and try to piece together what had happened.

'What would you be doing if . . .'

'If ah wasn't washed up here? Graphic design. I wasn't so bad like but I was into design, never computas, and it's all computas now.'

'You could learn them though, Phil . . .'

'Aye . . . maybe.'

I want to comfort him, to encourage him, to say it will be all right and mean it. But as we look at each other we cannot imagine new versions of ourselves, cleansed of our addictions, confident and strong, catching up with computers, matching the pace of the hurrying city. He has a drink, I have a joint, we laugh and shake our heads, and feel the world pulling ever further away.

★

Phil shut himself in his room with a bottle of vodka most nights, and occasionally with his girlfriend, Lynsey, another part-time bar worker, a Chelsea girl, daughter of an industrialist who lived nearby. She tried to keep him off the drink. Sandra, Scott of the Loveshack's German girlfriend, tried to keep him off the weed. They both failed.

Scott was from western Australia. He looked like a surfer, with huge arms, the hooked nose of a pirate and a pirate's grin. He could fix anything. Scotty was one of the few of us who were not in flight from something. He had come to England to look around and planned to go back to Australia, work as a fitter and machinist and build a house with a bar in it. Sandra was in flight from her friend, another German girl, who had gone weird on her.

Kelly, the other assistant manager, was in flight from New Zealand. She was gay, like Wanda and Louise, the Aussie cook. Kelly never explained why she had come to Britain, other than to travel and advance her career in the service industry, but she had about her the uneasy and untrusting friendliness of someone who had been bullied. Kelly had an optic clamped to a bottle in her room, loaded with her favourite, Jack Daniel's. She watched Wanda's drinking and commented on Phil's and Louise's. They all accused her of alcoholism in return. Who was taking too much of what by how much and the ruinous effect this was bound to have was a staple of conversation, as everyone else's overindulgence was a comfort to our own.

Lucia was our Ophelia, a willowy, pale Lombard, subject to sudden happiness and violent glooms. She was in love with Phil, she said. She painted him a picture, Phil's blue head in the corner looking up at a river of crimson pouring down a waterfall. She presented him with it and later tried to force her way into his room, weeping hysterically. 'Get her oot, get her oot, she's mad!' Phil roared, pushing her backwards. 'Oh Pheel! Pheel!' Lucia wailed pitifully, as he slammed the door. Lucia had trained as an architect but there had been some problem with her parents and now she said she would never go home. She cut down on her drinking when she found she was unable to hold a paintbrush steady.

Kattia, the Sicilian with spiky hair who had first welcomed me in, shared her room. For a while she tried to encourage Lucia, but when this failed she switched to persecuting her. They held terrible rows in Italian, Lucia's wailing operatics versus Kattia's spitting gangster chatter. Kattia looked and sounded, when angry, as though she ate locusts. The rows always ended with Lucia in tears and led to a vendetta. Because her English was not good Wanda relegated Lucia to the kitchen, as assistant cook and washer-upper. There she had rows with Louise.

Occupying his own space near the top but slightly to the side of this cock-eyed pyramid, was bartender Rob. He generally arrived, as befits any hero, somewhere between too late and the nick of time, after his shift had started, at peak hour, seven o'clock, when the punters were pouring in and whoever was manning the bar was beginning to flag. Rob was a jeweller by day but you would not have known that from his appearance.

If we were a platoon, hunkered down in our bottle-lined trench, surrounded by legions of foes – our fearful fantasies, the nightmare of the mystery customer, the wally who called himself the Area Manager, the spectre of the Health Inspector, the omnipresent menace of the Chelsea fans, the loon and deadbeat tide of punters and their pretensions, the lurking certainty that we were the bottom feeders, the bottlewashers in the luxury hotel of the western world – then Bartender Rob was our Achilles. He really had been a soldier, too, a Royal Marine. He hinted he had killed people: it seemed less unlikely than his interest in gems. He was short and broad, muscled and lecherous. He had taken much too much cocaine. His eyes were full of humour, huge affection, instant judgement and sudden, plunging moods. One of his irises had fragmented slightly, leaving a fleck of colour in the white of one eye.

Rob feared nothing except perhaps growing up – but then we all feared that. He liked to jam the jukebox with pounding rock and dance to it while he served; in the right humour he would shout and rave and laugh at private jokes so madly that even the thirstiest drone would step back half a pace and hope to be served by someone else. Rob would summon them imperiously, impatiently, barking 'Yes, Sir. What would you like? What can I get for you lovely people this lovely evening? HA!' He specialized in flirting with women under the noses of their bristling companions. He lived some distance away and liked to run to work. There he was now – his coming heralded by a disturbance in the traffic as he charged: 'Sorry I'm late RIGHT! WHO'S NEXT?'

We dread his appearance on nights when he is off duty.

'Phil . . .'

'Aye?'

'Rob's here.'

'Ah fook . . . here we go again . . .'

'ALL RIGHT, GENTS! Phil, hey Phil, all right, my Geordie lover! Horace! All right, Horace, you scamp! What would you like, boys? On me!'

He is wearing his suit and tie. To an observer he would have seemed another wealthy Chelsea yuppy.

'Not for me, mate.'

'No thanks, Rob. Got four more hours of this . . .'

'Boring bastards, here, stick my card behind the bar. I'll have a Guinness please, H . . .'

A clutch of pints later he is deep in conversation with a blonde whose friends obviously hate him. Every now and then he engages one of them, briefly, just for long enough to continue whatever debate he has sucked them into, and to remind them, subliminally, that if it comes to it he can certainly fight and beat the lot of them. The alarm and distress emanating from the table are palpable. I wonder whether it is a deliberate enactment of the bartender's ultimate revenge on customers – disguise yourself as one, then stick it to them. It is no fun being treated as a scrubber by young men we regard at best as equals, and for every one who asks nicely there are one and a half who look at their girlfriends and say, 'Pint of lager and what would you like? Pint of lager and a gin and tonic,' as if from a great height, to an idiot, and hold out the money with an air of impatient distaste, as if buying off a beggar.

When someone particularly riles us we have a range of petty but pride-saving measures. Ideally you dip your hand out of sight and produce a pint glass half full of flat, stale and mixed lagers, poured in error or salvaged from the drip trays, which you top with a fresh half of whatever the customer requires.

'In Australia they dye the drip trays blue so you can't do it, but you can get away with fucken anything in London, cantcha?' Scott observes.

'Let the customers buy our drinks,' is Wanda's dictum, encouraging us to put as much foam as possible on pints. We take this further than she intends it.

To the gin and tonic you start with a lot of ice (saving on the tonic, obviously) and add a slice of lemon from the left-hand fruit bowl, the one mysteriously favoured by the fruit flies, if possible garnished with a squashed insect. Scott's favourite is the alcohol-free, 'slimline' Bloody Mary. The beauty of vodka, the ignorant will tell you, is that it does not taste of anything. The beauty of the Bloody Mary is that it absolutely does not taste of vodka, unless the drinker is an expert and Bloody Mary drinkers, whatever they may claim, seldom are. With enough Tabasco, pepper and Worcester sauce no one ever notices the difference. Nor do they ask for more pepper, sauce or Tabasco, which is another advantage the slimline has over the kosher version. The additional beauty of these tactics is that they leave a shot of vodka in the bottle and half a pint in the barrel which the electronic till thinks have been sold.

We all spend a lot of time outwitting the till, but not nearly so much as Phil does. Phil and the till seem to hate one another, by the way he curses it. I resent the machine because it spies on us and tells people my ridiculous name, and also because I blame it for robbing me of my numeracy. The only mental exercise a barman might enjoy is adding up the brewery's idiosyncratic prices: with the coming of the electronic tills another of our abilities was obliterated. It can only be a matter of time before we are replaced with ID-activated drinks machines. A machine, while it would routinely cheat you, would at least spare you the outright abuse of vengeful staff.

'Ah was talking to Mark the other day,' Phil mutters, as we battle away. 'Ee's got a Paddy chef. This bloke, when he gets pissed off with someone, flops out his knob and rubs it in their sandwich. Mark said he caught him doing it and thought fair enough, he must be angry about something. Then he did it again, stirring mash potato and again, salad dip, and Mark rang me this morning and says I don't know about this any more, I see more of that man's knob than I do me *own*.'

There is a disturbance at the table next to Rob. He has fallen off his chair, knocking over several drinks, but not his. He apologizes lewdly and appears at the bar, demanding more drinks.

'No, mate, time to go home like, yer bladdered . . .'

'No no no, it's *fine*. Guinness and a double scotch for me, and whatever those *bastards* are having . . .'

'No mate, time to go home.'

'Come on, Phil!'

'Don't "come on" me, mate, that's it, all right? Now fook off home.'

Rob starts roaring and laughing. He weaves back to the table and resumes drinking. One of his unwilling companions appears.

'That bloke is way out of order. He won't leave us alone and he's being bloody rude.'

'Well, ah'm sorry like . . .'

'Can you ask him to leave, please?'

'Not really, no.'

'Why not?'

'We've asked him but he won't go.'

'Well, can't you chuck him out then?'

'Not really, no.'

'Why not?'

'Because he's actually the person who chucks people out and there's only one person who can control him and she isn't here.'

The customers make a frightened space around him. The plastered bartender appears to sleep.

The next day Wanda bans him from the pub, except when on duty. Rob takes it well: 'I don't care. I've given up drinking and I'm going to run the marathon, ha HAAA!'

Unless personally known to us, the staff regard all customers as potentially dodgy, sad and fraudulent. While the brewery wants as many as possible to come as often as possible and stay as long as possible, the staff sincerely wish they would all piss off. The bartender's welcoming smile and eye contact are laced with unspoken desires: just order quickly, pay up fast and disappear. I do not feel this way, at first. I looked with interest and enthusiasm at each new face.

There was New York Kevin, who looked like a rough-cut version of Michael Keaton. He had made his first million when he was twenty-one. 'Gym equipment,' he explained softly. 'I could see it was going to be big.' He seemed lonely, quietly eager to talk.

'I'm moving house,' he said, one evening. 'I like Chelsea but I prefer Belgravia. It's nicer, don't you think?'

'Definitely.'

'You should give me a call,' he said. 'If you ever need to get out of bartending.'

'What do you do now, Kevin?'

'Strategy. I kinda see opportunities and my people work on them.'

He would come in at about ten o'clock and order a couple of pints and maybe a cheeseburger until I took pity on him and advised against it.

Never, ever order pub food in the evenings, when the chef has gone. If you do you will be in the hands of a hurried and disgruntled bartender who has no stake in your surviving the next twenty-four hours.

The burgers came frozen, in green and white discs, like pottery dug out of icy ground. They went straight into the flame, or the fat, if you were feeling particularly resentful. Whatever they consisted of was not safe at normal earth temperatures. When one of the fridges failed some of them escaped, trickling out like cat sick.

Phil specialized in presenting platters so appalling that those of us on duty had to turn away to hide our laughter. He trained me in the use of the kitchen.

'Right, fat fryer. Just chuck whatever in there, throw it into a bun, handful of salad and serve.'

'How do you know when it's cooked?'

'When it floats.'

'Jesus, that's disgusting.'

'Yup, and with a smile it's ten pounds, mate.'

Those who knew the pub never ate there. Our longest serving customer is a man who appears to be in his late sixties but is much younger. He comes in looking shifty, as though he has just filched something from a corner shop. He makes for his usual seat at the end of the bar, the only stool we do not routinely hoy into the middle of the room. I never saw him irritated except when it was taken. We all adore him. In his ashy grey eyes is a disgusted look, an it's-all-going-to-hell look, and a great sympathy, which he tries to hide, because it does not do to be soft, and a humour, a mischievous and mocking glint. He is one of us, Dave, we all feel, a brother, a father, a dirty-joke-telling grandad. If Dave is at his post at the end of the bar you know all is well.

'What do you do, Dave?'

'Helicopter pilot.'

'You're not!'

'I am. I was over 'ere yesterday, hovering at 200 feet.'

'You weren't!'

'I was, you weren't looking or you would have seen me.'

We are compounds, the old man and I. I am an absorbent sludge – ash, chips from the kitchen, daydreams. Dave is memories, booze and cheese and onion sandwiches. He lives on them. 'Bullwinkle!' he shouts, waving one he has brought in a carrier bag. He talks of running a pub once, of a Swedish girl and a son he has never met, of holidays in Southend. 'You should go to Southend,' he says, mistily. 'Lovely day out.'

Young people adore him. He says he is one, really. 'Never grew up inside, see? Twenny-two in me heart!'

Dave drinks strong lager and the cheap house double with Coke. He is never charged for the Coke: being the oldest customer has its privileges.

'Remember when this was a proper pub. Bar in the middle, Flying Squad drank on this side, villains over there. They could all keep an eye on each other . . .'

He sips himself into a haze and likes being the last to leave. A friend who drives a black cab picks him up one night. Dave makes his exit like a drunken duke.

'My carriage has arrived, see – see! Goodnight, goodnight, ladies!' he bellows, and rocks back woozily in the seat as the vehicle moves off. Dave waves, looking triumphant.

In our world the triumph of the moment is all. We deal only in the present, in the witty come-back over the bar, in the half second it takes to decide not to serve someone, or the degree of friendliness with which you do, in the momentary eye contact with the pretty girl, out with her boyfriend, the second of consideration that will buoy you up for hours or the instant of dismissal which will drag your heart down to your sticky boots. The bar is a performance space and we are supposed to fill it with action, presence and humour. It is an audience-participation play and we are supposed to lead it. Be happy, be loose, be nice. Tonight is all there is.

'Smile, sveeties!' Wanda enjoins us. 'Go vild! Dance on the bar – vat ever you like. This is supposed to be fun, isn't it? Fun!'

She is right, I reflect. There is no way up and rock bottom is not at all far below: we might as well enjoy it. At first I am rather self-conscious, staring at the customers with too much curiosity, gauche and stiff. But I get into it.

'You an actor?' someone asks.

'Not tonight!'

Wanda overhears me calling someone 'Madam'. 'Sveetie!' she cries in delight. 'So polite! It's vonderful!'

I blush with pleasure. We all want Wanda to be happy, not because we are scared of losing our jobs or because we care about the business. We would not care if Scottish & Newcastle went bust tomorrow. But we like her and Phil, very much. We would never let them down. Four alcoholics, two dope heads, one recovering addict, one mad Sicilian and one weeping Milanese and various crocked customers: my family.

A Saturday morning in May. Summer has come suddenly this year; it has been champagne weather for a week. The delivery men are here, ludicrously early and cross because though they have been pressing the bell for ten minutes, vainly hoping for some sort of advantage over their schedule, nothing stirs in the pub. The bell used to work, they tell each other angrily, and press it again. They are right: in its heyday, the bell made a cowed whirring in our corridor but only last week we persuaded Scott to disconnect it, so we sleep on. The delivery men hang around outside, swearing and turning cold-eyed leers on the passing girls. Thanks to the King's Road we are guaranteed a daily stream of ignorant, virgin customers and pretty people parade constantly past our windows.

At eight thirty Carlos arrives. Carlos is a threadbare Colombian who is beginning to wizen. He smokes, hawks up a depraved-sounding cough-laugh and travels miles on the tube to hoover and mop our bar. I hate to think how little he is paid for this. The first thing he has to do when he arrives is face the lavatories. The Ladies is always a terrible prospect. (While men just pee everywhere, women habitually make a real pit of their loo: they scatter it with filthy tissues, flood the basin, foul the mirror and trample muck around the floors and skirting boards. The emergence of a gorgeous girl from our Ladies always makes me think of butterflies issuing out of corpses.) The Gents is simply the most evil-smelling little hole in London. As you go down the stairs the smell of piss gas, a blinding, putrid, ammoniac smell, assaults you, thrusting its reeking fingers up your nose as it simultaneously tongues your mouth. The Area Manager emerged retching, once, vowing to do something about it, but naturally nothing happened.

A little while after Carlos, Wanda arrives. A Slovene who fled what was then Yugoslavia after a scandalous affair with the daughter of a high-ranking Communist official, she came to London, liked the people and the parties and went into the entertainment business. She is a grey-eyed lady with the panache and manner of a female Gérard Depardieu. She hauls herself out of the small car she calls 'the French Porsche' and clips leads on the two tiny dogs she calls 'my monsters'. She sweeps into the pub in time to arrest the delivery men, who have just finished stacking a hundred frozen battery chickens in boxes at the foot of the stairs up to the kitchen.

'What's this, sweetie?' she demands of the nastier of the two.

'Your delivery,' he replies.

'Let me see it,' she commands.

He hands over the manifest. She glances at it for about a second and a half and thrusts it back at him.

'Why do you think I want hundred chickens? Can't you see this is a pub?'

'It's a kitchen order, innit? No good complaining to me anyway – you ordered them, or someone 'ere did.'

'Well yes, someone did. But not someone here. Someone at number 131 ordered them – this is number 113! I think 131 is a fried chicken restaurant.' She raises an imperious hand, and points to the road.

'Take all your chickens out before they melt! Out, out with these chickens!'

She keeps an eye on the cursing, humiliated delivery men as they lug the boxes back to their truck just in case they feel tempted to extract some sort of peevish compensation for their defeat. When they have gone she smiles, takes a deep breath and holds it as she descends the stairs to the cellar and the office. Carlos finishes cleaning, lights a fag and sets off back to the tube station.

At a quarter to ten the woman who empties the gambling machines appears with a clicking of heels. She is heavily made-up, manicured and accompanied by a bodyguard. The gamblers and the jukebox take a fortune. 'That's where the real money is,' Phil winks. 'Booze is just a front.'

The gamblers are fed by wordless, taut young men whose girl-friends sip Coke dutifully for hours while their lovers try conclusions with the spinning wheels. The money woman does a lot of arith-metic fast, the coins dancing under her fingertips, disappearing like magic into felt bags. Then she is gone.

At ten Assistant Manager Kelly descends and begins readying the bar. I hear her going downstairs. I lie on my mattress, looking up at the sunlight brightening the stained ceiling. Wade stayed out last night, so I have the room to myself. I wake up to my usual slow babble of voices. You may be at the bottom of the pile, but at least you have a room. You will eat. No worries, as Scott would say. Here, though! In this filthy pit. What are you, the best educated cockroach in London? What a waste. Shh. Don't fret. You're not on the streets. You might be a writer one day. There are worse things. Go back to sleep.

Downstairs Kelly is joined by Karen, one of our part-timers, a tall Swede from Gothenburg who is working as an au pair. She has a ring through her lower lip which looks painful. Sometimes I watch a male customer catch sight of her and see him thinking, 'Phwoar! Ooh . . . ouch.'

Karen and Kelly polish the brasses, put out the umbrellas, take the chairs off the tables, make themselves coffee and await Wanda's inspection. Wanda hates the umbrellas because they are blue and white: Chelsea colours. We are in the heart of Chelsea, Chelsea fans could bring us a lot of custom, but Wanda hates Chelsea fans.

'Ve are not a football pub,' she announces. 'Ve vill do the season. The boat race, Ascot, the flower show and Wimbledon. Ve vill not do football.'

The Area Manager cannot accept this strategy. He is young and thuggish in his wet-looking hair and shiny suit. He is in possession of a bare fraction of Wanda's understanding of the workings of pubs, and is, inevitably, her direct superior. She calls him 'Sveetie' to keep him in his place and he has no way around her because though she is an overt maverick Wanda is always the first in the area to complete the brewery's latest course, training package or other random hoop-jumping.

'Ve had a managers' brainstorming session in the park yesterday,' she confided. 'Takings are down everywhere. And you know what they decided? The big idea? Cut the vages! Ha ha ha! This is madness . . .'

They treat her as though they know she is up to something but cannot work out what it is. Wanda has let it be known that they can sack her any time they like: 'I have my own flat and I just got a new car – I vould thank them!' she cries.

Karen and Kelly polish the glass fronts of the fridges, wrap knives and forks in paper napkins and slice up lemons. They put ashtrays on the tables. All is prepared. Wanda appears.

'Good morning, my darlinks, how are we?'

'Hi, Wanda!' Karen grins.

'All right, my darling?' Kelly returns.

'Kelly, why haven't you opened the windows – open the windows quickly! The sun is shining, isn't it? Are you afraid of the light?'

Kelly colours.

'I'll have a leetle cup of tea please, sweetie. Thank you. Oh, hot isn't it? I think it's going to be very, very hot today. Thank you, darlink. What time is it? Eleven? Then open the doors, open the doors! Let's start the fun.' Wanda advances to the now open doors, sips her tea and gazes at the pavements, which are filling with potential trade.

'Ah. Look at all the leetle Kate Mosses,' she purrs. 'And here's Louisey! How are you, Louisey? Late as usual, sweetie.'

'Hey Wanda, hey Kel, hey Karen!'

Louise has a freckled face, thick dark hair and a ready laugh. She is often out of breath, as now, and shares with Scott and me an enthusiasm for dope, though she has nothing like our appetite. She and Wanda seem to like each other, though they are in permanent dispute over Louise's career, her hours, her breaks, her wages and menus. The cook feels the heat terribly – it is crushingly hot in the kitchen and sometime around mid-afternoon Louise generally suffers a collapse in morale.

'Chop chop, off to your kitchen, Louisey, we haf to talk about the stock sometime too . . . Ah, at last, a customer.' With that, Wanda processes up to her flat, reprimanding Kelly over her shoulder for forgetting to get the ice up. And Brian comes yawing in towards the bar. Brian is one of our dailies. He drinks the house double whisky, all day, sometimes with Coke, sometimes without, and if you charge him for the Coke he loses his temper. Otherwise he is a perfectly charming, shy alcoholic. His whole head is red, under the remains of his white hair, and speckled. He is not about to make the first customer of the weekend's mistake. He is not about to order a pint.

'Morning,' he says, bluffly. 'Ben Eagles please, with Coke, thank you.' He puts down the right amount (minus Coke).

Karen serves him, smiling her perfect smile. Brian stares back in a friendly but uncertain way: Karen's beauty trips him up, he is almost embarrassed to look at her.

He is followed by two young men who make the mistake twice. 'A lager and a bitter please.'

The thing is, we cleaned the lines last night, flushing out the pipes between the barrels and the taps with a nasty fluid called Sterit, then water. We were thorough but not over-rigorous. The first couple of pints out of every tap will look like beer but will consist of a mixture of water, beer, and if you are particularly unlucky, Sterit. Most pubs clean the lines on Friday or Saturday night when the staff can drink the pints left in each line, before they connect the Sterit. If you happen to be the first in on Saturday or Sunday, well, 'Serves the fookas right for bothering us,' as Phil puts it.

Upstairs, I have woken up again and made it to the bathroom and back. I have showered, dressed and done my teeth and the gloom that sometimes gets me in the mornings has receded. I am humming quietly to myself. It's a lovely, clean summer day outside and I was woken the second time by the sound of horses' hooves: a company of Life Guards came trotting down the road, breastplates glittering over their scarlet jackets and white plumes bobbing on their helmets. I make my way to the roof, passing Scott's door. Scott comes up the stairs and I deduce he has just said goodbye to Sandra. I know what he wants now.

'Seen the lady off?'

'Yeah.'

'Fancy one?'

'Yeah! Sandra just said to me, I know what you're going to do now, and I didn't lie. I said, well . . . [he pronounces it 'Oi sed, woll . . .'] I'm on a shitty split shift with Horatio from eleven till two, then six till close, what else am I gonna do!'

'Everyone blames me for everything,' I moan.

'Because you're always guilty,' Scott says, raising his nose and smiling down it.

We go out on to the roof, stooping a little as if to make ourselves smaller because the people who run the drying-out clinic have complained that the sight of us boozing and smoking distresses their patients. I produce my papers. Scott demurs.

'No, mate, I've got a better idea.' He goes back into the Loveshack and returns proudly with a horrible thing, a crushed, semi-burned beer can with a dent in the middle with holes in it.

'What the hell is that?'

'Pipe!'

'You're joking.'

'No, it's a pipe. You just stick the shit on there, burn it – and suck here.'

'No, Scotty. It looks horrific.'

'No tobacco, no paper, it's healthier.'

I gaze at this blackened, perforated, so-called health measure. Scott's dream is that one day he is going to invent something blindingly simple and make millions. This is not it.

'I can't face it. How about a bucket?'

'A bucket! Now?'

'Why not? We've got time, haven't we?'

He checks his watch. He's smiling. He shakes his head. 'Quarter to. You're one crazy bastard, mate. All right, let's do it, but we'll have to be quick.'

Five minutes later Scott has finished sawing a plastic lemonade bottle in half and I have filled a bucket with water and poked little holes into a piece of tinfoil with a pin from Lucia's sewing kit. We push the half bottle into the water so only the mouth shows, mould the foil over it and carefully load the perforated surface with weed. Now I hold a lighter over the weed until it catches, then slowly, steadily, draw the bottle upwards. As the body emerges from the water it fills with thick greeny-grey smoke.

'Ready, I reckon,' Scott says.

'You first?' I enquire, quietly. We are both staring with something like awe at the smoking half-torpedo.

'Nah, after you.'

I carefully peel the foil off the bottle top, empty the air from my lungs, fix my lips around the smoking hole and jack-knife forward in slow motion, driving the bottle back under the water and propelling its entire contents into my chest.

'Hah . . .' I gasp, smoke cascading through my head . . . 'Haah . . .' I am trying to hold the smoke in, but it's hard. 'Hwooaarph! Puh! Ek! Ek!'

I can hardly see Scott. I can hardly see anything. A crate of fireworks has gone off behind my eyes. My temporal lobes are in flames. What remained of my reasoning capacity is threshing its last in an orgasmic welter. My chest is collapsing. I am coughing and laughing, my sinuses, eyes and mouth are streaming. The sight of Scott carefully resetting the device has me in stitches.

Scott takes the plunge and emerges, smiling beatifically. Our eyes are bloodshot, our limbs are soggy. We can hardly think, see, stand or feel. Everything strikes us as outlandish, exaggerated and hilarious. We do one more each. We giggle. Scott, still holding down the smoke from his second bucket, shows me his watch. It's coming up to eleven.

'Time to go!' I say, gleefully. I can't remember ever looking forward to a shift before.

'Ready for work!' Scott squeaks, exhaling.

'We should get Louise to do one of these . . .'

'Fuck, yeah,' Scott nods. 'Can you imagine the chaos?'

'This afternoon, when she has her break . . .'

'Yeah, sweet, she'll be spewin'! I wouldn't want to eat one of her chicken nuggets after a couple of those.'

'I wouldn't want to eat one of her chicken nuggets full stop.'

'You reckon Wanda's down there?' Scott enquires, giving me a narrow look.

'I hope not.'

'Makes you paranoid, don't she?'

'Only when I'm wrecked.'

'Wrecked enough now, are ya, mate?'

'Oh yes . . . I've got Louisey's sweating chicken nuggets on the brain.'

'Roight! Let's do it!'

'Right! To the wars!'

Here we are, poised, two warriors on the brink of their charge into what they think is the battle. The enemy, they believe, awaits at the foot of the stairs. But they have it all wrong. Their enemies are within them and behind them. Indulgence, boredom and a dearth of challenges are their true foes, and they have already dealt our warriors mortal blows. The battle is over, the day lost. The warriors have maimed themselves, and so did so many of us betray ourselves, charging into battle backwards, our swords reversed, the points of our blades hovering over our own hearts. At least we were laughing.

I knew if I looked at Scott I would either guffaw raucously or well up with hot tears at the bathos of it all. The sight of this sweet, kind, utterly stoned Australian trying to smooth the passage of some self-conscious-looking Spanish señor through the essential steps of ordering and paying for what will prove to be awful food and trashy drink for his contrary, cantankerous family (the kids are playing up and the wife looks as though she's distilling grievances for a row) suddenly seemed too moving and tragic for words. I busied myself with the customers.

Ah, the customers. What did they really want? Surely not what they asked for, which was 'Piss', for the most part, as Scott calls it – 'Pinta piss, mate?' he asks me, after hours. He has a straightforward approach to the business.

'Bought a crate of piss for the fridge in the bathroom – put 80p in the bowl and help yourself. We'll make a little profit and buy more piss, then we'll have a party!'

Pub work puts me off booze. Booze is the constant currency. If someone wants to be nice to you they buy you booze. When we are rewarded it is in booze. Our perks are booze. Consolations are booze. We get people boozed up and later resent them for being boozy. Serving it for hours on end, emptying their wallets and distending their livers feels like taking unfair advantage, like clubbing baby seals. I drink far less as a barman than I had as a journalist.

'Oright, Horace, stoned again are ya, darling?'

Kelly's look was at once superior, patronizing and accusatory.

'No!' I said, churlishly.

'Yeah you are, darling, you're staring into space – look at ya!'

'I haven't woken up yet. How's your hangover?'

'What hangover, darling? I haven't got a hangover. I was a good girl last night?' Her sentences float upwards at the end but that is not what annoys me. What annoys me is that even here, so far down the social food chain that I am practically invisible, I am still not too small, too invisible or too worthless to be harried by someone with pretensions, when it suits her, to management.

There are four kinds of people in the world, I decide, suddenly: leaders, followers, managers and rebels. Let us put the rebels aside for a moment as they are a small subset and consider the leaders and followers, who make up the majority. These two get on very well, like dogs and fleas, but somehow a vast army of tentacled interlopers have managed to insert themselves between the two blocs, and they have taken over. Managers have designed our society to suit and reflect them. In the myriad pyramids they eternally build and rebuild for their own advantage the managers insert a leader here and there, to give the masses someone to respect, someone to work for, someone to place their hope and loyalty in, ensuring that anyone who could and should challenge them is too busy coping with humanity – for which leaders have a weakness not shared by managers – to threaten their beloved, infernal, self-serving management structures.

God was a leader, Adam was a follower, Eve was a rebel and Satan was a manager.

You have to be careful, I caution myself, before you assign anyone a place in this simple but infallible model: sometimes a leader will wear the badge of a manager and more often an inflated manager will be hailed everywhere as a leader. Managers like nothing better than to bring down leaders, whom they fear and envy, and replace them with one of their own. Once you have identified a manager and you are quite certain you are not mistaken, that this is not a leader who happens to have 'manager' in their job title, it is your moral duty to oppose him or her, cautiously but implacably and for ever. They recognize their own kind instantly and only with each other do they feel secure, as they all know where they stand in their amoral, vacuous pecking orders. Only with each other can they speak their tortured, euphemistic gibberish without fear that someone in the corner is thinking 'lies and bullshit'.

I want to go on, but I am suddenly aware that Kelly is staring at me, waiting for an answer or response to her statement-question, and I am gazing at her, wondering if I really believe that all managers should be electrocuted, and then clubbed.

'Completely stoned, right, darling?'

'Yes,' I decide. 'In the end – yes.'

I watch a triumphant smirk spread across her chops.

'But I could be as stoned as the Great Wall of China and I'd still take more orders than you, *darling.*'

'Go on then!' she says, her inner manager spotting an open goal.

I sigh. 'I can't be bothered. It's made me too apathetic.'

I will feel bad about this childish rudeness later, doubly bad when I watch Kelly obey the most terrifying order ever given in the pub. Later this afternoon fifty football fans will crowd in under the TV, drinking heavily and watching the Cup Final. Wanda will appear and demand it be switched off. She will make this demand of Kelly. And Kelly, knowing exactly what she is in for, will walk forward with the feeble remote control, stand directly below the TV and switch it off. And the football fans, with one furious, cursing roar, will demand it back but Kelly will shrug, smile and defy them. An act of amazing courage which makes spiteful gibberish of my formulations. I will take it all back.

But this is to come: now I feel so happily stoned I turn a beaming welcome on a pair of grey-haired tourists, man and wife, who look a little hot and tired.

'Good morning. Can I help?'

'Uh, yeah, we'd like a beer.'

Americans. We get a lot of Americans and on the whole I like them, though they do have an imperious attitude to service and struggle with 'please'. But they are not alone in that and they do, famously, tip. Mr fades back a step or two, and Mrs looks at me expectantly. She definitely wears the cargo pants in this relationship.

'Beer! Of course. What kind of beer would you like – Belgian? Australian? Dutch? English? Czech?'

'Anything,' says the woman. 'Anything as long as it's not Islamic. After what they did to us.'

Not so long ago bombs went off outside the American embassies in Kenya and Tanzania. Islamist terrorists are believed to have been behind them. I assume the American lady is referring to this, but she may not be. Given that she is apparently conducting a one-woman sanctions campaign on a non-existent substance in the hope that this will hamper a faction whose religion forbids it, she might just as well be referring to the Moorish conquest of Spain in the eighth century or the conversion of Cat Stevens.

I turn around slowly and consider the fridges. Which is the least Islamic beer in there? There are a couple of American beers but it is bad practice to offer travelling Americans their own swill. They want good, local, non-Islamic swill. Suddenly I am reluctant to impugn anyone, even the Belgians and Australians, with Islamophobia. But I have to serve Mrs Embargo something so I opt for two pints of Danish lager. The Danes are kind, tolerant, UN-supporting people. I am sure they will understand.

'Is this British?' asks the woman, with a shade of suspicion.

They withdraw to grieve over the minuscule, though accurate, amount of change and sip their beer. I watch them with a combination of amazed amusement and despair.

Soon the first lunch orders are coming in and Sal appears, carrying plates of food. Sal wears a dirty T-shirt and ludicrously sagging jeans.

A stained baseball cap rides backwards on oily black hair. His apron looks like a sheet in which someone has recently wrapped a road-killed rabbit. His face is pointed, his smile belongs to someone who has just thought of a particularly prurient sexual innuendo and his dark eyes conceal their intelligence under a veneer of deliberate stupidity. He regards the customers as potentially dangerous idiots and snitches: he sidles up to them, the food held well away from him as though he does not like its smell, and pushes it at them as though he is feeding animals through the bars of an invisible cage, smiling ingratiatingly, anxious to be away as quickly as possible. Now he comes to the bar, grinning at me.

'Eh Orazio, come stai?'

'Sto bene, Sal. You?'

'Molto bene, stronzo. Eh, you want to buy ticket?'

'Ticket to what?'

'Napoli.'

I laugh. 'I'd love to, but I have no money and no time off! Why are you selling tickets to Naples?'

Sal looks right and left in an overtly criminal manner and leans in.

'I have fake ticket,' he rasps. 'Will you see?'

'Sure.'

His hand dives into his jeans and comes out with a rumpled roll of paper, which he passes to me. I smooth it out and examine it. It appears to be a Eurolines coach ticket from London Victoria to Naples, open return.

'Are you sure this is fake?'

'Sí, sí, is fake.'

'Where did you get it?'

'My fren' makes it.'

'Well, he's very good. It looks absolutely fine to me. How much did it cost?'

'Twenty.'

'It really doesn't look fake. Are you sure he didn't just buy it?'

Sal looks offended and grabs the ticket back. 'Is fake!' he hisses. 'Eh, gimme coffee.'

I roll my eyes. Wanda does not mind us helping ourselves to coffee, on which the pub makes 800 per cent profit per cup, but there is no reason why I should make one for Sal, especially when we are busy. Sal knows this but he likes to be served. He leans against the bar with a disdainful air. I make him a cup, and present it. Sal raises his thick eyebrows in thanks. 'You have cigarette?' he enquires. He takes one, pouting, as if he is doing me a favour. I think he thinks of me as his bitch. He blows smoke at me and I decide to retaliate. I glance over his shoulder.

'Sal!' I whisper urgently. 'Wanda!'

He actually jumps, spins round, guilt and despair cartwheeling across his features. There is no Wanda. He curses. A customer looks alarmed. I serve the customer while Sal lolls against the bar, showing how relaxed he is. The customer places his wallet on the bar for a moment and Sal's gaze flicks over it. The customer clocks the look and pockets the wallet, offended. Sal sneers, then turns his attention on Karen.

The phone goes, making the one long ring which means it's an internal call.

'Hello?'

'H, have you got Sal down there?'

'Hey, Louise. Yes, we have.'

'Well, tell the lazy little bastard to get his arse back up here now! What's the point of cooking the fucken food if we can't serve it?'

I replace the phone. Sal is plying Karen with doe-eyed supplication.

'Salvatore! Louise wants you in the kitchen.'

He grins, as if to suggest that Louise wants him to service her in the kitchen, and slopes off.

Karen watches him go, and laughs. I grin and at that precise moment catch sight of Wanda, descending the stairs, looking right at me. She shakes her head at me and comes to the bar, running a rapid eye over the pub, as if photocopying, en masse, a selection of unimpressive CVs.

'Good afternoon, darlink. Tuck your shirt in, sveetie. Have you given up collecting glasses?'

'Hi, Wanda. How are you?' I respond, swinging myself out through the gap in the bar.

'Not bad, sveetie. Why were the takings so low last night? Nobody in or what?'

'It was pretty quiet.'

'We must sell more or they'll sack us all. This summer is no good. Oh God, there's that madman.'

A mumbling, halt, sunburned old tramp is making a sweep of the outside tables, yellowed claw extended, taking a collection from the customers.

'Ho!' Wanda cries, and bustles at him. He catches sight of her and scoots, mouthing something at her over his shoulder. She comes back, smiling.

'He's terrified of me, that one,' she says. 'A leetle glass of vine please, sveetie.' Scott fishes a bottle of our best white out of a fridge, stopping the pour precisely on the line marked on the glass. In inn-keeping that 'leetle' is everything; worlds in a sud of foam, profit and loss on a measure's edge. Wanda will raid the tip jar tomorrow morning to pay for her drink, we know, though we never complain.

'H,' Karen calls, 'can you change the Fosters?'

'Sure.' I grab the cellar keys. The smell rises to greet me as I descend the stairs. 'Holy moly,' I gasp. 'It's getting worse.' I need a pee, so I take the plunge into the Gents and relieve myself, running my eye over the jewel in our graffiti collection, a real beauty, the work of an anonymous hand holding a permanent black marker: it is called 'Faster Bastards'.

> *Faster Bastards*
> *Stole me bitches*
> *And lost me jobs*
> *So now I hate fast*
> *bastards who lie skive*
> *Take all the credit*
> *And still deny it*
> *The dirty cunts.*

We fear it will not survive the next visit of the Area Manager, but console ourselves that after his experience last time he may be reluctant to use the Gents. I will miss 'Faster Bastards' when it goes. I particularly love the penultimate line, the idea that Fast Bastards have been denying that universal 'it' for all time, and always will.

I return to the bar in time to see Wanda replacing the phone. She looks rattled.

'Oh God, Health Inspector is coming. I vill lose my licence for sure. Vere is Vade? Tell Vade to move all those papers by the fire exit, chop chop! Chop chop!'

It is a mystery how Wanda knows so much about the top floor: received wisdom says she is unable to pass between the fridge and the door jamb on the first landing. I sprint upstairs and tell Wade the bad news. Wade curses and adds another reason to his long list of why working in pubs sucks.

'Retail's where it's at,' he tells me soberly. 'You should go get a job in Gap. The money's way better, there's none of this shit on your day off and you get bonuses.'

It turns out that the pub telegraph is wrong in this instance. It is not the Health Inspector who walks through the door an hour later, but the Pest Control Officer. He descends into the cellar with a sinister liquid in a tank and a sprayer. He leaves later, after a terse conversation with Wanda. Shortly after that, Colin comes up through the floor. Colin and his entire extended family, Colin and all his doubles and doppelgangers, Colin and all his antennaed, armoured, many-legged multiples. He comes up along the pipes, up from the depths, up through the shelves of glasses. He charges drunkenly across the top of the bar, heading for the customers as if he means to fight them.

Best practice says you flick him out among the legs and feet and hope no one notices. I avert disgrace under the eyes of a pleasant couple by bringing a pint down smartly on his head and scraping him into a drip tray. Must try to remember not to sell the contents of that tray.

'Chroist, have you seen Colin!' Scott exclaims. 'Is he emigrating or what?'

'Moving to the Trafalgar. He wants to watch the football.'

At that moment a man in an immaculate morning suit and gleaming shoes with a white buttonhole sashays through the door. His hair is neatly brushed, his eyes shine and his teeth glint white.

'Nick!'

'Good mórrow. How *do*?' This is said with a sweep on the 'how' and an abrupt stop on the 'do', as if a judge had soared in and then tripped over his robe.

'Fighting on. How are you? What would you like?'

'I am in the very pink, thank you. I'll have a double whisky, if you please, and one for yourself.'

'Cheers, guv. I'll have to have it later, though. What have you been doing?'

'Well, his mother's staying, so I've been out looking for unblockers for her, and we need a mop.'

'You'd never walk through Chelsea carrying a mop!'

'Certainly *not*. I'll have it delivered. I don't know what has got into me today. A few too many last night perhaps. Took a gallon of Optrex to turn them from red to white. Then I felt like a brute this morning so I've had the staff up on ladders cleaning the light bulbs. When they'd done that I scattered some talcum powder about and told them to dust the plants . . . Lord . . .' he breaks off, eyeing some football-shirt wearers with comical disbelief, 'it's amazing what you see when you haven't got your gun.'

Nick is the butler of one of the richest men in Britain: he will not say who. This discretion allows a great deal of indiscretion. He seems to live in a world which is half P. G. Wodehouse, half Flann O'Brien. I first noticed him because he was the only person ever to stand at the bar reading a book and because he seemed amused by our antics. He stood opposite the till. 'When you want to be served in a pub where you are not known, you always make for the till,' he explained. 'It's the only place you lot are bound to go.'

He is full of such lessons. 'Eyes and teeth,' he reprimanded me, severely. 'Eyes and teeth are the secret of good presentation. What are you doing with that pint?'

'Serving it!'

'No, you are abusing it, and your customer.'

'How's that then?'

'Never, ever hold or touch the top third of the glass.'

'Right.'

Nick eats like a king and drinks like a pasha. He has his own Chelsea house, part of his employer's estate. His salary is paid into an account in the Channel Islands: he has adopted the habits of the super rich. He is training his employer in the art of correct dressing: 'We're getting there,' he remarks.

Nick worked for a Turkish billionaire and watched him manipulate the currency markets, to Turkey's considerable cost and the billionaire's commensurate gain. 'Did I tell you about the time we hosted a cruise for Princess Margaret? I was a junior then, apprenticed to an absolute master. Her Nibs chose to go swimming at exactly the same moment the ship's captain decided to pump out the bilges. A crescent of effluent began to surround her. What to do? You can't exactly shout "Come back, Mags! The water is filling with poo!" Fortunately my mentor was there. He leaned out and hollered, "Maam! *Photographers*, maam." She loathes them. Leapt out like a salmon.'

'But what's it like serving these people? Doesn't it drive you mad?'

'Not at all. You have seen *The Servant*, haven't you?' He looks pointedly around the pub. 'Better a lion's flea than a dog's business. It's a wonderful life. You could do it, Phyllis,' he says. (He knows I am not gay but treats me as an honorary member of his coterie, complete with *nom de guerre*.) 'You would start as an Under Butler. I could make an enquiry if you like. I'm sure we could get you in.'

(It was the most unusual offer I got, but not the most unlikely. That comes from a man who looks like an accountant and claims he owns a shipping line. They specialize in carrying nuclear waste from Japan to Sellafield for reprocessing, he says. He offers me a job, complete with an MBA which he will fund, then rather dilutes the compliment by offering everyone behind the bar jobs, especially the women. It becomes clear that the point is to sleep with one of them – any one of them.)

'That's very sweet of you, Nick, but I'm not sure I'm cut out to be an Under Butler.'

'Oh well. You can always change your mind – unless you find whatever it is you are cut out for.' His expression suggests this would be a peculiar and miraculous freak, which is understandable. 'Must get on. His wretched mother will be wanting her eggs. Toodle pip!'

He strides out, adding his remarkable presence to the faded colour of the King's Road, in which there are still outlines of the picture it must have been thirty years ago. Among all the shoppers there is the young man who wears a jewelled turban, the old woman in fabulous silks and sunglasses, there are models, art students and the occasional Hollywood star.

We do the bartender's jerky dance through the hours into the afternoon. At two, Phil appears and releases us. He communes with the till which tells him how much money we have taken. 'Not bad, H. Ye'll go *far*, my son.'

'Not that far. Me and Scott are back at six.'

'Sweet . . . Think of all that lovely coin ye'll be making.'

Phil has a hangover, which makes him furious with everything except us.

Phil: What would y'like?

Customer: Two orange juices please.

Phil (under his breath – because it means stooping): Ah *fooking* hell . . .

I slope back to my room, roll a joint and turn on my computer, which I got for £100 from a shipping company which was throwing it out. It makes loud whirring, groaning noises when asked to remember more than a paragraph. My novel flickers into life. It is about a Canadian girl, who is my first girlfriend, Lara, going to study for a year in France. She moves in with two wild French Communists, one of whom is clearly Theo, the other of whom is me, and finds herself caught up in a revolution. The pitch is simple: what would happen if one day the rioters won? What if all our peace and prosperity is a veil, like night, across our eyes? What if, out there somewhere, a huge wave is gathering? What if we are all riding the wave, this great blue swell of our privilege, surfing along, as it grows and grows, charging us towards an unseen, unimagined shore?

I have a recurring dream about a plane crash. One of those little white arrowheads falls off the shaft of its vapour trail and plunges down, twisting, like the squiggled arc of a breaking string. I go to the crash site and inside the fuselage there are the passengers, dazed and confounded but alive. I tell them to follow me out of the plane but they look at me strangely, suspiciously. They do not understand where I have come from or why I want them to leave. They seem to suspect I have caused the crash and I am unable to assure them that I have not. I am not sure that I have not.

The book is called *Falling Jumbos*. Everything around me seems to confirm that I am on to something. All the commuters, all the office workers, all the rich and anxious hurrying to their desks, making money, then coming in to get drunk, calling their dealers, sorting out drugs for the weekend. As though we are trying to blot something out. Hung up on fashion and lifestyle, mooning over magazines and celebrities, as though we are trying not to think. Like first class passengers in one of the beautiful white jets which soar, every two minutes, over the pub. Coddled and waited on, bowed and scraped to, but their palms are sweating. Nothing can go wrong, what could go wrong, nothing's wrong, we're all right now, and now, and now. So far so good, so far so good, as the film *La Haine* puts it: a man jumps off a building, so far so good, so far so good, he says, 'But it's not the fall, it's the landing.'

I do not know how the book works, but I know that there is a riot that cannot be quelled, and that our society, as mighty and complex and fragile and dirty as a jumbo, crashes. Everything about it assures me that *Falling Jumbos* will never be published. It seems to know things about me that I do not admit aloud, however. My character is constantly in trouble with the police.

'I love being arrested!' he cries. 'The police are my surrogate fathers. All this is about that. I am compelled to misbehave in order to get their attention, so that I can then be a model prisoner and make friends with them. I blame my dad . . .'

He is supposed to be being ironic. I switch it off in disgust. It is an anaemic, theoretical thing compared to the bloodied, panting life which surrounds me in the pub. I cannot work on it stoned anyway, so go out.

Across the road is a bookshop where I drift. The presence of books is comforting: I feel at home among them, as though here at least I know what I am doing. I spend a lot of time reading the writers' biographies on the first pages, comparing their paths with mine and anxiously doing sums, subtracting the date of birth from the publication year of their first book to see if I still have time. The high incidence of misery, alcoholism, poverty, marital breakdown and depression in their stories is not off-putting in the least. They ran across the wind, all sails out and stretched, and they made beauty, truth and sense from it, ships to carry us in. It is all I want, all I have ever wanted to do with my life, but I do not believe the boat I am building will ever float: it is driftwood barely nailed together.

It is agonizing not to be able to afford these books. I could just about stretch to one a fortnight, though I will finish it in two days. Which though? Conrad or Carver? It is miserable to have to choose. A young woman who has a proper job glides by. She has four books cradled in her arm: after a moment's consideration she adds a fifth. She is evidently dealing in insignificant sums. This is desperate. Jamie used to think it morally permissible to steal books, I remember: in fact, he went through a stage of stealing them in one shop and selling them in another. I am not made for that sort of crime. I plump for Carver's complete short stories and retreat.

Some madness overtakes the pub that night, one of those evenings when all London loses its temper, bucks its restraints, drops its mask and howls, many silently, through their eyes; some literally. You are most likely to be assaulted between seven and eight, according to a statistic in that evening's paper: when people have had their first two drinks and are irate at having to queue for their third, presumably.

Four men in raincoats demand service. Wanda is alert to them from the moment they walk in. Beery and flushed, they cast sneering looks around them like spit. 'We're the police,' their leader says. 'We might want to do a stakeout in here. Let's have a glass on the house.'

'You're drunk,' she says. 'You have authority for this? Let me see it then. What is the name of your inspector – you have his number? I know Chelsea police but I don't know you.'

The police fall silent. Their crests fall.

'Get out,' Wanda says. She advances on the leader as she would any drunk, offering him a choice between wrestling a large and angry woman, and flight. They flee.

Wanda growls and leaves shortly afterwards. 'Madness, madness, sveeties. Goodnight!'

A youth who works at the pub down the road comes in. 'Fucken 'ell,' Scott exclaims. 'There's that bastard. You're fucken dead, mate. I'm gonna break that bastard's neck.' Lee has slept with and impregnated Scott's sister, and been a bastard to her ever since. Scott has vowed to smash his face in if he ever sees him. Lee knows this and has apparently decided tonight is the night he wants it done.

Scott advances, Lee flees and shouts abuse from outside the pub, Scott advances again, Lee goes and comes back with a club of some sort, Scott charges, Lee hurls the club and disappears, vowing to return with some friends. Scott spends the rest of the evening peering past the customers, through the windows and down the road, pumped up and hopeful.

I demand proof of age from a party of six excited boys in short haircuts who do not even look old enough to smoke. 'Wha'?' one of them cries. 'We're Welsh Guards!'

Old enough to die for us but barely old enough to drink. They clutch their pints and stare at the women with frank amazement.

The rock star appears. He looks dreadful, staggering and slurring, dribbling. He clings to the bar as if to the rail of a ship in a heavy sea, downing the remains of other people's pints and clawing scraps of unwanted food off plates before we have the chance to bin them.

'Michael, are you all right?'

'Bronchitis,' he croaks, spilling another half over his chin and chest. 'Medication,' he whispers, waving a hand. Whether he wants medication, blames medication or, more likely, has been drinking on top of medication is not clear.

'I think you should go home . . . you don't look good . . .'

Michael falls over and makes no attempt to rise. Kelly and I rush to him. He seems pleased to see Kelly, pawing at her like a baby. When Kelly rejects his gestured invitation to join him on the floor he closes his eyes and looks as though he is going to sleep, or die. She calls an ambulance which arrives amazingly quickly – they park up the road and wait for this sort of thing. The crew check him out, pronounce him unworthy of their help, and leave. We haul him up. Several taxis refuse to take him. Eventually a police car stops, and the officers say they will drive him home. We never see him again.

A young American pulls up a stool and tells me he commutes between Boston and London, working in computers, of course. 'I was with the military in the Gulf War,' he says. 'Just before we went in we took down all their systems. We made them *blind*.'

He asks for a cheeseburger. Sighing, I go up to the kitchen to make the thing. I retune the radio from Louise's Heart FM to Radio 4. It's an arts programme, Mark Lawson is interviewing Alex Garland, author of *The Beach*, about his second novel. The writer is about my age. His father also works for the *Daily Telegraph*. He likes PlayStation and, I read somewhere, a spliff. He is a quiet-sounding, hesitant superstar and I have just dropped a burger into the fat fryer by mistake. I want to say it is unfair, but it is not unfair. It is what it is.

Back in the bar a very drunk woman jabs me in the chest with her finger.

'You're beautiful!' she cries.

'No, you are,' I return. 'I'm a barman.'

'Are we 'avin *foon* yet?' Phil enquires.

Soaked in the smell of lemons boiled in the detergent of the glass wash, subject to at least three anxious bordering on dirty looks from waiting customers, my ears ringing with the jukebox (people are still playing Oasis, who recorded their CDs at a higher level than everyone else) and stinking of sweat, stale beer and smoke, I start laughing.

A young man takes a break from arguing with his girlfriend and promises to kick my head in.

'But why?' I demand, plaintively. 'I've done nothing.'

'Because I eat bar staff,' he replies. Phil is busy, Scott is on his break and if I try to throw him out this boy is definitely going to punch me. I will just have to live with it. He knows this, and sneers at me for the next half hour.

Finally the blessed hour comes and we ring time at the bar. Phil takes away the tills. We throw them all out and clean up. Dave hunches on his stool, his face warm with pissed smiles. We sweep and stack as the jukebox plays Pink Floyd's 'Wish You Were Here' and we all sing along, separately at first, then tentatively together, then all together . . . *just two lost souls swimming in a fish bowl – year after year – running over the same old ground – What have we fou-nd? The same old fears?* . . . *wish you were here* . . .

Our voices are out of tune but we are all in harmony: men who do not discuss their feelings or much reveal themselves, just for an instant, a tired, end of the night, half the lights out, chairs on tables moment, all thinking of someone secret and something indistinct, smiling and shy, when it finishes.

Phil reappears.

'Does it add up?'

'Nothing adds up, mate, but the till's ten pence to the good.'

Finishing the floor I discover a bag of weed and a five pound note.

'Look at this, Christmas!'

'Nice one. Be sure to enjoy it, ye'll no get better than that,' Phil comments.

He was right.

Much later on, exhausted but too wired to sleep, I go for a walk up a near-empty King's Road, stalked by taxis. There is the pub where Rossetti and his pre-Raphaelites used to drink, now a cocktail bar. There is Carol Reed's house. Orson Welles walks beside me, looking over his shoulder at shadows. Here is the shop where Vivienne Westwood met Malcolm McLaren: apparently Billy Idol used to work there. There is the pizza place which used to be a ballet school where Alicia Markova danced. There is Markham Square where James Bond was supposed to live, opposite Bywater Street, home to George Smiley. Mary Quant's shop still sells clothes but they are going to turn it into a coffee shop. McDonald's used to be a hippy place with topless waitresses.

I wander down to Jerome K. Jerome's flat and on to Chelsea Bridge where there is an all-night food stand, a cab-driver's favourite. Sipping sweet tea I watch empty trains clattering on to the bridge to Victoria, their electric flashes throwing lightning on to the walls of the titanic ghost of the power station. Low orange clouds scud eastwards, torn sails, and the river laps black. Far away down the river my father's office glows, Canary Wharf, stubby steel and bright little lights like the prow on the ship of the whole city, like a future beyond my reach, beyond my lifetime.

She walked into the pub smiling that smile which seemed to curl between affection and scepticism, with rich amusement in her puffin's eyes, as though nothing had happened.

'All right?'

'Jane!'

Wanda adored her immediately. 'Go on, go on, take her upstairs! Show her around . . .'

I showed Jane the room, embarrassed.

'Don't be embarrassed. You've done well. Look at you, all set up.'

'Done *well*?'

'Yeah!'

'It's dreadful.'

'No it's not, I think it's great.'

'What are you doing?'

She shrugged. 'Scenic art. Making nonsense for TV.'

'What sort of nonsense?'

'You know *Live and Kicking*? Jamie and Zoe – that sort of nonsense.'

'Like what?'

'Whatever. Whenever Mr Blobby smashes something up, well – someone's got to make it first.'

'What's it like?'

'It's comedy. Hilarious.' She rolled her eyes. 'I like Zoe Ball though. She's great. I think I might be a bit obsessed with her.'

'What else are you obsessed with?'

'Well, er,' (wincing) 'All Saints?'

'All Saints! Those girls! Why?'

'I dunno, I just like them. I like their clothes.'

'You're mad.'

'Coming from you, buster . . .'

We walked down the King's Road that night, through warm and syrupy air. I saw myself coming the other way, aged seventeen with Ben and the boys, laughing, defiant and immortal. We kissed on the

Albert Bridge, which looks like an iced wedding cake, as celebrating football fans went by, flying flags and whistling. As the summer glowed and faded and glowed again we walked in Battersea Park and picnicked by the river. There was a young man there one afternoon, running around his girlfriend with his shirt off.

'Chamberlaine!'

'Clare!'

Olly was selling advertising for the *News of the World*. He was as buoyant and assured as ever. 'What are you doing, mad head?'

'Writing a novel . . . working in a pub.'

'Nice one!'

'Cheers . . .'

As the summer aged we all made plans for change. Rob switched day jobs and found he was an excellent estate agent. Scott and Sandra booked tickets to Australia. Phil was preparing to apply for his own licence. Wanda opened a bar in Streatham on the sly and bought tickets for a gay cruise up the west coast to Alaska. 'Me and five hundred lesbians, sveetie, can you imagine that!'

I gave up dope and cigarettes. With the attrition of bar life as a prompt I found it quite easy to stop: I wanted to be with Jane and I wanted to be more than a barman, so I quit. Stopping dope is comparatively easy. When you are into it you cannot imagine letting your stock run out, you will go any distance to score. I walked to Brixton from Chelsea and back, after a long shift, several times, quite happily: the idea of not having it is too fearful.

But when one day you decide to stop you are amazed that you did not do so before. Compared to giving up cigarettes it barely counts as quitting. You do go into withdrawal but you do not do it immediately, as with nicotine, but gently, as befits marijuana. You may find yourself in a miserable sweat a few weeks later but at least you have some time to adjust. Stopping cigarettes at the same time entirely subsumed it, and thanks to Jane I was not able to indulge the various grim delights of that.

Scott woke me one morning. 'Telephone for ya, mate.'

I stumbled down and took it in the kitchen.

'Es that oreeshoo claaair?'

Ben, calling from New York, putting on a ridiculous voice. It was 5 a.m. there and no way was he just waking up. I resisted a sudden parental impulse to ask him if he was on drugs. We compared notes.

'I got nothin', man,' he said, with a comic self-disgust.

'Yes you do, you bastard. You have a flat and a job.'

'Not for long . . .'

'Your dad was in earlier.'

'My dad? What did he want?'

'Looking for you.'

I went to see him. We sat on the lawn of his house, drinking white wine with his wife. They asked gently how I was. I said I was fine. He was smoking a pipe and she her cigarettes.

'I've stopped,' I said.

'Oh? Well done. What prompted that?'

'I don't know. One thing I could do to improve things.'

His wife, the psychiatrist, nodded. She specialized in eating disorders. 'People often deny themselves things as a measure of control, when they feel they lack control in other areas of their lives.'

'That's me all right!'

We talked about fears. 'What do you fear?' my father asked.

'Ending up on the street.'

He nodded.

In the early autumn my birthday approached.

''Ow old are you going to be, 'Ornblower?'

'Twenty-five, Dave.'

'Gor, twenty-five and you're washing glasses! Should've made your mark by now.'

Dave was one of my surrogate fathers. He had adopted one or two of us, and he believed, like my real father, in tough love when necessary.

'I'll make my mark, don't worry!'

'Yeeah . . .' Dave said, part scornful.

'I've got to leave, Wanda.'

'Why, darlink?'

'I'm going to be twenty-five, I can't stay for ever.'
'Twenty-five!' she laughed. 'But you are so young!'

They threw a party. With a staple gun they made my bed stand up in a corner of the room, duvet, sheets and pillow all in place. Then they wheeled out the booze and a camera. The pictures show us in clumps, hugging, our arms around each other, dozens of glasses of wine, champagne and pints going down. Phil is pissed, his eyes rolling, and people keep stroking his head. Wanda is always talking, except in the one where she is hugging Scott, her eyes closed, her expression blissful. Scott looks wry. Rob's huge arms are widespread, embracing four people at once. In the last photo the pub is empty, golden daylight falling through the windows, the extravagant orchid-shaped lights still on. It looks strangely beautiful, and even there, without a soul in it, you can see the secret. Wanda's secret, the magic key, the trick which makes it all work, which allows you to spin money from overpriced drink, terrible food and no more entertainment than a few unstable bar staff. The secret is atmosphere, of course.

In seven months I had never been a minute late for a shift. I knew hard team work, I knew loyalty. I had learned some understanding of people. I reckoned I was all but unemployable but I had managed to save a small sum and now barely drinking, because not smoking, I was barely spending, thanks to Jane, who took me in. What little I had was my own: my father had been absolutely right, and I entirely wrong. With no pressure to grow up I might never have grown up. Seven months in a pub had changed me more than three years at university.

Two months of writing letters and filling in forms landed just one interview, for the best of the jobs, a post at the bottom of the Arts Unit at BBC Radio. I knew it was hopeless and would not have bothered had Jane not insisted. There were two men in baggy jumpers in the corridor, communicating in quiet half-sentences as though the main current of the conversation was telepathic. The interviewers did not seem to think that most of a year in a pub trying to write a novel was a waste of time. Knowing all sorts of obscure trivia about writers' lives was an advantage. The tabloid training and local journalism were positively desirable. They called me back.

'You can't do the job we've advertised because you don't know the technical stuff yet, but would you be interested in being a researcher?'

In the lift going down I whispered 'I've got a job! I've got a job!' over and over again. Wanda phoned. 'They called and asked me for a reference, sveetie. I said you are lucky, lucky, you BBC! I gave you such a reference, you vould not believe it!'

I sat at my desk on the seventh floor of Broadcasting House, the home of radio, and looked out over half the roofs of London. I would come to love the work, if not the admin, and I would adore many of the people: they became another family to me. The hours were long and the pay was low, and though we moaned we did not really care. 'Oh well, lucky we're not in it for the money,' we sighed, proudly.

In the BBC I found something to believe in, at last, a cause beyond myself, something good. For the first time since the International School I belonged to something which allowed me to look myself in the eye. The BBC is an idea, like the International School, encapsulated in very few words: international understanding, said the school; inform, educate, entertain, said the corporation. People to admire and an idea to believe in: all it takes to tame mad elephants.

And I thought it glamorous, too. It granted recognition.

'What do you do?' asked one of Jane's friends.

'As of this morning, I'm a researcher for the BBC,' I said.

'Wow!' she said.

I blushed with the purest pride.

I would not give up on my novel, though it would not be published. I would be there for the next seven years. It was almost a fairytale ending, or at least a fairytale beginning.

But not quite. Drug addiction is not a simple arc; the road to wisdom via excess is not straight. There is no direct route from innocence, through trauma, to enlightenment.

10

Mania

We stood on the banks of the Thames with a million people. There was a happy community atmosphere: the biggest crowd I had ever seen was motivated by nothing more than celebration and a vague expectation that the end of the twentieth century might be worth watching. Deafening fireworks produced clouds of thick smoke but there was no other spectacle. We were the show: men, women and children in vast numbers, like a carnival without floats. Our leaders went to their ridiculous Dome. Television showed them holding hands and gulping in a fishy way as they sang 'Auld Lang Syne' as loudly as they could. The millennium bug did not bite and the apocalypse was cancelled. 'The river didn't burn, the wheel didn't turn, this is New Labour, this is New Britain!' concluded Joel, Robin's brother.

We drank brandy and champagne and took dirty coke in a house in Kennington where Theo lived. He and Toby had been doing hard time for a crummy management consultancy.

'Weeks in the Marriott in Nottingham, deciding how many people to fire at a fire extinguisher factory,' they described it. Dope had helped. They had moved on to better tech sector jobs. Theo seethed and jabbered: he seemed to like the work, in an impatient way, as though the electronic universe was just about big enough to contain his ideas and rich enough to reward him sufficiently.

Toby had made the jump from betting on dogs (he had a system, of course, which paid its way) to owning a dog. Work did not appear to pain him; life, if you asked, was 'fine really': nothing seemed to pain him. He was still living with Robin.

Robin had been flourishing at his architectural school: a star student, president of the union, founder of a magazine, organizer of legendary parties, triumphant until his final year, when a weak project and a lot of skunk had brought him down.

I had seen him then, working late into the nights, fuelled by coffee and skunk. I knew he did not believe in his project: when I asked him to explain it to me he had rambled and shrugged and fiddled with his computer. A better friend would have sat him down and forced him to face himself, as he had with me, at York. But I had failed him. I had shared the skunk, laughed at his jokes and impersonations, and hoped he would pull himself out of it. Now he was working for a fashion chain as an in-house architect, and hating it. He was drinking a lot.

Enquiries about his state of mind triggered blasting torrents of comically foul curses at the 'absolutely repugnant' c-word he was working for, the hordes of festering c-words who made up the fashion world, the horrible bullshit the label sold, except for the high-end stuff, which was viciously expensive, and the inexpressible misery of commuting from the East to the West End of London.

'Back in Torpy looking after me mum!' reported Michelle. She was not really doing anything, but she sounded happy. She had done well at Goldsmiths, in environmental design, but she had not followed up her success, returning to Torpington, her family and skunk.

Christian pursued further study in Vancouver, then Sheffield, and had met a girl whom he followed to Liverpool.

'So what are you doing tonight, Christian?' I asked him on the phone, looking for an impression of his life.

'Well, I've got to tidy up this place, because it's a complete dump – and there are some people coming round later. Then we'll probably get pissed, I would imagine.'

'And what are you doing for cash?'

'Temping. Data entry.'

'What's that like?'

'Thrilling stuff, mate . . .'

He was not seen much: people who met him said he drank a lot, shouted and passed out. One of the brightest of us, temping.

Wilson had stayed with the Territorial Army. He was living in Clapham, the great ghetto of the young and upwardly hopeful, a dutiful son and brother, returning often to his family in north

London, and a hard worker. Having been an encyclopaedia salesman in America and an estate agent in Pimlico he was now working for an internet company which handled the web account of a luxury car business. He was the only one of us who had had no significant relationship with drugs: the young unmarried man's diversions, drinking and women, seemed enough. There was a roving dissatisfaction about him, I thought, as he hurtled from one booze-up to the next, but he made no complaint.

We went kite flying with his father and younger sisters on Hampstead Heath. The kite strings became tangled into a series of labyrinthine knots. Wilson's father pushed his glasses up his nose, crouched down and patiently began to go through them. He studied and tugged, picked, prodded and muttered. Chris tried to be patient, but it did not last long.

'Shall I have a go?'

'Let me just . . .' his father said.

'You're not going to do it, I'm afraid,' Chris announced, drawing his Swiss Army knife with a flourish. 'Here . . .'

'No, Christopher!' cried Mr Wilson. 'We can unpick it. Be patient.'

'No you can't. Let me cut it.'

'The army way is not the only way. Or necessarily the best way, in this case.'

'It's the efficient way,' Chris grated.

It went on for some time. I thought Chris was going to stab something. In the end he was right: they had to cut it. By the time they did they were both slightly potty. It was like watching that exercise rugby players do, when they lock shoulders and push, bodies heaving, feet scrabbling, until one gives slightly and they both, inevitably, collapse.

I arranged to meet Maria in a Soho pub. She came in, slipping between drinking men who sensed her before they saw her. She was as small and slender as I remembered; hair so dark it was almost blue; rapid eyes.

Now she was working for a trendy advertising firm, had a boyfriend and a flat in King's Cross and she was in the middle of destroying it all.

'I'm manic again,' she said, jiggling her ankle. She was chewing gum hard, the way people on acid do, and smiling uneasily through it. There was a held, cautious air about her, as though she was conscious of concealing things she was not proud of. She was together but fraying, almost before my eyes.

'It's such a strange thing. It's like you can do anything – everything! All at once. You have so many ideas, and you can hold so much in your head, and you really can just do *anything*.'

'Like being on speed or something?'

'Yeah! Well, no, I mean, it's fast like that, really fast, but they're good ideas, it's all so easy . . . they can't believe it at work. And people can sense it. Men can really sense it.'

'Are you seeing many?'

'Well . . .' She shot me a glance.

'Right! What's that like?'

'Messy!' She laughed, her burbling, slightly dirty laugh. 'No, great, really, I liked it, but I shouldn't have done it . . .'

'Can you slow it down?'

'I don't think I can. I try. I do try. But it's just unbelievable, it's like a ride. And I know how it's going to . . . crash. But I can't stop it.'

'Drugs?'

'No! Knocked it on the head. Doesn't make any difference though, it's too late!'

When we had finished she slipped away, with a quick kiss and a tiny wave, a small, dark sylph, engulfed in seconds. The next time I spoke to her she had lost the job, the boyfriend, the flat and her strength. She was at her parents' home, doing the rounds of doctors, and she had been prescribed lithium. A couple of years later, a couple of years of slowly, carefully knitting her life back together, her doctors gave her the wrong dose of the wrong substance and tipped her over the edge. She tried to kill herself in the house she had been brought up in, surrounded by pictures, trinkets, bits of everything she had been. Had her mother not come home early, had the latch not slipped on the bathroom door, and had her mother not been a doctor, I would have been to Maria's funeral by now.

*

The only time he ever went down the stairs to the Gents sober, Dave slipped and broke his ankle. The injury refused to heal properly. During tests they found cancer in his throat and lungs. I went to see him in his flat in Battersea. There was no fear in his eyes and no bitterness; instead there was something childlike, a sort of amazement, as though he was looking at the world in wonder from a long way off.

''Ornblower,' he whispered, 'can you get me some dope?'

'You can't smoke, Dave.'

'Put it in me tea. Go on, you bugger. I can't drink, can't smoke, it'd be nice.'

I went to Brixton for it, then we sat in his flat together, smiling, listening to Pink Floyd. It was like watching my father die, though my actual father was perfectly well. We did it regularly, until Dave died in the first flush of summer 2000. The whole gang went to his funeral. It was a heartbreaking, golden day, the birds at the crematorium singing at the top of their voices, hysterical with excitement, and the men hot in their suits and the women in their black.

We were a strange crew, raffish, young and old, mostly single, sliders, wheelers and survivors. The vicar took a look at the funeral party and preached a stiff homily on sobriety, family and responsibility. People who had been crying stopped. Congregation and vicar bristled at each other.

'And now,' said the vicar, 'a piece of music which I am told David was very fond of.' No one had told him what the CD was. As the first chords rang out we began to smile. 'Hotel California' – a song about devil worship, debauchery and addiction.

We cried like children. Then we went to the pub for the wake. Wisps of the life he had never talked about swirled around us in the cigarette smoke. The time his estate had been menaced by gangsters, whom Dave had confronted with a shotgun: the gangsters moved house. The mystery Scandinavian woman. His work as a plumber, and the time he had spent with a circus. His sister gave me a mug marked Cirkus Merano. 'He wanted you to have this,' she said. The mug was made in Norway, though his sister said he had been with them in Hungary. The design shows a dancing pink elephant in a top hat, bow tie, frilly girdle and ankle bracelets.

We went to Battersea Park that night and scattered his ashes around a young tree. Then we threw the casket into the Thames, in the spate of an outgoing tide, and wished it bon voyage.

We composed a plaque for Dave's place at the bar. It is still there, almost the only thing which remains of the pub we knew: after Wanda left they ripped out all the old features and furnishings, leaving it looking and feeling like the alcoholic wing of Starbucks.

Dave

Friend, helicopter pilot (?)

Wish you were here

This is the moment to walk away from it. A man is dead, twenty years before his time. Dope played no part, but dreaming and regretting and burnishing one while numbing the other certainly had. Statistics show that as people reach their late twenties and early thirties drug use drops dramatically. We grow out of it. If we are lucky enough to find proper jobs there is less time for it. Horizons and priorities shift: our highs come from relationships, achievements, children. We are too busy, too tired and less fearless. But I did not simply walk away from it, and nor did my friends. Just because we were ready to drop it did not mean that it was ready to drop us.

Jane said she dreaded the month of March. 'The spring comes, you start listening to Bob Dylan, then you start smoking dope, then you come home late, then you don't come at all, then you're off, fucking on . . .'

We were together, then I started smoking and 'fucking on' and we fell apart, then I stopped and we got together again. After two years we broke up. Jane wanted children and stability. I wanted to stop hurting her. She did not believe I would ever give up dope.

'Can't you just smoke a little bit sometimes, like everyone else?'

'Yes . . . No. I can't. I've given up . . .'

I always thought I would; whenever I did I thought I had. But it only ever took one or two slips and then I would find myself heading for Brixton again.

Giving in to addiction is like this. There is a tremor in your limbs; your hands shake slightly. You are light on your feet, much faster than your normal self. You flow up flights of steps and ski around corners. Your eyes are sharp and curious. In your stomach the snare drum of your calling beats hard and hot, in your head symbols kiss-kiss-kiss. Every glimpsed face is intriguing, you are removed and present at once, it is all hyper-real and not real at all. You are desperate to get there but at the same time anticipation, the impatient wait, squirms like desire in your guts. It is all foreplay now. The euphoria of surrender comes in waves. You have wilfully given in, you are dirty and licking your lips. As each wave recedes, as the traffic stalls or the queue jams or the train halts you feel sick, exhausted, disgusted with yourself. You force your morals under. You will justify anything now. One side of you is aroused and another miserable. Something of you, something lucid and decent, is heading the other way, going home.

What a terrible thing it must be to love a drug addict. Some stoners can carry it off and remain faithful, present and true. I know good fathers and husbands who smoke constantly. But there are many more who are more like me, who become distant and introverted, evasive and inconstant. Almost the worst of it was that I could see out, through the dopey veils of my internal worlds, and watch the woman I loved peering in, past my selfishness and my endless lies, looking for and sometimes glimpsing something good, something kind and hopeful which would listen to her, which would respond to her, which did not give itself only to take itself away.

I hurt for months and years after I lost Jane. I cannot calculate the pain I must have caused her. Remorse collected inside me like fat in the arteries, I could feel it in my pulse. But I was certain that letting her go was the right thing to do. That is the worst of it – turning away from someone you love, and turning them away, because you know in your heart, though you know it sounds melodramatic and narcissistic to say it aloud, that they really will be better off without you, because you are too lazy and too hungry for something else to change your ways.

I move in with Robin and Toby, into the Hackney Palace, a former crack den, now an accommodation Withnail would have rejected. There is mould on the walls, water runs down the light fittings in the bathroom, there is a strange black stickiness on the sofa which refuses to be wiped off, there are oily diesel particles on all the window sills, it is freezing, the woman upstairs is insane, the mirror on the bathroom wall falls into the shower when Toby is using it, the hall ceiling comes down and you can tell what time it is in the morning by the frequency of the Number 38 buses outside, only narrowly missing the collapsing wall by the front door. Topping up the electricity supply means tiptoeing down to the cupboard under the stairs where the floor is covered in faeces which seep up from somewhere. Outwardly we are happy. It is a relief to have stopped hurting Jane, or at least, to be free of the sight of that hurt.

The opening notes of the *Jackass* theme tune play constantly on the telly: Robin is addicted to it. When he is not watching men slamming their nuts in doors, Toby is watching dogs. There are five thousand copies of his *Racing Post* under the dining room table. I keep us all supplied with dope.

'God, I hate the journey to work,' Robin moans.

'Oh, I don't mind it!' I say, cheerfully.

'Of course you don't. You set off at about half past nine, stoned!' he replies.

Which is often true. When I do not have a programme looming, when I am under no direct pressure, I have a joint before I go. I plan it carefully: I have the joint as soon as possible after I wake up so that in the hour it takes me to get to work it wears off. The admin, the planning meetings and the endless telephone calls are all much more challenging and entertaining in these conditions. In the summer I sometimes have one at lunchtime too, in the park, again as near to one o'clock as possible, so that it will be fading at two, when I go back. I take off my shirt so that the smell will not stain it and lie down with my back to the wind so the smoke will be blown away from me. I can hardly wait for the one I will have when the day is done, skinning up in the gents and then hurrying to one of my places, alleys, a mews or a quiet square, where I can get another fix before the bus ride home.

The drug addict with a criminal record is my secret self, the part which feeds and feeds on the novel I am still writing. It never goes away: not a day passes when I do not fear that my stained character will be revealed, that there will be a call from our boss, come to my office, and Human Resources will be there with a piece of paper, and they will usher me out of the building.

I will never be free of it. The record, stored on computers, will outlive me. Whenever the papers talk about ID cards, cameras, microphones, facial recognition technology, linked databases and microchipped passports my guts tighten. The idea of admitting your crime, taking your punishment and paying your debt seems quaintly antiquated, now that both crime and punishment are ever present, barely a key-stroke away. When they swipe my passport at an airport I believe they can see it. Every time I walk under a surveillance camera I imagine that there is someone looking down and sneering – there goes another one.

Sometimes it feels as though there are two societies: all of you, whom the police are there to protect, and then us, a subset which ranges from insignificant twits like me to the most lethal and brutal, whom you have to be protected against. Whenever I read or hear an account of a crime I feel all the usual impulses of the distant observer – detachment or amazement, sorrow, horror or revulsion, depending on the incident – and something else besides. A wonder at the twists and slips, at the mistakes and desires, surrenders and self-indulgences, at the imps and demons, at the misfortunes, complexes, maladies or delusions which greased the perpetrator's descent. And pity, for even the very worst, even as the newspapers exult in their 'evil', their remorselessness, their sickness.

I hug the dope to me like a comfort blanket. It is my business, it is my sop against boredom, my private accelerator and magnifier to intensify and soften time, my little secret, my indulgence. It is the way I switch off after work and the way I tune up in the morning, so that the bus route is scattered with ideas, associations and blurred insight.

It is terrifying, standing in the lift with someone, thinking my God, they can see it. They can smell it. It must be showing in my glassy eyes. I must be bloodshot. I'm caught, this time, surely, I'm caught.

I do not get caught. I am so soaked in it, so inured to it that each joint does little more than flick me up, a few minutes' fillip before normality returns. But however assiduously I hide it from my colleagues the effect tells in my work. In stoned periods I am disorganized, lazy and inefficient: suicide, in such a competitive environment. The more pressure I am under the less I use it, but in the quiet periods I am often only semi-present, head in the green clouds, career stalling. It takes me years to achieve promotion to producer: when finally it happens the dope is relegated to weekends and holidays.

You get good at hiding it, but the ones you have to hurry are never as much fun as the ones you can take your time over, at home or on holiday. The wooden desk is warm under my wrists, the surface glowing orange-tan; every object on it casts a shadow. The little light blue folder which contains the rolling papers looks cheerful; the box of cigarettes shines like forbidden advertising; the cube of light brown resin in its plastic wallet looks rich with promise and illegality, as if already bagged as a prosecution exhibit.

The papers come out with crisp snicking sounds: I lick the last third of one and stick the other to it, so they form a broken L, the short leg at 145 degrees to the longer one. I make a diagonal fold which crosses both papers and put them on the desk in front of me. The hashish comes out of its bag and I smell it: there is that rich, delicious odour, a dark tang of Africa, and a lighter, sweeter flavour: nutty, chocolatey, floral. This is Moroccan 'Double Zero' – excellent hash, which makes you feel giggly and imaginative; enthusiastic, warm and sexy. It hints at mystery and romance: if you are disposed to stare at sunsets or gaze at moonrises, even moonrises over Dalston Junction, doing it with this can move you to awe and euphoria.

I fire the lighter and play the flame over a corner of the cube until it begins to smoke blue-white. Dropping the lighter I begin to crumble the hash into the trough in the white papers. It softens and flakes quickly under the flame but then the particles stick together: this is annoying but a good sign, indicating quality. Soon the trough contains a line of light brown crumbs. I pinch the end off a cigarette and scatter the tobacco over them. I tear a strip of card off the end of the cigarette paper packet, roll it into a tight tube and place it at the thin end of the papers. If I have to, I can do all this in ninety seconds in a pub toilet. I can do it, without looking, in a bag, my hands out of sight, while I carry on a conversation with someone on the other side of the table. I can do it in my palm, walking along a busy street. I can do it in the back of a taxi without letting the driver catch the scent. I can do it, and smoke it, in a train toilet at 125 miles an hour and neither the ticket inspector standing outside, nor the next user, coming in straight after me, will know anything about it.

But now I take my time, because I am in Marrakech, on holiday, a year after breaking up with Jane, with a new girlfriend. We have not been away together before. This is the first flowering of our relationship. I do the whole thing slowly, precisely, drawing out the pleasure. It is a form of foreplay.

Now all is ready and I pick the thing up and roll it, tight but not too tight. I twist the spare paper at the end into a twizzle, hold it between my finger and thumb and give it two shakes. I raise an eyebrow at my girlfriend. She is sitting with her back to the headboard of the bed, her legs only partly covered by a bright cotton wrap, and she grins at me. I tear off the twizzle and present the spliff to her with a flourish. She shakes her head.

'You start it,' she says.

Silently grateful, I do. We smoke it together, taking turns. Soon we are both talking volubly, and listening, with bright-eyed, impatient attention. We want more, more of each other and more of the dope. I make another one. We swig whisky. It gets dark outside. I make a third and leave her with it while I leave the room – the arches and lamps along the gallery impossibly romantic, the scooped pools of shadow and silence around the courtyard redolent of films and dreams – and take the stairs to the roof. It is flat, dark, and deserted. Over one parapet is a narrow alley; all around are the minarets of mosques, and the murmur of the voices and doings of the medina. There is a big yellow-white moon, reclining, as if propped on one elbow.

I return to the room to fetch her. I take her hand and lead her up the dark stair to the roof. She comes, treading quietly. I can sense her excitement in her breathing. She is almost timid, she is turned on, eager yet almost fearful; I feel – I can hear – her anticipation; I sense her guessing. We smoke the spliff, watching quiet figures making their way along the alley below us. Dogs bark, not far away. When it is finished I flick away the glowing butt and move behind her, putting my arms around her. She presses her body against me and tilts her head back; I kiss her neck. Her eyes close and open slowly; she watches clouds unrolling across the moon. I undo her shirt, exposing her to the pale light. She steps away from the wall. She kisses me, pressing hard against me, her mouth soft and hot. I can feel tremors in her.

The next day we went up into the Atlas, to the Tin Maal, one of two mosques in Morocco to which non-Muslims are admitted. It is in a high valley where the blue air seems thin, in a pass between giant mountains, on the bank of a cold stream which flows through boulders and pale, lunar dust. Inside the Tin Maal are ranks of Moorish arches and a breath-held silence, ruffled only by the wind. The Tin Maal has no roof. You stand between stone, silence and sky. It was once the seat of a warrior imam who gathered the hard, devout people of the mountains around him, formed an army of ascetic believers and marched on Marrakech. No sultan could defeat him, no force could match his warriors, but instead of conquering the kingdom he retreated back to the high valley.

Something about the Tin Maal spoke to me, obscurely but unmistakeably. My sense of the divine, which had always been linked to the wild places, to the majesty and indifference of nature, was profoundly touched. I seemed to feel something in this supposedly deconsecrated place, which was half man's, half God's and almost lost. But whatever had happened here, whatever was worshipped here and argued here, its creed of submission and doctrine of rejection, its urge to rebellion and its unity of purpose, whatever it was, it was still there. It was intensely moving, almost frightening. We tiptoed back to the car and drove away.

We gave a lift to one genial young man who had been working for his uncle in the mountains and was now going back to school, all his possessions in a small bag. His enterprise and strength shamed me. I was embarrassed, when he asked me what I did, to say I worked for the BBC. How hard would he work if he had my job. How beautifully his paperwork would be done, what long hours he would put in, and how gratefully. I resolved to grow up, to cut the dope and to be much, much better at work.

*

Four days after we returned to London I was making tea in the canteen, humming the Clash song, 'Career Opportunities' – *do you wanna make tea at the BBC – do you wanna be – do you really wanna be a cop?* – when I noticed a small group of people gathered around one of the televisions. There was a perfect blue sky, a familiar silhouette and a smear of smoke. It looked as though something had happened to the World Trade Center.

That was the end of it, though we did not realize it at the time. 'This will change everything,' we said, not knowing quite what we meant. But it was the end of what had been for us protracted, political adolescence, the childish security in which we had grown up. Never again would we ever say there were no causes to fight for or against, or that history had ended, or that capitalism was the only game in town. It could never be assumed or pretended that our way was the only one. The thousands or hundreds of thousands who had reason or excuse to envy us, to begrudge us or to hate us were never again out of mind.

Since we had 'won' the Cold War we had supposed we were invincible. What followed, an absence of war, television war, the Balkans and Chechnya, we could effectively ignore. War had been something our leaders could choose to unleash on other people, far away. No longer. 'We are all Americans today,' people said, and we were. In the hegemony of the West and the eyes of the world we had all been Americans for a very long time. Now, it seemed, our war had come.

I tried to get hold of Ben but it was useless. I finally spoke to him days later.

'I walked out of my flat, looked down the street, and saw the first tower come down,' he said.

'Are you OK?'

'Yeah, I guess.'

'How are you?'

'Well . . . I wish they'd just stop fuckin' bombing us, y'know? I mean, what the *fuck*?'

'Mmm . . .'

'Well – do you know what it's all about?'

I thought of the Tin Maal, of Falling Jumbos, of my ravings about blowing up the mushroom at university, of setting fire to those bags. Frustrated young men, fantasists, a cause, death and glory.

'Well, you know, foreign policy . . . the Middle East . . .' I mumbled.

In the summer of 2002, a few days after our ten-year college reunion, my friends gathered in a restaurant in Soho. We had come together from all over the world for a blissful weekend in our Welsh castle. Everyone was relaxed and happy, confident and fully themselves. A lot of us had become doctors, and quite a few had made money. One or two were in politics, others were teachers, environmentalists, research scientists. There was a vet, there were lawyers, one or two had children. Gambo was running an outdoor pursuits centre in west Wales. Robin was freelancing as an architect. Toby was making money in a technology firm. He had a son.

Now a few of us were dragging it out, meeting in London for a meal. I was very happy and excited. And I was greedy. It was all so good, but I thought I would make it just a tiny bit better. I popped out while the others were waiting for the waiters to prepare a table and ducked into a narrow alley. I was talking on my phone and smoking a joint when I turned and saw a file of white-shirted policemen hurrying towards me. They looked as though they were expecting me to run and were not worried about catching me if I did. They were already too close. *Goddamit!* I thought. *Not again, not now!* I had a small bag of weed in my pocket.

'Right, I am arresting you for the possession of cannabis, you do not have to say anything, but anything you do say can be used in evidence against you. Do you understand?'

'Yes,' I sighed. 'Look, all my friends are in that restaurant and they don't know where I am. Could we tell them?'

'Not now. Have you got anything else on you that you shouldn't have?'

'No, I haven't. The thing is, it's my ten-year reunion, they've come from all over the world and I won't see them again for years . . .'

'Don't worry, it won't take long. This way, please.'

We climbed into a white police van at the other end of the alley. It was a lovely late summer evening, fading blue sky streaked with pink. Soho looked as enticing as I had ever seen it; women dressed for the heat, men all brushed up and eager. The police were in an excellent mood, particularly the young one who had arrested me.

'He shoots, he scores!' he exulted, smacking a fist into a palm. 'Only been out ten minutes and . . . wham!'

At the station there was a moment when it looked as though I would be put in a cell but it passed and they sat me on a bench. I could have cheered. After a while, a silver-haired man with a lot of silver knobs on his lapels, a man with a lined face and tired eyes, sat down beside me. He held a piece of paper in his hands. He was looking at it, frowning. I knew what he was seeing. Caution for this. Caution for that. Conviction for A. Conviction for B. Conviction for C. (Conviction for C: Theft of a 300-tonne crane barge, the *Robin Hood*. Pled guilty, small fine. It was an accident. Nathan and I were trying to rescue a rugby ball from a river. We did not mean to untie both mooring ropes, only one. We had had rather too much vodka.)

'So. What do you do, Mr Clare?'

'I'm a journalist.'

'Who do you work for?'

'Uh, I'm freelance.' Whatever happened, I was going to keep my employers out of this. 'I've been working steadily for five years, though.'

'I see. Looking at this . . .' I looked at my feet, as he pursed his lips and twisted them to one side. 'You had a few wild years, bit of a bad time, and you've been good since then, is that right?'

'Yes, yes, exactly.'

'How much cannabis did you have on you?'

'About ten quid's worth.'

'Where did you get it?'

'Brixton.'

'OK. I'm going to give you a caution and let you go. You've been lucky. And you've learned a lesson. Don't smoke drugs in Soho. We don't care what you do at home, but not in Soho, right?'

Oh, the relief. It swept me like a warm wave, it was physical, I felt it blush through my muscles like heroin.

'Right. Yes. Thank you.'

★

Ten minutes later I was back in the restaurant. My friends were on pudding. There was a derisory cheer as I appeared. I explained what had happened, mortified. They already knew. They had guessed the whole story. They shook their heads and called me an idiot. I looked around the table. There was Lara, from Canada, my first girlfriend, and her fiancé, who seemed very clean and was being carefully nice to me. There was Nate from California, who had passed through dope and alcohol to anti-depressants and therapy: the first of us, then, to get that far. There was Robin, a stoner and drinker, now suffering periodic and terrible depression, and Toby, moderate in all things except when he was drinking. There was Antonia, who had taken God-knew how many drugs. She was quite manic but one felt she might always have been so. There was Marco, an Italian, svelte and cool as midnight, a stoner. Kevin, former stoner, from Ohio, now living in San Francisco, also in therapy and probably on pills. There was Kjetl, Norwegian, a titanic drinker, addicted to snus, the tobacco and ground-glass composite certain Scandinavians stuff between their gums and lips.

Beyond them, against the blur of the restaurant, I imagined the ranks of faces of all my friends, and I knew what they had all taken and roughly how much, and something of what it had done to them. So many faces, all colours, creeds, classes, nationalities, with nothing but our intake and our time in common. Most damaged, some prospering. And there was me. Officially declared clear, minutes ago, of my wild years. They shook their heads and smiled. I loved them, with huge gratitude for their forbearance and understanding. But none of them knew how bad, how wild, the consequences of the wild years were. And as I sat there, laughing, blushing and finishing the wine with them, I did not know either. All this time, blundering along, I had not really seen it. If I had stopped then I might not have seen it. I wish had stopped then, but I did not. Perhaps I was never going to stop until I had no choice.

Mania, Psychotic Episode, Manic High, Bipolar: we have a lexicon for it now, a glossary of mental health which has come with advances in medicine and psychiatry, as so many advances have come, from America. In September 1996 while I was starting in Devon, the

Guardian reprinted a piece from *Cosmopolitan*, 'a guide to getting to grips with shrink-speak' which was then beginning to become widely popular here, along with shrinks. I had heard Ben speak of 'issues' in the eighties, always with a grin. By the time I walked out of my father's house in 1997 I had assimilated the idea and was demanding the manifestation of 'unconditional love'.

A decade later 'dysfunctional' and 'passive-aggressive' are part of mainstream vocabulary. Tackling 'behavioural disorders' through being 'pro-active' is government policy. All these terms are in the *Cosmo / Guardian* guide but it has taken them more than ten years to filter into the ways we think. It is therefore not surprising that I did not know what it was when it hit me. Indeed, you have absolutely no idea what it is when it strikes and you do not care. You are having far too much fun and you have much too much to think about. You have never felt better in your life: what is all the fuss?

I had taken a couple of months off from work to write. I was happy, but jumpy. I never started smoking because I was miserable and wanted to hide, but rather because I was content or excited and wanted to celebrate, to make happiness stretch a little, to deepen and broaden its cloth. So I had one or two joints. I felt fine. And then I had more, and played Dylan, and sang along, and played the Pogues, and danced in my room, and told myself that was fine: if I wrote in the mornings with a clear head I could have a joint in the afternoons. Writers have a drink at lunchtime, do they not, some of them? Well then.

When the evening came I settled down with the computer or a book, and a joint, and tapped away. No harm there: if it is gibberish you can delete it tomorrow. But at three in the morning I am still there, and still smoking. And instead of slowing me down it seems to speed me up. Suddenly I am interested in new things.

Clothes, why have I never been interested in clothes before? I start wearing a leather jacket and an Ethiopian scarf and swaggering like a knight. I am a knight. All my male friends are knights. Look at their armour, see how much it says about them, look at their faces, imagine them in helmets and chain mail, imagine them if they had lived five hundred years ago, Sir Robin, Sir Toby and Sir Chris! I giggle wildly, then my attention darts to something else. There is a jewellery shop on a street near where I live. I stare in at the window, bewitched. Jewellery: how could I have missed it? Such an intricate, complex art, full of history and travel and treasure, an art as old as mankind, talismanic, occult, full of symbols. Now I notice jewellery on people and study it like an anthropologist reading the markings of a tribe. What does that ring mean? What do the materials mean? Where does that necklace come from, what story attaches to it? I would like to make jewellery. I would love to make jewellery. I will: I start collecting things which might be useful. I buy a book about gold. I make friends with the jeweller and buy a little tool and commission all sorts of things from him. He is very easy with me, patient, and takes no notice at all, but I am on to something else now: tobacconists! Why have I never thought about that before, the different rolls and blends of tobacco? How stupid I have been, just buying their poison and sucking it down, thoughtlessly. I start trying different blends of tobacco, rolled with filters. You do not have to take things as they are, you see, you can customize everything, with a little invention and imagination you can make everything fit, somehow, fit, it is very important that everything fits, because everything can be just so, ought to be, really, the world is a trove of bits and they all have their place, if you see what I mean – do you? Do you see what I mean? In a corner shop, buying tobacco, my gaze catches on the rack of miniature bottles of spirits. Miniatures! How beautiful they are, how beguiling! Look at their lovely little shapes, their gorgeous colours! They're worth having just for the bottles. And so cheap, really, aren't they? 'I'll have a miniature Captain Morgan, and a little Jamieson, and a little Martel, and three little vodkas, please.'

'I was a barman once, you see, quite a good one,' I tell the shopkeeper, and he nods and smiles, how nice it is to make people smile, what a nice man, I could hug him, and what a waste, not to use those bar skills. I bet I could have taken them further, I bet I could have invented some really amazing cocktails, there is so much I have forgotten, not done and not tried but it is all coming back, it is all coming now. Everything you have been is everything you are and really you have to keep it all alive, you have to use it all, you have to do everything well and at the same time. God, it's thirsty work all this thinking, exhausting, all this life! I drink the contents, hoard the bottles and buy more miniatures, miniatures by the score. I press them on confused friends. I rattle around my room, eye lighting on . . . lighting! Lighting is so important. I buy lots of lights and experiment with different combinations, as you have to, you have to think about it, pay close attention, because lighting makes atmosphere and atmosphere makes spirit and spirit makes mind and mind, mind is all!

Passing a model shop I stop dead. I used to love that, as a child. Why have I let it go? I dash in and gaze at all the kits. They are beautiful things, with their Biggles scenes painted on the lids, and they are homage too, aren't they, to the brilliant designers of the Blom und Voss flying boat, and the Sunderland flying boat, what amazing machines, and here they are collecting dust, no one is interested any more they're all too busy playing computer games but I am, I am very interested! Now why have I come in here? Something told me I ought to come in here – listen to it – think – there is a reason – there is always a reason – they are beautiful though – they use models in films, don't they, or they did, they did in *Star Wars* – films! That's it, films! I will make a flying boat and I will use it as a prop in a film. Films! I never did make that film. I buy two flying boat kits and model torpedo boat, because you cannot not really, what on earth is better than a torpedo boat? And so cheap! And now we need paints and brushes and glue, all this lovely, antiquated, useful stuff, and let's rush back to my room to put the kits together and plan the film and start working on the script, quick! Quick! Time is so precious and I have wasted so much time.

I pound out a script for a spoof James Bond and buy a video camera, because you have to start somewhere, and ring up friends who I want to cast. My old friend Richard the actor from university is doing very well. Maybe he will help, I'm sure he'll love to help, I can see him already, I know just the part for him and it will be so much fun making it – oh will we ever have a laugh! – and he'll do such a beautiful job and at the end he'll say well done Horace and I'll hug him and I'll say thank you so much dear Richard I know it seemed a bit mad at the time but you trusted me didn't you and we did it, didn't we, didn't we do it well? I ring him up. I ring everyone up. All these people I love, their names listed in my phone, and

I never see them! I never even speak to them! I have been so blind and lazy and stupid, thank God I'm awake now.

'All right, Horace, mate. Of course I'll do anything, you know that. Just send me the script.'

'Thank you, dear Richard, thank you so much! I'll send it soon I promise, you're going to love it!'

I will set the film in Algeria. Algeria! An Algerian hotel porter in Paddington tells me about the French exploding nuclear bombs in the desert in the sixties.

'People are still dying from it and no one cares,' he says.

I do. I care. I study books about Algeria, buy detailed maps, ring people I know who have contacts in north Africa and start planning a trip. My friend from Newcastle is working on the *Sun*. I ring him up.

'. . . and just imagine it, Tom, no one's ever really got the story, a few pages in a few books but basically it's the French testing their nukes in the desert and people are still dying and apparently the sand was turned to glass we could get pictures and everything. And maybe we could get the French to talk? Maybe the Algerian government will talk, they'll have to say something, won't they? Well that's what I'm going to do anyway, that's the plan, I know a guy who runs camel trips into the Sahara and another guy who says he might be interested, and no one goes to Algeria, do they? Right there on our doorstep and all that suffering and we ignore it – and it's a great story! – what do you think?'

'I'm not really sure what you want, and I can't really understand what you're saying.'

'Ha ha! Look, don't worry I'll get on with this and I'll call you when I've got something.'

'OK . . .'

There are hardly enough hours in the day to fit it all in but I will fit it in, I will. Stopping for meals is a bore but I am interested in cooking. Cooking is wonderful. I cook like a demon, buying all sorts of ingredients I have never tried and hurling random combinations into a huge pot.

And then it goes further. Suddenly I cannot bear to throw things away. Every object seems to have a further use. I become a manic recycler but I am not gathering things in order to have the council take them away, I am gathering them because they all have existences, essences, uses, if only you can hang on to them until their purpose suggests itself. Bottle tops for jewellery or collage (I am into collage, I have made one from a tabloid picture of a model called Sophie Anderton and lots of copper wire, silver staples and beads: I have given her earrings and a necklace and bracelets and an amulet and she looks wonderful and rather frightening, a totemic sort of Jezebel, I say hello Sophie to her when I come in and goodbye Sophie to her when I go out) and because once you have a few bottle tops you might as well have a few more to build a collection and matchboxes in case I find a match, bottles because you can always use bottles, broken pens and lighters because you can fix them or cannibalize them, discarded television aerials because they will probably still work, newspapers because every one seems to have an article or a picture I want to keep, old radios (I am obsessed with radios, I need to keep up with the news all the time, I take a radio with me in all the taxis I am taking now that I am busy so that I never miss anything, I never go out without dozens of things in case I need them), old razors for the blades, pins for the colours, pen tops for the pens, bits of wire, beads, feathers, keys with no locks, padlocks with no keys, broken toys, buttons, dead batteries (if you warm them on a radiator they come back to life), bits of wood, discarded CDs, cheap DVDs (because they are a bargain and because watching one stoned is the only time my brain actually seems to switch off) and cartons and boxes to keep all this stuff in . . . My room looks extraordinary, a tangled reef of strange shapes, bright colours: all this beautiful, useful, suggestive loot.

It goes further. Objects start to speak to me, not literally but clearly, as though each thing carries a freight of inference. Pound coins, for example. What a life a coin leads. How magical it is, how miraculous that they come to you, crossing your palm, just now, at this instant, just here, linking your path to others: you are suddenly physically connected, in the press of metal in your fingers, with other lives. Distant people, people you will never know, maybe people you do or will, dead people, unborn people perhaps. How amazing it would be to have a map of the journey of a coin, through time and space, with all its owners marked. They asked me to write a story like that once, at primary school, now I think of it, but what a thing that would be, a map of chance and fate. Imagine you could see it in the coin, or feel it like a clairvoyant – listen! You can almost hear the voices it has heard. A thing as mundane as a coin *and it could unlock the universe!* Like these, this gleaming Irish coin like real gold and this Scottish one and this beautiful Welsh coin with a dragon on it. Dragons are lucky! I never ignore a symbol now. I hoard the dragons and check my change for shamrocks which I will use for pool (the luck of the Irish) and drink a lot of Guinness because it is good for you and it seems good for the skin, too. And you can drink it in a special way and feel wonderful for hours, pumped up for all the things you have to do.

A friend witnesses a typical morning from this period.

'You said I'm going to go out and buy breakfast, do you want some, and I said sure, that would be nice. After an hour you hadn't come back. After an hour and a half, lunchtime, I thought oh well and went to the pub, and there you were, with a packet of bacon in a bag, eating a tomato like an apple and drinking Guinness with a raw egg in it! And you were saying it's great, it's great, you should try it! The landlady said, is he all right? I said yeah, he's just a bit mad at the moment.'

My girlfriend and her friends and I are going to see a play. I arrive at the interval with a cup of magic mushroom tea in case they want some and my girlfriend looks down from a terrace and sees me sitting outside washing my hands in Guinness. She comes down to me with her friends. They decline the mushroom tea. I can see the pain and worry in her face but I cannot quite understand it. What is there to worry about? What harm am I doing? I am just interested in a lot of things and trying to make up for lost time and maybe I am not behaving in quite the same way as everyone else, but who says that is wrong?

'I'm really worried about you, H,' she says.

'Don't be!' I say, with increasing anger each time it comes up.

What has got into everyone? Why are they looking at me like that? I go back to my room, my universe of signs and symbols, my secret totems and touchstones. For nights and nights I do not sleep, crashing out eventually around four or five when the robin outside my window begins to sing, only to leap up again, a few hours later, ready to go again.

Sometimes it is very frightening, late at night. It starts when I imagine all the good things I could do. I could work harder and make better radio programmes when I go back to work. I could write a good book. I could make a good film, marry a good woman, make her happy, raise good children. God, if there is a God, wants me to do these productive things. And the Devil, if there is a Devil, wants me to have another cigarette, another joint, because they will stop me doing good and make me die. It is like converting to Calvinism in a flash. Suddenly every action, however tiny, every thought, however unformed, is a step along a cliff top, a teetering between grace and sin. And if sin exists and grace exists and the Devil exists and God exists then they are all here, now. The Devil is in the bathroom! I go crashing into the bathroom, fists clenched, laughing fearfully, knowing there is nothing in there except the tailor's dummy belonging to my landlady which I have thrown into the bath, but half expecting some monstrous black and scaly thing, darkly shining, bloodied claws outstretched.

'Good. You stay in there, you,' I tell the dummy. Then there is a noise from outside the window and I whirl around, terrified.

We go to Wales for the weekend to see my mum with Michael the Marsh Harrier, as I call him now, my friend from York. After dinner, when my mother has gone to bed, I put on a party.

'I know what, let's put on our best clothes! I'll put my suit on, Michael, I've got a suit for you – and you've got a dress haven't you, love?'

'O-K,' Michael grins slowly. 'Are we allowed to ask why?'

'It'll be great! Let's look our best!'

So we all get changed. We look smashing. In a small living room in the middle of the night somewhere in the depths of Wales, we are dressed for Monte Carlo.

'Fantastic! That's what we want, a bit of class. Now, let's have a drink . . .'

I raid the shelves for everything and the cupboard for one each of all the mismatched glasses. I arrange the glasses on a bookshelf and fill them all with something. Vodka, gin, whisky, lager, a Welsh version of Bailey's, stout, red wine, white wine, port, sherry, Drambuie, and a shot glass full of olive oil.

'Now, we all have to drink one of everything!'

We do, though my girlfriend refuses the olive oil.

'Now let's dance!'

My girlfriend taught me to dance the Charleston that night, to the faster of Paul Simon's songs.

Watching her, imitating her then doing it with her, I caught the rhythm of it and it actually worked, for a moment or two, she in her beautiful black dress, me in my suit, our hands dancing, feet flashing, and Michael clapping and cheering, 'Yes, that's it! Yes!'

Why deny the obvious, child, why deny the ob-vious . . . Paul Simon sang, and for as long as it lasted it was perfect: love, movement, rhythm and joy, as though these two I trusted had trusted me and come with me into this place, this haphazard, truant place, as though we could all feel it together, this thing I had been trying to find and longing to show and share, as though I was a serially failed conjuror at last whipping away a veil to reveal real magic, and this wonderful woman had responded, conjuring this dance in answer as if she were casting a spell, as if love, movement, rhythm and joy were silver balls, and we could throw them to each other around the little room.

I could not sleep afterwards. When the light came I poked a microphone out of the window and recorded the dawn chorus. My girlfriend and I went for a dawn walk, or rather, I insisted on going for a walk and she came with me despite her exhaustion, keeping an eye on me as I strode ahead in a long coat, brandishing an air rifle for no reason. The next day we went canoeing in a rough, shallow stream. Michael and I did it in bow ties.

My friends looked it up on NHS Direct, a website of symptoms and ailments. This is what it said: 'Being happy, elated or euphoric. Talking very quickly. Feeling full of energy. Feeling full of self-importance. Feeling full of "great" new ideas and having "important" plans. Being easily distracted. Being easily irritated or agitated. Not sleeping. Not eating. Doing lots of pleasurable things which often have disastrous consequences – e.g. spending lots of money which you cannot afford. Increased libido.'

Bipolar disorder.

I had the full set. I did not do much about the last: just enough. I flirted with someone, not for sex but for pleasure, excitement and affection, which was more than enough to hurt my girlfriend and convince her, after weeks of this madness, that she should leave. It happened in Soho, in the rain. She told me over dinner, and again over drinks, but I would not take it in. We set off to the tube station. Suddenly I stopped.

'Look at that! Amazing!'

A shiny stalk of metal, twisted and bowed, the remains of an exotic lamp stand in a heap of rubbish thrown out of a fashion shop.

'Put it down, H,' she said.

'No way, are you kidding? It's wonderful. Just the thing. I'm taking it home.'

'Please put it down, H,' she begged.

'No!'

'Don't you understand? I'm leaving you.'

'Well, if that's what you want to do.'

'Of course it's not what I want to do!'

'Don't then, come home with me.'

'No, because you won't stop and I can't go on like this.'

'Stop what?'

And so she left. And I loved her. I burned the pain with marijuana and doused the loss in rum. In a two-month spree I did not give myself a second to look it in the eye. Captain Morgan became my wrestling partner. Every time he had the upper hand I tripped him over a joint. When anyone asked I said it was miserable but right. We were not meant to be, I said. She'll be better off . . .

It is like carrying the mark of Cain. People can see it, can almost smell it on you: it is reflected and compounded by the expressions in their eyes as they look at you. Assessing, curious, wary and instinctively repelled, as though madness is catching and they want no part of it. You talk and they say you are babbling, talking too fast. You think aloud and they look amused or confused, or frightened. You make a suggestion – let's do this, or that, or . . . and they back away, angry and upset. They try to tell you how you come across and now you are angry and upset. You try to govern yourself, to slow down, but you cannot.

Toby came to see me. He sat at my desk surrounded by my piles of coloured rubbish and half-made models and asked me again if I really was all right, and shouldn't I go and see someone?

'I'm fine!'

'You don't seem fine.'

'Well, I'm miserable because I've just been dumped and I'm stoned, but apart from that . . .'

'Well, I really think you should see someone but it's up to you, of course.'

Then Chris came, in his white shirt and smart tie with his motor-cycle helmet under his arm, like a very upmarket paramedic. He had a look in his eye which his colleagues must have seen at work, a thoughtful, careful, problem-solving look. He tried a Samaritans approach first.

'What do you think is wrong?'

'Nothing really . . .'

So we did that for a while. Then he said: 'OK, what do you think you could do about it?'

'Well, obviously I should stop smoking dope, get drunk, cry about my lost relationship, throw up, feel better, move on . . .'

After a bit of this he said, gently, 'Look, supposing you are bipo-lar or manic depressive or whatever. It's a condition, and if you don't treat it it will get worse, and the hardest thing about it is admitting you have it, that must take huge courage, huge courage, but once you do admit it there are well-established, practical ways of managing it.'

'Lithium.'

'Well, whatever. The point is you need to see a doctor.'

'I don't want to see a doctor!'

'Look, tomorrow, or as soon as you make the appointment I'll come with you. Whatever time it is, doesn't matter. You don't have to do anything, you don't have to take anything, just let's go and see someone – and talk.'

'Talk about what? I don't know what I would say.'

'Just what you are feeling.'

'I feel fine!'

'H! You're not fine!' He wants to shake me. He clenches his fists in frustration.

'Do you honestly think I'm bipolar?'

'*Yes*, H! Yes.'

'OK, look, here's what I think. I have had some mad episodes, definitely. Obviously! I mean look at my flipping record. But they have never come, the madness has never come, and the depression has never come without drugs. Always the same – take drugs, act mad, stop drugs, get depression, get better, take drugs. So this is the deal. I'm going to stop the drugs, for good. If it ever comes back, out of a clear blue sky, then I will go and see a doctor and take the pills and do whatever they say. But until I am sure I am not going to do it.'

He sat back and shook his head.

'I think you should go and see someone.'

'Why? What's wrong with that?'

'It's not necessarily the drugs. You might be taking the drugs in response to the symptoms. Self-medicating.'

'No way. I was never manic before the drugs.'

He looks doubtful.

'Well, come on, Wilson, how long have we known each other? I wasn't manic at college. I was never manic.'

'St Etienne.'

'We smoked dope in St Etienne! And you were as bad as me!'

I was terrified of the doctors and terrified of the label. Once they pin that on you, I thought, you have had it. Diagnosed Manic Depressive. 'Oh, he's Manic Depressive,' they will say. And then it will be on your medical records, on your employment records, on your ID card one day, on your electronic passport for all we know. How is that going to look on my CV, alongside the criminal record? How is that going to play when it comes to BBC selection boards? I would rather be just another nutter. And there was something much more frightening about drugs someone else prescribes and controls than drugs you take yourself. Drugs that were meant to mess you up, that were known anecdotally or directly by your friends I could handle. Drugs that were supposed to make you better but might mess you up on the side, drugs you had to keep taking indefinitely, drugs given to you by someone who is not taking them, powerful, fundamentally altering drugs that had been through clinical trials, that were manufactured by pharmaceutical giants, which had unpredictable side-effects, some requiring further drugs to counteract them: I did not have the guts for those.

At Christmas that year the mania ran out, around the time I finished the latest batch of dope and did not go for more. The mania left and took half of me with it. It took my ideas and inspirations first, then my words, so that I could barely speak a line. Then it took my optimism and my hope, then my momentum, all my energy. It took my confidence and my clarity. It took my interests and my appetite. It took my comfort: I went for walks up the hills and could see nothing beautiful, only a strange figure, stumbling over tussocks, head down or staring around, blankly panicked. It took my horizons away. My mother and brother treated me carefully. They could see things were not right but we all knew there was nothing they could do. They had wanted me to go and see someone and I had refused. I was still refusing: not because I thought nothing was wrong, now, but because I knew everything was. I thought they would be bound to section me.

I looked at everything I had written and saw rubbish. I deleted it all. I stared at all my treasure and saw rubbish. I remembered snatches of things I had said, the random telephone calls, the vital ideas, all the plans: all rubbish. Grimacing, as if the boxfuls of junk were the deposits of some wild animal which had been nesting in my room, I binned the kits and the models and closed the film script. I thought of my ex-girlfriend and the girl I had been seeing. Several times an hour I stopped suddenly, struck by a thought, by a memory, wincing at it, groaning or cursing if I was alone. Oh God, what have I done,

I thought, hour after hour. I lay awake at night, sticky in the sheets, as though the mania was sweating out of me, staring at the parade again, the trudging parade, stretching all the way back to university and beyond.

Your mind runs away from you: you think the most terrible things. You look at all you love and see it broken. You look at people you love and see them hurt, damaged, in pain. You think things no one should ever think: as if your mind is hunting for the worst, most horrific things that could happen, then tilting the thoughts, imagining you did them, showing you doing them. I have seen myself commit atrocities.

If my thought dreams could be seen, they'd probably put my head in a guillotine, but it's alright Ma, it's life and life only . . . sings Dylan.

I could barely stand it and did not have much time: the depression would be debilitating very soon and I had to go back to work. At least I had a job to go back to. I dreaded to think what would have happened if I had hit the mania at work. And I needed the money, too. I had thrown away thousands and thousands of pounds.

I woke and felt the fell of dark, not day. Going to work with depression is much harder than going stoned. You have failed to dress properly, wearing a weird assortment again, half of it dirty or damp, because you have not organized your washing. You have showered but you are sure you smell. The mirrors in the lift show you how frightened you are, how strange and how dislikeable. You squirm in meetings, fighting panic and fear. You cannot think of anything. You cannot remember anything. The material of your chair seems to prickle against your back, horribly warm and scratchy through your shirt. You gaze in amazement at your colleagues: how clever they are, how good their memories are, how quick and funny they can be. And you sit there, a sweating statue, feeling your burdened presence eating the joy and optimism out of the air. Radio production is full of pressure, chance and things that go wrong: you need to be quick and calm, and to live easily with your nerves. But now I am not and I cannot. It demands good judgement and strong ideas but I am empty and insecure. Instead I work late, day after day, trying to nail things down, trying to take chance out of it. Minor setbacks feel like disasters. I make my programmes in my dreams and wake up to find I have to do them again. My colleagues see my stony face and think I am angry or frustrated, but I am not. I am frightened.

It is both worse and better than before because I cannot hide away with it in a student room. I take it to work and try not to fall apart in public. And I am not alone with it: my girlfriend comes back. She helps to carry it and helps to carry me, and what I have done to us. And I am not alone in it. I can recognize it on other people, as quickly and as certainly as the smell of the cells. The terror and the misery behind the mask, the 'seeming a bit down', the 'acting a bit weird lately': it is much more widespread than the statistics indicate because so many of us do not confess it. It is probably in every office and street in the land. They say it is becoming more common.

It lasts three months: by the end of the third I feel like a recovering addict on day release, walking a narrow line.

Robin is glad to have me back: he shied away from my mania. He and Toby told me to stop dope and to 'see someone' so many times that there was no point repeating it. He waited for me to surface and welcomed me when I did. He owns a narrowboat: further evidence, in my eyes, that everyone in my circle has handled life better than I. (I own nothing but books and an old and beautiful Citroën.) He does not agree. The boat causes him endless worry and expense.

It is strange to find ourselves where we are, as we sit smoking in the narrow cabin, confronted with ourselves in each other. Seeing him always reminds me of how invincible we felt, how mighty we were, and though I know he still is mighty, he does not believe it. Even after all this, he still believes me capable of things I am not at all sure I can do: making a good life with someone, settling down, earning a steady living. We have more confidence in each other than in ourselves.

We listen to Nina Simone. *Oh-oh child, things are gonna get easier, oh child, things'll be brighter . . . One day we'll walk together in a beautiful sun, one day when the world is much lighter . . .*

Robin has survived black depression. He looked hunted when it was on him, would not easily meet your eye, would quietly talk about it when pressed, simply, relating the surface conditions but only hinting at the depths. If you did not know him well you would never have been able to tell. In company he is always ebullient, apparently confident, witty and outgoing. He confronted the monster in ways I did not dare.

'I know you're suspicious of anti-depressants,' he says, 'but they really helped me. They helped me work and function. Otherwise I could not get out of bed. I could not do anything.'

He went from having no job to having four: as well as voluntary work he teaches at a special school, he lectures and he paints, excelling in all. He tells miserable stories in the funniest way. Of instant despair at the first beep of the alarm clock. Of fear of the post, of bills. Of hearing yourself talk, and knowing it's bullshit, of seeing the way people look at you and being sure they think you are mad, lost and bluffing. Of only ever being one step ahead of the black dog, of feeling that if you trip over the merest thing it will be on you. Of dealing with the Inland Revenue when you are absolutely broke.

'You have to be really, really stupid. And completely helpless,' he explains. He assumes a kind of wailing tone: ' "I've just been really, really stupid, I've been so stupid, I'm so, *sooo sorry*. You have to under-stand – I can't do *anything*, it makes me panic, I don't *understand* it, I don't understand *anything*, I haven't got *any* money, if you want to send the bailiffs that's fine, absolutely fine, I haven't *got* anything anyway, I've been hiding your letters, I haven't *received* your letters in fact – I can't think straight – I'm feeling really panicky! I don't know who I am any more – hang on, who – who are – who is this? *Are you my mum?*"

' "Er no, Mr Jenkins, this is the tax office."

' "Oh thank God! *H-e-e-help meee!*" . . .and then they're really nice.'

We talk about the drugs. 'Well,' he says, 'four of my friends died from drugs. Three from heroin, one from acid.'

'And if you knew then what you know now?'

He shakes his head. 'I can't believe people who say they wouldn't change anything if they could do it all again. I would change so much. I'd do almost everything differently.'

'Do you think dope was the problem?'

'Yes, up to a point. I think it was always there, the tendency, but . . . I'm not denying dope played a massive part in it. We know it did.'

★

Maria is living with her parents, keeping busy. 'When I let myself stop and think, the spiral starts,' she says. 'I'm so tired of being careful!' she exclaims. She is desperate to rejoin the world but she has to nurse herself, to handle herself gently. 'They did not give us enough to do,' she says of university, 'but we were idle and immature.' I asked her if she thought dope was partly responsible for her predicament. 'Oh yes, unquestionably,' she said, surprised that I had to ask. She had a two-year head start on me with dope, having smoked in her sixth form. I think those two clean years at the International School may have saved me, giving my brain a little more time, before I began to batter it.

Nathan eventually quit the Ministry of Agriculture, Fisheries and Food. He writes songs and practises, but no longer with George: they do not do gigs now. George is not easily persuaded to leave the house. Nathan trained to be a tree surgeon. He loved it, though he claimed to be scared of heights. Now he is a tree inspector. He has a strong relationship with his girlfriend, and many friends. I went to see them. Instead of taking acid, drinking vodka, eating road-killed geese, pounding up dope stalks, scoring eighths of hash or stealing boats we spent most of the day in York Minster, just looking, like everyone else. We laughed at the old stories. Two friends of his were crossing the ring road on acid. Halfway over one of them decides he is an orange. He curls up in the middle of the carriageway. Disaster! Except the other one is simultaneously struck by the conviction that he is Superman. Palm raised with absolute authority, backed by a body of indestructible steel, he stops the traffic. Then the guy I heard about working in a hotel kitchen on ecstasy, called upon to prepare a fruit salad.

'No, I won't do it.'

'What, why not?'

'I can't kill the banana!'

We laugh and laugh and shake our heads.

Christian is a facilities manager for a large institution in London. He had to conceal half his academic record in order not to appear overqualified for the job. Michelle is still in Torpington, still smoking. Wangechi is a highly successful artist, becoming famous, living in

Brooklyn. When I saw her recently we talked about our last encounter. I had forgotten quite how boorish and mad I had been: I had blanked out my most repellent behaviour. As she talked it all came back. I writhed and winced. In the end she accepted my humiliated apology, graciously. 'You didn't understand that they [New Yorkers like her housemate whom I insulted] thought I was a freak,' she said. 'I was only just clinging on. And then this lunatic turns up, challenging everyone, practically picking fights, saying he's my friend!'

Chris, Theo and Toby have done well. They all have happy relationships: Chris is married, Theo is married with one son; Toby has a son and a daughter. They all made money. It may not be a coincidence that they were the least dreamy of us, the most realistic. It may not be a coincidence that they took the fewest drugs.

Chris has reached a stage of unimpeachable respectability.

'I've been shouting at the police recently,' he says.

'What?'

'I saw two of them, community police officers, with their hands tucked into their flak jackets. "Are we cold, officers?" I said. Then there was a policewoman with her hands in her pockets. I said, "Er, excuse me, are you a traffic warden?" "No," she said. "Metropolitan Police." I said, "Right, it's just that with your hands in your pockets . . ." Ha! You should have seen her jump. It reminds them of their training college.'

He goes to public debates, where he speaks from the floor. He attends political meetings. He is involved.

Jane met a lovely man, warden of an island off the Welsh coast. They have a daughter and the stewardship of six hundred pairs of puffins. They plan to move to Shetland.

I vowed to stop the dope in 2004. One of my dreams came true: I was offered a book contract. My poor novel is still unpublished but it did get me an agent, and taught me enough to write a better book. I slipped once since, in the euphoria of publication, and fell into dope for a couple of months: long enough to lose the girl I loved, again and for good. I did not want to write about it. This is not a book about love. But I promised to tell the truth.

★

Paddling her through a tunnel on the Regent's Canal, in our first days, the water reeking and poison black, tampons, syringes and invisible rats eddying around the canoe, things turning just below the unseen surface, a summer evening the size of a coin ahead of us, I sang to her, though I do not sing well, sang low but with all the music I had.

It was Christmas Eve babe
In the drunk tank

Singing it all into existence, that hot, hot summer, and holding her feet the first time she came to supper. I could not have known: she said I just love it, it makes me feel so safe. I'll marry the man who'll hold my feet all night. Right! I said. All joy and intent! It sounded easy. Just hold her feet all night and marry her, make this love complete, answer this, this wonderful question, this possibility, with all completeness, and all and all will be well.

An old man said to me, I won't see another one

Slowly slowly catchy eely, I texted – she was an eel, you see.
Slowly slowly eely decides! she sent back.

And then he sang a song
The Rare Old Mountain Dew

And our amazing expeditions, from Soho in the rain that night to Marseilles, and all those hotels I could not afford, and her motto: maximize, maximize! And the way she taught me always to go on just a bit further, all the way to the end, just to see what's there. And our normal evenings, a bit of old chicken in the fridge: we laughed and hugged. It's all I need really, we said, a bit of old chicken and you.

I turned my face away
And dreamed about you

At night I held her and when I turned over she said sadly oh, you're going away. I'm not going away darling, I always said. I put my feet on hers, or held them between mine. I tried like that.

Got on a lucky one
Came in eighteen to one
I've got a feeling
This year's for me and you

And her joy, the way she jumped and whirred, and her thinking look as she pulled her hair as if searching for split ends, frowning through to the sudden clearing, the decision, almost always right.

So Happy Christmas
I love you baby
I can see a better time
When all our dreams come true

You donkey, she said, when I got it wrong – no, donkey! With such affection. She loved donkeys. And owls, and capers. I like a caper, she said. And peas. Does a wonderful impression of a pea on a fork. And our mornings. What a beautiful day! I said, at a soft grey rainfall, and she touched me. You've taught me to see beauty like that, she said.

The boys of the NYPD choir
Were singing Galway Bay
And the bells were ringing out
For Christmas Day

She kept things in boxes, so many boxes. Whenever she loses anything – have you tried looking in a box? I shout, Yes! she shouts, or oh bugger off, you. I love those jokes, the ones you can roll from one room to another, hearing the laughter in the other's voice.

I could have been someone
Well so could anyone

The way she made cards and never forgot to send one. The way she cleaned up for the cleaner because she thought it wrong not to. The boxes were full of treasure, beautiful things from all the countries in the world she had seen, saved up for her life to come. The first time we broke up she did the Trans-Siberian alone, in the depths of winter.

You took my dreams from me
When I first found you

And then together again. And in the open at work: three years it took some of them to see it. She was always so professional about work, though that was not all the reason we hid it. More a shyness, and her not wanting to be asked where I was. I love working with her, said someone who did not know about us, because she's completely calm and there's nothing she can't handle. I was never more proud. Two studies, we said. We'll have two studies.

I kept them with me babe

We were set fair, until I went away again. Hiding the dope from her, hiding the effect from her, thinking if I delay forty minutes I'll be late but it will have worn off a bit, I'll be able to act straight. Tearing something away from her, to gorge on it myself. How that must have hurt.

I put them with my own

I was wearing a canoe helmet in our room in the guest house in the middle of Wales, where they seemed to love us, the way the world sometimes loves lovers, and blowing up the second flotation bag, trying out the kit for our launch tomorrow, a week on the river and the happiest of my life, when she bashed me on the head suddenly with the other bag and I was speechless for love of her, so small in her helmet, starting a blow-up bag fight with me, with that gleeful challenge in her eely eye.

Can't make it all alone

And I thought I'll marry you, I'll marry you for ever, as I whacked her back, and I'll tell them all, when the time comes, this was the moment I knew it.

I've built my dreams around you

Of all the things I lost my love, God forgive me . . .

The boys from the NYPD choir

If I could have not hurt you.

Were singing Galway Bay

If I could have not lost you.

And the bells were ringing out

For Christmas Day.

I I

The Palace of Wisdom

L ONG BEFORE I saw him I heard rumours about Ben. 'He's on the wagon, you know,' someone said. 'He's given up.'

'What? Everything?'

'Not cigarettes.'

He is living and working in San Francisco now. He has a proper job: design director of a trendy magazine. After five years we met twice, the first time in London, on a cold sunny day in Sloane Square. Suddenly he is standing next to me, grinning, wearing shades. He is almost exactly the same, perhaps a little broader, filled out. We walk down the King's Road again and take a table at a café where the army barracks used to be.

We talk about rehab.

'You remember we used to joke about it!' I laugh. 'We figured you'd get free drugs and they'd feed you . . .'

'Uh huh. Well, I haven't had a drink or any drugs for two and a half years now . . .'

'What happened?'

'It all got to be too much, drinking and cocaine. Work said go and sort yourself out and my brother said he'd checked out a few places, a few good places, and I was thinking Christ, I thought I'd just go and walk in the woods for a few days . . . but no. And my other brother had hired an orange Mustang to drive me there. I felt such an ass.'

We order coffee and water and orange juice and salad, after a while, and chain-smoke.

'And you know you think you're special? Like you're fucked up in your very own individual way? But you're not. They have this book, dates back to the beginning of the AA, hundreds and hundreds of stories of all these people. And they're all your story. You read it and think well shit, looks like I'm just a number after all. And they know how it's going to go. They say: "On day three you'll think you're cured and you'll be ready to leave. But you're not." Sure enough . . .'

We sit at the table, surrounded by ladies who lunch and do not look at the price list, like two old soldiers discussing a war. We talk about who got injured, who was crippled, who died and who survived.

We talk about acid. After I was thrown out Ben got into it at school.

'The first time I took it it was so good I thought my God, this is all I want to do! I ended up, the last time, lying in a bath under a neon strip light in cold water thinking *I wish this would just stop*. I'd gone in there for *comfort*, you know,' he says, with a half-smile.

I do know. It is agonizing to imagine it.

'Why did we do it?'

'I dunno, some fascination with the dark side?'

We talk about not drinking. How it changes your social life (eradicates it at first) and saves you a fortune. He says it is not that hard. I cannot believe him.

'What do you do now, when you would have drunk?'

'Once in a while I stay up really late, watch shit TV, feel terrible the next day – that sort of thing. Walk by the ocean with my girlfriend. You know, they say don't deal in the past, it's all gone, and the future is imaginary. Be in the present. Watch the bird. Exist.'

He reports it dispassionately, not with the convert's earnestness nor the cynic's parenthesis. He means it literally: live in the moment, watch the bird, be happy with what is. How ironic it seems to me, as he talks, that a treatment counsellor should use watching a bird as an example. Bird watching was always one of my greatest pleasures, before drugs. We talk about self-sabotage. We grin. I tell him I think his strength is extraordinary.

'I feel embarrassed about it in a way,' he says quietly, 'like I was the one who went too far, couldn't handle it.'

'I feel that way about dope.'

The second time I meet Ben in San Francisco. On the last night we go out for a meal with friends. There is a party of young people in the bar, raucous and excited, they look like high school students. Gradually the reason for the party becomes clear. Two of them are going to Iraq tomorrow. I order beer, unthinking. Ben asks for water. He is obviously used to that moment when another's eyes flick over him, involuntarily guilty, lest we have tempted him, and curious, looking for an outward sign of struggle, a hint of denial, a ripple of the act of will. There is not even a flicker. How extraordinary, I think, to believe that destruction rests on the rim of every bottle, that a single sip contains an oblivion of cocaine, alcohol, breakdown, skid row and possibly death. What do I know about willpower, compared to this? I know nothing. He makes it look easy. He always made everything look easy.

I do not want the beer, I realize. Peer pressure is not about being seen to do the same thing as your friends so much as wanting to be in the same place as them.

Later we discuss my plans for the flight which leaves at dawn. I say I think I will go to the airport and sleep there. Ben is not convinced and we agree I will stay with him and get an early taxi. On the way home he says,

'It's a bit romantic but you're into all that. You should see this.'

He points the car up a series of hills, arriving eventually at the head of a steep cul-de-sac. We get out and climb up a rock outcrop. The whole of San Francisco is spread out in bright lights and dim shapes at our feet.

'My God, it's beautiful!'

'It's good, isn't it?'

We sit down. It is a warm night, soft air rises up the ridge on one side. The city glitters almost silently below. We argue about lights in the northern sky – stars or aeroplanes? He points out different districts – Cole Valley on one side, the Mission and the Castro on the other, SoMa and Market Street ahead, running downtown to the shining towers. Ships come slowly into the dark bay and Alcatraz flashes. As we talk, a bank of fog steals in from the Pacific, lower than the red lights on top of the Golden Gate.

We talk about school, about what we thought we were, about how we thought we fitted in. How he was a rebel, and I was a mad romantic, because those were things we could be, identities which suited us, which we could sustain.

'Remember jumping into that duck pond?' I laugh.

'I still can't believe we did that. We coulda been killed, paralysed at least. What were we thinking!'

We talk about our English class, and Blake.

'So can you explain about the wise man seeing not the same tree as the fool sees?' he asks. 'Are we just fools?'

'Well, it's like the road of excess leads to the palace of wisdom. We thought the pursuit of wisdom was an excuse for excess.'

'A requirement!'

'And wisdom was the thing to go for, but if we had been really wise we would not have needed to travel the road, do you think?'

'Mmm . . .'

'Maybe it's like that Calvinist idea of predestination. That some are born saved and some damned and all you can do is determine the nature of your damnation, like Hamlet.'

'So were we damned, then?'

'I don't know.'

'But not born wise, huh.'

'No. But Dante says the only way out of hell is straight through it. We've proved that!'

The fog sends a long finger in from the west but when it reaches City Hall it hesitates, hovers for a time and then divides itself into many thin bars, spreading in parallel southwards, towards us. We talk for hours, watching it all, the wide night, the fog and the city, as beautiful and perfect, from a little height and a little distance, as anything man can make. We talk about our fathers and about women. Vanessa Paradis comes up, somehow.

'Gad, Johnny Depp,' Ben murmurs. 'That man had all my women.'

We smoke fifteen cigarettes each, at least. The air changes, eventually, from a warm draught to a cooler one. Ben checks the time – 4.30 a.m.

'No idea it had gotten so late. We should go.'

'Yes.'

We get up and take a last look at the view. Some of the best minds of our generation are asleep down there, not far from their laptops, dreaming all our futures. Just before we leave Ben turns and picks all

his cigarette stubs out of a crack in the rock where he has been carefully hoarding them.

'Hell, Hardiman! I can't believe it – you're so good! I flicked all
mine away, like an idiot. I am sorry.'

'Yeah, well,' he says, 'we'll let you off. You're just a tourist,
after all.'

He is right: I have been just a tourist, after all. 'Hardcore!' we used
to say, impressed and slightly scared when someone overdid it. I am
not very hardcore. Many of my generation went much further into
excess, and into dope. Most handled it much better but many
destroyed their lives. Some died.

Some of the souvenirs of the journey I carry on my face: lots of
lines and tiny broken veins; smoker's skin; a burst capillary under one
eye; two suspicious little dots in one iris. Laughter lines. My teeth are
a mess. I try not to think about the damage to my lungs, heart and
arteries. I have an idea that my gaze used to be very open and that
now it is more guarded. There is a question in it. Not 'Can I trust
you?' so much as 'Can you trust me?' I have hidden so much. At one
time or another I have hidden or tried to hide all of this. I have told
a great many lies.

When I smell or see marijuana now I feel a little sick, partly with
nerves, partly with excitement. I turn it down. In the last year I had
two drags, on New Year's eve, but even that was over my limit. I am
not safe around it: I will never be.

I loved it once. The word is not too strong: I thought about it,
desired it, looked for it, hoarded stories in which it featured.
Throughout this long affair I still loved it, despite all it did to me and
those I love. I never blamed it. We never do. We leave that to the
squares, the puritans, the wholesome, moralizing killjoys who never
smoked a quarter of an ounce in a day and therefore do not really
know what they are talking about; certainly do not know dope as
we did.

I was always so grateful to my dealers. Many of them were friends:
they 'sorted me out', sold me what I craved, and I blessed them. The
people they bought it from I never met, nor the people above them.
I supposed, in a woolly way, that somewhere near the top of the tree

there were ruthless, possibly frightening people who trafficked all sorts of drugs, but if I ever imagined a professional dope dealer I pictured a cross between Robin Hood and Bob Marley, a merchant adventurer, a reggae-loving, bongo-playing anti-hero. Someone who took risks for us and grew rich: someone like that smiley, skanky Mr Nice, Howard Marks. Good luck to him, I would have said, setting him far above the tobacco barons, who were simply out to take as much of our money as they could before they killed us. We and our dealers were on the same side, surely? After all, anyone can grow it. The only difference between us and them was that they could be bothered, or were smart enough to ship it in. Surely they were like us, surely they were smoking it too? The tobacco barons, heroin traffickers and cocaine magnates are obviously the gangrene of humanity: but pot peddlers? They could not be the same breed of men, could they?

When they sold us stalks and seeds or cut the hash with shoe polish we were never angry with them. We shrugged. Times must be hard. There must be a drought. The pigs must have made a bust.

We heard they were experimenting with new, ever stronger strains; we heard they were looking for ways to make it more potent and addictive but we did not blame them. Was it not always our choice to smoke? They were just giving us what we wanted, all those kind, clever Mr Nices.

If we never blamed the dealers we certainly did not blame the drug. 'Herb . . .' I once heard a man say, with huge incredulity, 'is . . . a *plant!*'

He was dumbfounded that anyone should have it in for such a gentle, inoffensive thing. Less addictive than nicotine, not even as dangerous as alcohol! What a wonderful sales pitch that is. And what a supreme logo it has, that naughty little five or seven-leaved frond, with its wicked, jagged little leaves: pretty, organic, devilish cool. It must be approaching the brand recognition of McDonald's golden arches and Mickey Mouse. (And what have the other drugs got: a syringe? A rolled up banknote? A crack pipe? You do not see them on many hats, T-shirts, nose pins or earrings.)

Loveable cannabis! That funny, friendly, naughty green giant, hiding its cancers behind tobacco, concealing its madness and wastage behind correlations, minority adverse reactions, genetic predispositions, ignored evidence and 'mounting' incomplete research. The gentle opiate, which gives so much pleasure as it takes happiness away. Some of the most hopeful, pleasured, idealistic and – I felt at the time – inspired moments of my life happened alone in a small dim room, with nothing but a bag of weed and some music, conjuring up gorgeous illusions as my jobs, relationships and prospects fell apart outside.

Clever cannabis. They said it was more carcinogenic than tobacco but the stat that stuck was that it is less addictive than nicotine, much less: it is merely habit forming. Which makes it sound like a naughty lifestyle choice, like fat or sugar. But every salesman knows that a man's brain affords just as good a grip as his body. Coca-Cola has not been selling less since they stopped putting cocaine in it. The comparison with cigarettes does cannabis huge favours, but smoke forty joints a day and your mind and soul will be long, long gone by the time you hawk your lungs up.

Gentle cannabis. Not really in the same league as all those nasty killers further down the road: smack, crack, coke and crystal meth. Queen Victoria took it for her period pains. Hemp seeds are good for you. It has all sorts of medicinal properties. All the best people have tried it; in 1997 the great and the good signed the *Independent on Sunday*'s 'legalize it' petition in their hundreds. This is a soft drug!

Soft cannabis. Is it a gateway or a stepping stone? The debate is too boring for anyone to care how it ends. Cannabis has outlasted it. Cannabis is not a gateway so much as a huge signpost: kicks this way! Just step over the supine law and ignore the mumbling politicians and – oh, you have already. Cannabis, in its hazy, neither here nor there, they don't know what to do with it, no man's land / everyman's land, bridges the law. You could not conceive of a better way to lead people to the deathly summits of drugs than by blurring their foothills with this flowery, funky, ubiquitous little weed. Just illegal enough to seem naughty, just tolerated enough to seem safe. Our leaders and legislators could not have made marijuana more attractive to the young if they had tried.

It took so much from me, and from my kind. And it made vicious, callous people rich, from the dealers to those mischievous marketeers who sell the rolling paper. You see it advertised on bus shelters:

'Rizla – It's what you make of it.' Wink wink. There is only one thing you can make of it: something you suck on and die from. You can add dope to it, or not. Rizla very much hope you do. Stoners are worth a fortune to them. 'They tried to ban the king skins,' we used to tell each other, laughing about the extra long ones, 'but the manufacturers say they're for long-distance lorry drivers, so they don't have to keep stopping to roll.' It is amazing how many sixteen-year-old lorry drivers you see buying them in every corner shop and supermarket. When I arrived in Rotterdam central station clutching a fistful of wages and hungry to score, the first thing I saw, flashing, high above the withered little heroin addict begging for my change, was a huge neon sign, on the top of a building: RIZLA +.

On another trip to Morocco, in Chechaouen in the Rif mountains, the first person to approach us was a sallow young man with red eyes and no shoes, with nothing but a shiny little lump of dud hash which he had been rolling and rolling in his palm for hours, perhaps days, as he waited for a tourist clueless enough to buy it. It was New Year, there were a lot of dope tourists about, young Spanish and Portuguese, but they were looking for the good stuff, available in huge, cheap bricks. Nobody was interested in this desperado. We did not want it either. I was in a non-smoking phase. We asked him if he might help us find a hotel. He tried. I tried to tip him, but he did not want a tip. He wanted me to buy the hash so that he could be rid of it, buy some more, go back to the bus stop and wait again. I wondered if he would eat or smoke the tiny profit he would take. Smoke, of course. Times with dope and no money pass easier than times with money and no dope, as we used to say. It was the only time I have ever bought it as an act of charity and one of the very few times I have seen a seller of marijuana brought as low by it as so many buyers are, one of the few times I have seen the damage my habit did to strangers.

What I have done and where I have been does not qualify me to make recommendations: or, it qualifies me no more than any one of thousands of us. However I have tried to be an observant tourist. I made lots of notes and I did reach the end of the road. This journey ends with a letter from there: from here.

★

Dear S,

I first see you on a lovely, dirty winter night in south
London, rain bouncing off the pavements like grease spitting
in a pan.

The route from the tube has become so familiar over the years
that every step is now a stage in the ritual, a ceremony I love, a
rite which kills and deranges me by irresistible degrees. Up the
steps, past the gatekeeper, the old Rasta droning 'Incense . . .
incense . . .' Brixton's watchman, whose dark and reddened eyes
catch all the working day's victims as they are disgorged by the
Underground. Down the High Street I go, past the police station,
past the bus stop and on, into the estates.

The eyes of the tower blocks shine with the warm lights of
kitchens and halls. Orange street lamps cast wavering halos in the
stippling rain. On down I go, across the smear of grass and on
towards the arches below the railway line, staring up at the
procession of aeroplanes, loud and low on their glide paths, flying
dragons, lights glaring through the murk. Trains clank and heave
along the viaduct, the bowed heads of the commuters yellow-lit in
their glass boxes. I have worked today, I too was tired at six o'clock,
but I am wide awake now.

I bear left past the arches: each is a garage spewing light, music
and machine noise. I glance into them, meeting the suddenly blank,
incurious eyes of the mechanics. I weave through their work –
disembowelled skeletons, gleaming shells, smashed, cannibalized
wrecks – and reach the road. Right again and now I am counting off
the cameras. I know where all of them are and which ways each of
them looks. This is Coldharbour Lane, 'the front line'; every yard of
it belongs to one gang of dealers or another; occasionally they shoot
each other. Left at the junction, under the first bridge and on
towards the last camera, the one that knows all about me. Tonight is
a lucky one: it is staring towards me as I approach which means it
will not see me as I go in. I pass underneath it and turn, looking
hard up the road. No patrol cars, no police vans, or at least none
marked. A few more paces and I am on another camera, only this
one, of the millions in London, is on my side. At the last moment I
turn left, push open the glass-panelled door and pass inside.

It is the reception area of a taxi service. Drivers hang around, lounging on low black plastic armchairs. Video games beep and burble. I nod at the woman behind the counter and reach for the door to her right. She presses a button, the door opens. Now we are on a narrow landing. At the end is another door guarded by another camera. There is no need to push the bell: someone downstairs is ready for me, there is a buzz and I pull the door open. Hard on my right side a flight of narrow stairs leads steeply down. I can hear the noise, the deep voices raised in argument, the laughter and the crack of pool balls. And I can smell the drug. The thick, blue-green reek of it rises to greet me as I descend.

The Taxi Service never closes: you can score here any time, any night, any day, including Christmas. For an addict this is wonderful: no doubt, no waiting around for dealers and no disappointments because they never run out. The deal you get varies in quality and quantity but you always get something. They only sell dope. They do not tolerate the use of other drugs, the presence of guns, fighting or excessive aggression. The casual customer will never feel safe here, will never linger – it used to be a heart-pounding thrill for me to dip in and out, secretly scared, trying to be cool, praying I would not be caught, robbed or beaten up – but the regulars know they are as safe here as anywhere in Brixton.

The rules are written on the wall: What you do here, what you see here, what you hear here, what you say here, let it stay here or don't come back here. This charter is decorated with an image of Mickey Mouse. The rest of the pictures are more in keeping: Marley, ever young; Biggie and Tupac together at last; Lil' Kim in her underwear; Lauryn Hill, Nelson Mandela, Martin Luther King. There is a gambling machine, a large television which shows quiz programmes, news and sport (horses all afternoon) and around it a stack of smaller monitors which show everything the upstairs cameras see. I have just walked across their screens. There is a fridge full of soft drinks and booze, even champagne. The carpeted floor tilts, the ceiling is low, the walls are a bright, unlikely shade of blue. At one end of the room is a large table. The duty dealer sits at its head as if holding court. The rest of it is generally occupied by the card players. At the other end of the room is the pool table. There is a bench and a few chairs; there is one copy each of the *Daily Star* and the *Racing Post* which tonight's dealer, Joe, will lend you, and there are normally between five and thirty men, standing around, sitting, playing cards or pool, drinking and smoking dope.

Although more than half of the customers who tramp down the stairs and then hurry back up are white, mostly young men and women, the regulars – the members, as I think of them – are all black men. Though they are all Londoners now (the dealers are second or third generation Londoners) the members come from West Africa, from Nigeria, Senegal and Ivory Coast; others are from the Caribbean, from Jamaica, Barbados and the Dominican Republic. There is an intercity train driver. There is a man who used to be in the army: when he was stationed near Hereford in the sixties he says the locals wanted to know if he had a tail. He is putting miniature cameras on model aeroplanes now.

'Next time there's a riot,' he says, 'we'll have evidence! Whoever controls the cameras controls everything!'

I remember how we used to talk like that at university, muttering about conspiracy, about how it suited the government that dangerous revolutionaries like us spent all our days stoned.

There is my friend Shola, who works for local government. He is a man of high social standing in Nigeria.

'You again!' I say, severely. 'In a place like this?'

'Ah! But you know I'm baaaad!'

You hear many languages and a lot of different patois. The air is hot and heavy with noise, dope-smoke and the smell of men's sweat. I feel more at home here, happier here, simultaneously at ease and on edge, than I do almost anywhere else. Neither my name, my job, my background, my accent, my story, my class, my failures, records or achievements, nothing and none of it counts down here. I am treated exactly as I am found. Time and the rest of London are suspended. Here is all. However wrecked you are though, you concentrate, because though it is a relaxed and polite place there is no law except the kind made instantly. I stand out because I am white but I blend in too because I am an addict and because, through sheer repetition, I have almost become part of the furniture.

Apart from the traffic wardens, one of whom was a woman who used to drop by for a fix in the afternoons, and a tall, beautifully made-up young girl like a butterfly who used to appear sometimes, who I thought was a daughter of the mysterious ruling family who ran the place, there were no women among the regulars until that night.

You were already there when I arrived, at the pool table, but in my first, rapid glance, I did not see you. Or rather I thought I saw a boy, a young man, tall, in baggy jeans, big trainers, hooded top pulled over a baseball cap, wrap-around shades, key chain like a dog lead dangling from the belt, brown hands holding a pool cue.

I approached the dealer. Joe is a phlegmatic man who has honed his natural cynicism into a sophisticated instrument. It can be very funny, very damning or very aggressive. I had seen him throw someone out with it: his flat and total dismissal of everything the man was, everything he said and anything he might do as effective as a series of punches. There was a lot of noise that night. The card game sporadically erupted into furious dispute. It is sometimes difficult to tell whether the disagreement is always as serious as it sounds. Two players were on their feet now, eyes popping, flailing out furious tentacles of sound, claim and counterclaim, waving their arms.

'OYY!' roared Joe. '*FUCK'S* SAKE!'

There was a pause.

'*Thank* you. Yes, mate?'

'Two, please.'

He passed me two little bags, half full of green weed, and I gave him a twenty.

'Thanks, Joe.'

'Thank *you*,' he said and glowered at the argument, which was swelling again.

'Could I have a beer as well?'

My favourite perch was the end of the bench, by the pool table, a high seat with room for three or four and a perfect view of the game. I started the ceremony with the Rizlas, the dope and tobacco. The joint complete, I tore off its twizzle of waste paper, sparked it and cracked open the can. The beer ran cold into the pit of my stomach and my head filled with the first cloudburst of marijuana. I sighed and turned my attention to the game.

You had two reds remaining and were taking a shot at one of them. The man on yellow had only one left but he seemed tense. You did not stoop properly, I noticed; the dark glasses were nowhere near the cue but hovering some way above them. One long finger, splayed on the baize, tapped once, the cue licked forward and struck. The white flew down the table, glancing a red into a middle pocket, struck two cushions and stopped, neatly aligned with a corner and the remaining red. The black was against the cushion at the other end. With the next pot the white glided the length of the table and stopped dead on the back cushion. The opponent put down his cue, expressionless. The black was dispatched with a soft, unhesitating prod and a slight curve of a lip which may have been a smile and you shook hands. The loser put his hand in his back pocket but you said:

'Good game. Unlucky. You want double or quits, yeah?'

The loser did not hesitate. 'Yeah, a'right.'

'Set them up then. Jus' let me make a zoot, yeah?'

I frowned slightly. It was not that embarrassing to have mistaken you for a boy: the baggy clothes, hood, cap and glasses could have been designed to provoke the mistake. It was not that you played so well or that you were so relaxed down here: what struck me was that you appeared to be hustling and that your victim was one of the best I had lost to, a canny expert of the game, miles out of my league.

I awaited the next contest with interest, as did several others. We had plenty of time to anticipate it. You took ages making your joint, which you crammed, I noticed, with bright green skunk – the kind which flattens you, which makes you feel as though you are tripping on waves of paranoia if you are not used to it. They did not sell that down here. At last it was ready and you lit it, punctuating deep drags with swigs of cider from a black bottle.

★

I reckoned by the time you had finished with the queue of willing victims you had taken at least ninety quid, roughly the amount I had earned that day at work, though yours was tax-free and harvested in a quarter of the time, apparently with a tenth of the effort. I watched you put your big headphones on and bid laughing goodbyes to the challengers. I wondered, as you climbed the stairs, what you looked like and whether I would ever have the chance to play you. I left a while later. I loved walking back. It was a glide through a transformed world.

The next time I went to the taxi service I was earlier, it was only just getting dark and I expected the place to be quiet. It was; only three people at cards and two at pool, but one of them was you. When I saw the big hooded top and your slim arms I felt a jolt of pleasure in my stomach, a happy little twisting. I bought my dope, settled down with a joint and watched as you routed another opponent. He was desperate to play you again and again; laughing, you let him. Finally, halfway through my second joint, I felt ready. I stood up, put a coin on the table and retreated, pulse awakened, anticipating the match. You won again.

'You wanna game, yeah?' you said.

'Sure.'

'The thing is,' you said, turning towards the corner so that only I could hear as you spoke out of the side of your mouth, 'I'm playing for money, yeah?'

'I'm not really into betting . . .' I said, reluctantly.

'Ten?' you said.

'Five.'

'All right then,' you said, soothingly. 'Set them up, yeah? If you win I'll pay you back.'

Which is how you took the first six quid off me.

'D'you want double or quits, Horatio?'

I was not sure how you knew my name.

'OK,' I sighed. 'What's your name?'

One of the boys who was attached to the establishment, who occasionally did shifts as a dealer, swung down. He saw us talking and snorted.

'Ratted 'ickle bloodsucker got 'er teeth into you!' he cried. 'Always looking for another one to eat!'

You giggled.

In the following weeks and months I never heard the sound of footsteps coming down the stairs without looking up to see if they were yours. I was never happier than when they were. I think I fell in love with you, in a way. I thought idly and speculatively in the back of my mind about what it might be like to kiss you but I would never have tried it. You were twenty-two, eight years younger than me. We liked each other; we became trusting friends. And there was something else. If we flirted we did it without intent. When one day you told me you were gay I was neither surprised nor disappointed.

I lost a fortune to you, of course. And I learned a bit about pool and a lot more about other things. We had some wonderful nights, laughing, joyful evenings in the taxi service. 'It seems like a happy time, Joe,' I ventured once. 'Good atmosphere, at the moment . . .'

'Pfff – you think so? Enjoy it while it lasts. It's all turning to shit soon.'

You said you did not like it much down there and the amount of money you could make decreased as the players became wise to you. The spell never broke; there was always someone willing to have a go, even those like me who could hope for little more than the pleasure of losing to you: most men are optimists where girls like you are concerned. You milked them. I watched you play some beautiful games; when you met your match the spectacle would hold a circle of us in breathless attention.

I asked you where you had learned to be so good at pool and you told me the story of the man in Uganda who humiliated you, and how you swore you would go away and practise until you could beat him. I would have loved to have seen it when you did. You explained that you did not stoop all the way down over the table when you took your shots so that your opponents, always men, could not see down your top.

You told me about yourself: that you are Sudanese, that cap and hood are not style, or not just style, but in accordance with your religion. I understood that though you smoked and drank and had sex you also had a sincere relationship with Islam and a vexed one with your community, that the disguise was supposed to ensure you were not recognized on the street by anyone who might tell your parents that you were up to things in rough parts of town. You told me you were going to study criminal psychology at university.

People said you should turn professional and (aside from the fact that you already were, effectively) you said you were thinking about it. After a while, after that shooting (crackheads with a gun trying to rob the taxi service) we swapped numbers and met for games in other places, pubs and snooker clubs. As I was and had been for a long time, you were smoking much too much dope: we were both addicts.

I lost contact with you sometimes, when I gave up, or toppled into one of the depressions. I thought it would be an imposition on our friendship and deeply hypocritical if I were to lecture you but we talked often about the prices we paid – that we would pay – if we did not give up the drug.

At last, after those particularly awful months during which I met the mania and stopped, making that vow, when I had not seen you for nearly a year (I knew that if I did I would not be strong enough not to smoke with you), we met one late autumn afternoon in Victoria.

We walked together and talked. 'It's been bad, really bad,' you said.

You told me that you had been smoking crack, that you had done it for days on end and given up caring whether you ate or drank, whether you slept or where, how you looked, whether you washed or not, had given up everything except the thought of the next rock. You cautioned me:

'Don't ever, you get me, Horatio? Don't think you'll just have one, or one drag, or whatever. It's not like that. It gets you straight away.'

'But you must have known – why did you . . .'

'I didn't know how bad it was.'

We had both tried pretty well everything: except for crack and crystal meth I cannot think of a street drug I have not taken at least once. I thought it was sweet of you to warn me but I realized afterwards that the only thing which had protected me from crack was circumstance: had I not said yes to everything else I had ever been offered? We had often marvelled that across all our differences, our vastly separate experiences of the world, you and I are strongly similar people. You were right to warn me.

'How did you afford it?' I asked.

'I was really lucky, yeah? This guy just gave it to me, he just wanted to take it with me,' you said.

'How did you stop?'

'It was making me really horrible, really aggressive, it was turning me into someone else. I just thought this isn't me. This is not who I am. This is not my religion, I have to stop. And the guy tried to – one night he wouldn't go, yeah, he wouldn't stop, in the end I attacked him. I mean really nasty. And I don't do that. It was not me.'

We went into a pool club. It was horrible: a video jukebox blaring bad music as fat white men sat around clutching their phones and pints and stared at you: as you said, the atmosphere messed up our game. I beat you for about the third time in my life playing no more than competently. You took off your glasses and I saw your eyes. You looked as if you had been punched. Shattered dark circles hung below them. You went to the loo to put on some make-up and when you emerged you rolled a joint. You and your friends are much less cautious about it than I was: I would have rolled it in the lavatory. Among you the drug is barely worth concealing. We went outside to smoke. I knew it would blow me away, my first for a year. We walked up and down a roofed-in alley, a strange box-like concrete space like the forgotten wing of a multi-storey car park. There were bins along one wall and the nest of a homeless person on the floor. At one end there was a petrol station, at the other men with short hair came and went, in and out of some door we could not quite see. We walked up and down and talked. The weed was screwing you up, you said. You said you did not know how to stop. And the booze was a problem: you were definitely drinking too much. There was a bottle of cheap vodka in your bag. On the good side, you had a lovely girlfriend and you were hopeful about going back to university, having dropped out at the end of your second year.

The smoke from the joint was incredibly strong – you could smell it at a hundred metres, I guessed.

'Sweetheart,' I said, as we left, 'I'm seeing police everywhere.'

'Yeah, darlin'!' you said. 'It's the back of the police station, innit?'

Later, waiting for your girlfriend to change her clothes, we sat shivering on the concrete steps of a block of flats with the November wind blowing through the open sections of the stairwell above and below us. While you ate fish and chips I told you what I was going to do.

'I'm going to write it all down, everything.'

'Yeah?'

'Yeah. Every bloody thing. I'm going to tell the truth about us – about me and everyone I know – about what happened to us, about what we did and why – and what it did to us.'

'A'right,' you said, thoughtfully. 'That's going to be the book?'

'Yes.'

You thought about it, picking a few more chips. You finished and scrunched the remains into a greasy ball. You wiped your lips delicately on a paper napkin and stood up. 'I hope you do it,' you said. 'I hope you do. Do it for me, yeah?' you said, with a half-laugh in your voice.

'I will,' I said. 'I'll try.'

As I said goodbye to you later, after another joint, I had a terrified, paranoid feeling that I might not see you again. You seemed suspended above hell by the slimmest thread. It was easy to imagine that something might happen to you. And you reminded me of myself again: Ben felt the same way about me once, as we said goodbye.

★

Dear S, I know how well you have done since then. The room you found; the work you do; the degree you have returned to; not smoking so much. But I am still scared, too. So many people told me to stop and although I knew they were right it made no difference. As you can see, I have been very stupid and also very lucky. No one can count on luck. Though we both know lots of people who seem to be able to get away with it (I know successful professionals who smoke every day) we also know they are the exceptions: we are the rule.

I feel very guilty when I think of the number of times we smoked together, the number of times, after the taxi service was busted, that I made use of you and your contacts in order to get my fix. I was too weak and too addicted to say what I should have said or to set the right example. We used to talk about it sometimes, once we had our joints in our fingers: then we would talk about stopping, living healthily and going straight.

I needed to tell this story, but were it not for you I would not have known how to tell it or why it should be shared. I would not have had a reason for telling it now or the courage to do it. It seems strange to have laid out half my life in order to get to this, the point, in order to be able to write this letter to you.

But looking at you and worrying about you made me see myself. I always felt that my story was a guilty secret, that I should be ashamed of many of my deeds and habits. But when I looked at you I did not feel that at all. I did not feel that you ought to be ashamed or guilty about what had happened to you. I felt that you were a victim of many circumstances, and that the trouble you were in was as much a curse as a sin. Yes, we did what we should not have done many times: we always knew drugs were a bad idea. And we giggled as we did it, we quite liked being bad. But you made me see that our mistakes are not inexplicable or irreversible, and not necessarily a damnation.

But, dear friend, damnation is out there, hovering, not at all far away. Not just depression, which you know all about: it is even worse than that. I have seen it. I left you that night, self-conscious, awkward, feeling stupid and regretful, worried about you and paranoid, all the usual things, head rattling like a box of broken glass. I tried to pull myself together. It was Christmas and I was going home to Wales. And then it happened.

Ten minutes later I knew holy dread. I knew true fear. I saw through everything and in an instant, in terror, knew what it is to lose your mind, your grip and reason. I saw how thin are the skins between death and the dream of life, between sanity and the shrieking void. In that moment all the divisions dissolved. I will never forget it. I was terrified and humbled, mortally afraid for my immortal soul. I felt the eye of God was upon me, as though just for an instant I had been afforded a glimpse, an echo, an intimation, and I was blinded, deafened, cowering. I knew then, completely, how I should live, and I knew too that from that moment there were no excuses.

Of all places, it happened in Victoria, on a bus.

I kept very still. I fixed my eyes on the yellow handrail in front of me, and kept breathing. I remember wondering if I was now mad, if the next time I spoke I would rave and rave for ever. I felt I might scream, I felt I might be screaming: inside I was screaming and at the same time keeping very quiet and very still. It went on and on. Trivial things became obvious to me and I was a trivial, trivial thing.

I have heard it said that nothing lasts for ever. This I now know is wrong. Everything – everything is for ever. Nothing is just the stuff, the everyday, train to catch, life and death, home for Christmas nothing, in which we write our contracts with forever. Nothing may seem as if it will last, but everything actually will.

It was as though I was being put to the question, tortured for an answer. And while it seemed that there was no question still I knew the answer and I gave it, with all my heart. I said yes. I said it humbly, gratefully, and I meant it. I was a soiled and soiling thing, shamed and seen. I made some vow then, to something, about something.

My existence was suddenly a long way away, an impossible distance below and behind me. I knew, vaguely, who and what I had thought I was: a young writer on a London bus, heading home for Christmas. But now I understood it was all a construct of my

vain imagination, and that I was a tiny, insignificant mote of
nothing which up until that moment had been spinning a story for
itself and others, a story of being and significance. I could suddenly
see the awful, lunatic presumption with which I had assumed I
mattered. Now it was as if I had been awakened suddenly from a
long and complicated dream. In those moments before I said yes,
moments in which I realized time and space were merely part of the
dream, I knew what hell was. Hell was simple: it was the promise
and the threat that this would not stop, that I would float above my
own existence, a witness and a consequence of all its flaws, dirt, lies
and pettiness, until eternity was done and darkness fell. I had known
mania but this was madness. The bus was proceeding up the
Vauxhall Bridge Road, but it would never reach Victoria.

Now you might say that a revelation on drugs is not a revelation at
all, merely a function of intoxication. But we have been on drugs a
thousand times, much stronger drugs, and this was nothing, nothing
like anything I had known, heard of or even vaguely apprehended.
If taking drugs took you where I went then people would not take
them more than once. You can drink a bottle of whisky and feel and
see and think some strange things, but if you meet the archangel
Gabriel in a field on your way home the fact of your having drunk
the whisky will suddenly become irrelevant. Of course, technically
the skunk was to blame: had I been straight I doubt I would have
seen eternity on the Vauxhall Bridge Road. But for me the
fundamental point of taking drugs was to peel away the road, to see
through dark glass, to find and open invisible doors.

'There are more things in heaven and earth,' Hamlet tells my
namesake, 'than are dreamt of in your philosophy.' And in those
moments, in minutes become light years, I saw all the proof of
those more things that I will ever require. I mean to leave it all
alone. The surface of the world is more than enough for me.

I do not know how I reached Paddington. I was too scared to take
the tube in case it happened again and I broke down amongst all
the people and terrified them.

★

It is snowing as we leave London; by the time the train reaches Swindon half the night is white. I huddle in my seat, sober and shaken. It is like surviving a car crash. My God, I keep thinking, my God. We change trains twice as the snow thickens. All the way across England it feels as though my pulse is slowing, coming down from a racing peak.

I start flashing back through it all, all these incidents, and beyond them. Was I always slightly deranged? Was wearing that poncho a mad thing to do, when I was fifteen? And everything since? Where was the line? Does canoeing in a bow tie make you mad, if you know at the time it is mad, if you are doing it because it is mad, and funny? Perhaps it has all been mad, right from the beginning. New York, Torpington, Newcastle, yes: half the choices that have made me, made by a maniac. But what about the bits in between? The natural perspective is to imagine yourself normal and good and to see the rest as aberrations. But suppose for you madness is the norm, and what everyone else regards as normal is, for you, remarkable? Suppose you are and have long been mentally ill, deranged by your own hand. What then?

No excuses, I keep thinking, no more excuses. You cannot afford the mania again and you cannot put everyone else through it. And the depression. You may not survive a next time, you cannot go there again. Pray you do not have to. And that – that, whatever it was, on the bus, that is the end of it. That has to be the end. Please, let that be the end.

When I reach Abergavenny no taxis are running out into the black and white beyond. I call my brother to tell him I will still be a while yet.

I go into the pub by the station like a traveller coming home from the far side of the world. A large man at the bar turns round, looks me up and down, taking me in, my battered Moroccan satchel, my shaken and tired air, like a lone survivor, I think, someone who has finished with something, at last.

'Nice *handbag*, mate,' he says.

Finally, at midnight, a taxi appears, slipping and skidding.

'Are you sure you're OK to go up the valley?' I ask the driver, cautiously.

He is a young man, about twenty-four. 'Oh yeah!' he exclaims, alight with a humour and excitement I recognize. 'It's bloody brilliant. Been having great fun tonight!'

When he drops me off I admonish him to go very carefully.

'Yeah! No worries!' he says, and speeds away.

The yard is very dark and the front door opens to even thicker darkness and the smell of damp. I bolt it behind me. The kitchen door fits very snugly, separating the tumbledown half of the house from the habitable bit. I pop it open and there is warmth and the smell of pine needles and cooking. There is a scrabble of claws on the tiles and there are the dogs, jumping up delightedly, pushing their wet noses into my hands.

There is the Christmas tree our mother has put up, as she does every year, there is the warm light by the cooker, and there is my dear brother, who came on an earlier train, who has never been into drugs and has seen me come home in so many states that I can tell how I am just by the way he looks at me.

'Hullo,' he says, grinning, 'how are you? You sounded a bit weird on the phone.'

'Hullo, mate. I'm OK. Overdid it a bit, that's all. Long journey. How are you?'

'Good,' he says. 'Fine.'

'And how's Mum?'

'She's fine. She's gone to bed. Are you hungry? There's some really good soup left. Delicious. Would you like some?'

'Mmm, yes. I would.'

'Was it a bad journey then? It took ages, didn't it?'

'It was a long one,' I nod, dumping my bags and gently fighting off one of the dogs, who is trying to kiss my face.

'God, it's *great* to be home!' he says suddenly, as I ladle out some soup. I know that jump of conviction he gets, that sudden buck of joy, and here we are, two men in our thirties, grinning at each other like children with all the glee of Christmas in our smiles. 'Just wonderful, isn't it?' he says. 'Isn't it?'

★

Later I went up to my room and thought about you, about my friends and this thing I planned to write for you, this story of a slide from choice to necessity. How different it might have been. Maria spared hell. Robin saved depression and misery. His four friends still alive. Ben free of wreckage, rehab and the wagon. Crime I might not have committed and madness I might not have known. All the people, like Nathan's friend George, not hiding in their rooms. All those friends of friends, not drug casualties, no less than they might have been. The families less agonized. The actual difference we might have made, the things done in place of smoke and fantasy. The hundreds of thousands of pounds not wasted. How much less alone, how much less 'boxed', how much less bolted into our own heads we might have been. The pain not caused. The love not lost. How much saved.

What would we have missed, if we had taken another path? All this story and more like it: judge for yourself. We do not blame dope and the other drugs for everything, but they attacked us at our most vulnerable point: at the level of our dreams. When you talk about winning a big-money pool championship, about modelling, about leapfrogging the everyday into a higher, richer, happier realm, you remind me so strongly of myself, rolling another one and dreaming of being a writer.

I think you will see parallels here with your own life, though I know it has been very different and in many ways harder. I hope you will forgive me for not being a better friend. (Opposition, Blake says, is true friendship.) And now you have seen where I have been since that day I sat on a swing, on a mountain, thinking about a racing pigeon and a girl and all the adventures I wanted to have, and now you know where that road took me, I hope – because you still have time – I hope you will choose another.

H.

Acknowledgements

The author and publishers would like to thank the following, and gratefully acknowledge permission to reprint copyright material as follows:

Common People
Words by Jarvis Cocker
© Copyright 1994 Island Music Limited. Universal/Island Music Limited. Used by permission of Music Sales Limited. All Rights Reserved. International Copyright Secured.

Career Opportunities
Words & Music by Mick Jones & Joe Strummer
© Copyright 1977 Nineden Limited. Universal Music Publishing Limited. Used by permission of Music Sales Limited. All Rights Reserved. International Copyright Secured.

The Guns of Brixton
Words & Music by Paul Simonon
© Copyright 1979 Nineden Limited. Universal Music Publishing Limited. Used by permission of Music Sales Limited. All Rights Reserved. International Copyright Secured.

Bankrobber
Words & Music by Mick Jones & Joe Strummer
© Copyright 1980 Nineden Limited. Universal Music Publishing Limited. Used by permission of Music Sales Limited. All Rights Reserved. International Copyright Secured.

Fairytale of New York
Words & Music by Shane MacGowan and Jem Finer
© Copyright 1987 Stiff Records/Island. All Rights Reserved. International Copyright Secured.

Naked
By Mike Leigh
© Copyright 1995 Mike Leigh/Faber and Faber. All Rights Reserved. International Copyright Secured.

Every effort has been made to clear permissions. If permission has
not been granted please contact the publisher who will include a
credit in subsequent printings and editions.

Read more ...

Horatio Clare

RUNNING FOR THE HILLS: A FAMILY STORY

The *Daily Mail* described this best-selling childhood memoir as 'so beautifully written that you almost hold your breath'

When Jenny and Robert fall in love in the late 1960s they decide to build a new future together, away from the city. They escape to an isolated sheep farm nestled on a mountainside. It has no running water but it is beautiful and rugged. Their young sons can roam wild.

As their flock struggles, money runs low and rain drives in horizontally across the fields, inside the ancient house their marriage begins to unravel. Wilful and romantic, Jenny refuses to abandon her farm. She will bring her boys up single-handedly on the mountain. Together they embark on a perilous adventure.

Running for the Hills is an astonishing family memoir – Horatio Clare vividly recreates his mother's extraordinary way of life and his own bewitching childhood in a magical story of love and struggle.

'A joy . . . heartening, raw, tender' John Carey, *Sunday Times*

'Touching, funny and extremely well written' *Daily Telegraph*

'It should be required reading' *Guardian*

ISBN 978-0-7195-6539-7
Order your copy now by calling Bookpoint on 01235 827716 or visit your local bookshop
www.johnmurray.co.uk